FEDERAL AVIATION REGULATIONS
EXPLAINED

Parts 1 and 135

Kent S. Jackson
Joseph T. Brennan

55 Inverness Drive East, Englewood, CO 80112-5498
ISBN 0-88487-174-6

JS319013A

The Authors

Kent S. Jackson is an attorney in Overland Park, Kansas who practices primarily in aviation law. He has represented numerous pilots, flight departments, and corporations in FAA enforcement proceedings. He is a contributor to *Flight Training* magazine. An active commercial pilot and flight instructor, Mr. Jackson is a member of the National Transportation Safety Board Bar Association, the Lawyer Pilots Bar Association, the National Association of Flight Instructors, the Aircraft Owners and Pilots Association, and the Experimental Aircraft Association. He is also an Adjunct Professor of Aviation Law at Central Missouri State University.

Joseph T. Brennan is an attorney in Kansas City, Missouri who practices primarily in aviation law. He was an attorney for the Federal Aviation Administration for 27 years, and has instructed FAA inspectors on enforcement procedures. During his career with the FAA, Mr. Brennan served as Regional Counsel, Great Lakes Region; Aeronautical Center Counsel, Mike Monroney Aeronautical Center; and Deputy Assistant Chief Counsel, Central Region. Mr. Brennan is a member of the National Transportation Safety Board Bar Association and the Lawyer Pilots Bar Association. He is also an associate staff member of the Transportation Safety Institute.

The authors welcome comments, suggestions, and information which will aid in the development of the *Federal Aviation Regulations Explained*. Information may be sent to the authors in care of

Jeppesen
55 Inverness Drive East
Englewood, CO 80112-5498
Tel: (303) 799-9090

or, the authors may be contacted directly at

(913) 338-1700
FAX: (913) 338-1755

Acknowledgements

The authors wish to thank their friends at the Federal Aviation Administration, the National Transportation Safety Board, and in the aviation industry whose help and support made this book possible. The authors would especially like to thank:

Richard W. Carlson, Operations Inspector
Federal Aviation Administration

Frederick P. Dibble, Regional Director, Airline Sales
Saab Aircraft of America Inc.

Fred W. Kirby, Manager, Technical Services
National Business Aircraft Association

Paul E. Newman, First Officer
USAir

Nel Sanders, Senior Manager, State and Tax Issues
National Business Aircraft Association

Joseph Sprague, Specialist, Government Affairs
National Air Transportation Association

The Authers would also especially like to thank:

Phyllis Brennan
Michaela Eady
Cathy Jackson
Schuyler Jackson
Susan McKeon
Jim Mowery
Michael Peck
Elizabeth Wallace

Preface

When Captain Jeppesen began writing letdown procedures in his "little black book," flying was less complicated and far less reliable. The demand for dependable schedules and safety in increasingly congested airspace has forced pilots to give up the romance of silk scarves and face the realities of complex, and sometimes confusing, regulations.

Intended to increase safety and make common sense of the law, the Federal Aviation Regulations have become so detailed and complex that pilots have found themselves saying "I know what it says, but what does it mean?" To help pilots answer the question "what does it mean?" the *Federal Aviation Regulations Explained* looks at FAA Advisory Circulars, the *Airman's Information Manual*, NTSB decisions, FAA Chief Counsel opinions, and regulatory background. *Federal Aviation Regulations Explained* is the only publication that also provides cross references and an index to help pilots see the regulatory "big picture."

This book contains the regulations for FAR Part 135. FAR Part 1 is included as a reference source for the other regulations. Each regulation has the following interpretative resources:

- The regulation itself
- An explanation, unless it is self-explanatory
- Cross-references to other regulations
- Related advisory circulars
- The location in the *Airman's Information Manual* where related information can be found
- NTSB case excerpts associated with the regulation
- FAA Chief Counsel opinion excerpts

Not all the areas are covered in each regulation, only those areas which are pertinent are included.

Although it would be nearly impossible to locate **every** FAA interpretation of every issue presented by the FARs, the authors have endeavored to select NTSB decisions and FAA opinions that are representative of common interpretations. The authors have also selected some of the more conservative FAA interpretations to inform pilots of the FAA's position.

A Word of Caution

No book can replace the advice and counsel of an attorney experienced in aviation law. *Federal Aviation Regulations Explained* is intended to help pilots understand how the FAA and the NTSB have interpreted the regulations based on past incidences and circumstances. Since not every Flight Standards District Office interprets regulations in precisely the same way, a simple phone call to the local FSDO can often prevent expensive and time-consuming misunderstandings.

FEDERAL AVIATION REGULATIONS

PART 1 DEFINITIONS AND ABBREVIATIONS

TABLE OF CONTENTS

1.1 GENERAL DEFINITIONS

As used in Subchapters A through K of this chapter unless the context requires otherwise:

"Administrator" means the Federal Aviation Administrator or any person to whom he has delegated his authority in the matter concerned.

"Aerodynamic coefficients" means nondimensional coefficients for aerodynamic forces and moments.

"Air carrier" means a person who undertakes directly by lease, or other arrangement, to engage in air transportation.

"Air commerce" means interstate, overseas, or foreign air commerce or the transportation of mail by aircraft or any operation or navigation of aircraft within the limits of any Federal airway or any operation or navigation of aircraft which directly affects, or which may endanger safety in, interstate, overseas, or foreign air commerce.

"Aircraft" means a device that is used or intended to be used for flight in the air.

"Aircraft engine" means an engine that is used or intended to be used for propelling aircraft. It includes turbosuperchargers, appurtenances, and accessories necessary for its functioning, but does not include propellers.

"Airframe" means the fuselage, booms, nacelles, cowlings, fairings, airfoil surfaces (including rotors but excluding propellers and rotating airfoils of engines), and landing gear of an aircraft and their accessories and controls.

"Airplane" means an engine-driven fixed-wing aircraft heavier than air, that is supported in flight by the dynamic reaction of the air against its wings.

"Airport" means an area of land or water that is used or intended to be used for the landing and takeoff of aircraft, and includes its buildings and facilities, if any.

"Airship" means an engine-driven lighter-than-air aircraft that can be steered.

"Air traffic" means aircraft operating in the air or on an airport surface, exclusive of loading ramps and parking areas.

"Air traffic clearance" means an authorization by air traffic control, for the purpose of preventing collision between known aircraft, for an aircraft to proceed under specified traffic conditions within controlled airspace.

"Air traffic control" means a service operated by appropriate authority to promote the safe, orderly, and expeditious flow of air traffic.

"Air transportation" means interstate, overseas, or foreign air transportation or the transportation of mail by aircraft.

"Alternate airport" means an airport at which an aircraft may land if a landing at the intended airport becomes inadvisable.

"Altitude engine" means a reciprocating aircraft engine having a rated takeoff power that is producible from sea level to an established higher altitude.

"Appliance" means any instrument, mechanism, equipment, part, apparatus, appurtenance, or accessory, including communications equipment, that is used or intended to be used in operating or controlling an aircraft in flight, is installed in or attached to the aircraft, and is not part of an airframe, engine, or propeller.

"Approved," unless used with reference to another person, means approved by the Administrator.

"Area navigation (RNAV)" means a method of navigation that permits aircraft operations on any desired course within the coverage of station-referenced navigation signals or within the limits of self-contained system capability.

"Area navigation high route" means an area navigation route within the airspace extending upward from, and including, 18,000 feet MSL to flight level 450.

"Area navigation low route" means an area navigation route within the airspace extending upward from 1,200 feet above the surface of the earth to, but not including, 18,000 feet MSL.

"Armed Forces" means the Army, Navy, Air Force, Marine Corps, and Coast Guard, including their regular and reserve components and members serving without component status.

"Autorotation" means a rotorcraft flight condition in which the lifting rotor is driven entirely by action of the air when the rotorcraft is in motion.

"Auxiliary rotor" means a rotor that serves either to counteract the effect of the main rotor torque on a rotorcraft or to maneuver the rotorcraft about one or more of its three principal axes.

"Balloon" means a lighter-than-air aircraft that is not engine-driven.

"Brake horsepower" means the power delivered at the propeller shaft (main drive or main output) of an aircraft engine.

"Calibrated airspeed" means indicated airspeed of an aircraft, corrected for position and instrument error. Calibrated airspeed is equal to true airspeed in standard atmosphere at sea level.

"Canard" means the forward wing of a canard configuration and may be a fixed, movable, or variable geometry surface, with or without control surfaces.

"Canard configuration" means a configuration in which the span of the forward wing is substantially less than that of the main wing.

"Category" —

(1) As used with respect to the certification, ratings, privileges, and limitations of airmen, means a broad classification of aircraft. Examples include: airplane; rotorcraft; glider; and lighter-than-air; and

(2) As used with respect to the certification of aircraft, means a grouping of aircraft based upon intended use or operating limitations. Examples include: transport; normal; utility; acrobatic; limited; restricted; and provisional.

"Category II operations," with respect to the operation of aircraft, means a straight-in ILS approach to the runway of an airport under a Category II ILS instrument approach procedure issued by the Administrator or other appropriate authority.

"Category III operations," with respect to the operation of aircraft, means an ILS approach to, and landing on, the runway of an airport using a Category III ILS instrument approach procedure issued by the Administrator or other appropriate authority.

"Category A," with respect to transport category rotorcraft, means multiengine rotorcraft designed with engine and system isolation features specified in *Part 29 and utilizing scheduled takeoff and landing operations under a critical engine failure concept which assures adequate designated surface area and adequate performance capability for continued safe flight in the event of engine failure.

"Category B," with respect to transport category rotorcraft, means single-engine or multiengine rotorcraft which do not fully meet all Category A standards. Category B rotorcraft have no guaranteed stay-up ability in the event of engine failure and unscheduled landing is assumed.

"Ceiling" means the height above the earth's surface of the lowest layer of clouds or obscuring phenomena that is reported as "broken," "overcast," or "obscuration" and not classified as "thin" or "partial."

"Civil aircraft" means aircraft other than public aircraft.

"Class" —

(1) As used with respect to the certification, ratings, privileges, and limitations of airmen, means a classification of aircraft within a category having similar operating characteristics. Examples include: single engine; multiengine; land; water; gyroplane; helicopter; airship; and free balloon; and

(2) As used with respect to the certification of aircraft, means a broad grouping of aircraft having similar characteristics of propulsion, flight or landing. Examples include: airplane; rotorcraft; glider; balloon; landplane and seaplane.

"Clearway" means:

(1) For turbine engine powered airplanes certificated after August 29, 1959, an area beyond the runway, not less than 500 feet wide, centrally located about the extended centerline of the runway, and under the control of the airport authorities. The clearway is expressed in terms of a clearway plane, extending from the end of the runway with an upward slope not exceeding 1.25 percent, above which no object nor any terrain protrudes. However, threshold lights may protrude above the plane if their height above the end of the runway is 26 inches or less and if they are located to each side of the runway.

(2) For turbine engine powered airplanes certificated after September 30, 1958, but before August 30, 1959, an area beyond the takeoff runway extending no less than 300 feet on either side of the extended centerline of the runway, at an elevation no higher than the elevation of the end of the runway, clear of all fixed obstacles, and under the control of the airport authorities.

"Climbout speed," with respect to rotorcraft, means a referenced airspeed which results in a flight path clear of the height-velocity envelope during initial climbout.

"Commercial operator" means a person who, for compensation or hire, engages in the carriage by aircraft in air commerce of persons or property, other than as an air carrier or foreign air carrier or under the authority of *Part 375 of this Title. Where it is doubtful that an operation is for "compensation or hire," the test applied is whether the carriage by air is merely incidental to the person's other business or is, in itself, a major enterprise for profit.

"Controlled airspace" means an airspace of defined dimensions within which air traffic control service is provided to IFR flights and to VFR flights in accordance with the airspace classification.

Note — Controlled airspace is a generic term that covers Class A, Class B, Class C, Class D, and Class E airspace.

"Crewmember" means a person assigned to perform duty in an aircraft during flight time.

"Critical altitude" means the maximum altitude at which, in standard atmosphere, it is possible to maintain, at a specified rotational speed, a specified power or a specified manifold pressure. Unless otherwise stated, the critical altitude is the maximum altitude at which it is possible to maintain, at the maximum continuous rotational speed, one of the following:

(1) The maximum continuous power, in the case of engines for which this power rating is the same at sea level and at the rated altitude.

(2) The maximum continuous rated manifold pressure, in the case of engines, the maximum continuous power of which is governed by a constant manifold pressure.

"Critical engine" means the engine whose failure would most adversely affect the performance or handling qualities of an aircraft.

"Decision height," with respect to the operation of aircraft, means the height at which a decision must be made, during an ILS or PAR instrument approach, to either continue the approach or to execute a missed approach.

"Equivalent airspeed" means the calibrated airspeed of an aircraft corrected for adiabatic compressible flow for the particular altitude. Equivalent airspeed is equal to calibrated airspeed in standard atmosphere at sea level.

"Extended over-water operation" means —

(1) With respect to aircraft other than helicopters, an operation over water at a horizontal distance of more than 50 nautical miles from the nearest shoreline; and

(2) With respect to helicopters, an operation over water at a horizontal distance of more than 50 nautical miles from the nearest shoreline and more than 50 nautical miles from an off-shore heliport structure.

"External load" means a load that is carried, or extends, outside of the aircraft fuselage.

"External-load attaching means" means the structural components used to attach an external load to an aircraft, including external-load containers, the backup structure at the attachment points, and any quick-release device used to jettison the external load.

"Fireproof" —

(1) With respect to materials and parts used to confine fire in a designated fire zone, means the capacity to withstand at least as well as steel in dimensions appropriate for the purpose for which they are used, the heat produced when there is a severe fire of extended duration in that zone; and

(2) With respect to other materials and parts, means the capacity to withstand the heat associated with fire at least as well as steel in dimensions appropriate for the purpose for which they are used.

"Fire resistant" —

(1) With respect to heat or structural members means the capacity to withstand the heat associated with fire at least as well as aluminum alloy in dimensions appropriate for the purpose for which they are used; and

(2) With respect to fluid-carrying lines, fluid system parts, wiring, air ducts, fittings, and powerplant controls, means the capacity to perform the intended functions under the heat and other conditions likely to occur when there is a fire at the place concerned.

"Flame resistant" means not susceptible to combustion to the point of propagating a flame, beyond safe limits, after the ignition source is removed.

"Flammable", with respect to a fluid or gas, means susceptible to igniting readily or to exploding.

"Flap extended speed" means the highest speed permissible with wing flaps in a prescribed extended position.

"Flash resistant" means not susceptible to burning violently when ignited.

"Flight crewmember" means a pilot, flight engineer, or flight navigator assigned to duty in an aircraft during flight time.

"Flight level" means a level of constant atmospheric pressure related to a reference datum of 29.92 inches of mercury. Each is stated in three digits that represent hundreds of feet. For example, flight level 250 represents a barometric altimeter indication of 25,000 feet; flight level 255, an indication of 25,500 feet.

"Flight plan" means specified information, relating to the intended flight of an aircraft, that is filed orally or in writing with air traffic control.

"Flight time" means the time from the moment the aircraft first moves under its own power for the purpose of flight until the moment it comes to rest at the next point of landing. ("Block-to-block" time.)

"Flight visibility" means the average forward horizontal distance, from the cockpit of an aircraft in flight, at which prominent unlighted objects may be seen and identified by day and prominent lighted objects may be seen and identified by night.

"Foreign air carrier" means any person other than a citizen of the United States, who undertakes directly, by lease or other arrangement, to engage in air transportation.

"Foreign air commerce" means the carriage by aircraft of persons or property for compensation or hire, or the carriage of mail by aircraft, or the operation or navigation of aircraft in the conduct or furtherance of a business or vocation, in commerce between a place in the United States and any place outside thereof; whether such commerce moves wholly by aircraft or partly by aircraft and partly by other forms of transportation.

"Foreign air transportation" means the carriage by aircraft of persons or property as a common carrier for compensation or hire, or the carriage of mail by aircraft, in commerce between a place in the United States and any place outside of the United States, whether that commerce moves wholly by aircraft or partly by aircraft and partly by other forms of transportation.

"Forward wing" means a forward lifting surface of a canard configuration or tandem-wing configuration airplane. The surface may be a fixed, movable, or variable geometry surface, with or without control surfaces.

"Glider" means a heavier-than-air aircraft that is supported in flight by the dynamic reaction of the air against its lifting surfaces and whose free flight does not depend principally on an engine.

"Ground visibility" means prevailing horizontal visibility near the earth's surface as reported by the United States National Weather Service or an accredited observer.

"Gyrodyne" means a rotorcraft whose rotors are normally engine-driven for takeoff, hovering, and landing, and for forward flight through part of its speed range, and whose means of propulsion, consisting usually of conventional propellers, is independent of the rotor system.

"Gyroplane" means a rotorcraft whose rotors are not engine-driven except for initial starting, but are made to rotate by action of the air when the rotorcraft is moving; and whose means of propulsion, consisting usually of conventional propellers, is independent of the rotor system.

"Helicopter" means a rotorcraft that, for its horizontal motion, depends principally on its engine-driven rotors.

"Heliport" means an area of land, water, or structure used or intended to be used for the landing and takeoff of helicopters.

"Idle thrust" means the jet thrust obtained with the engine power control lever set at the stop for the least thrust position at which it can be placed.

"IFR conditions" means weather conditions below the minimum for flight under visual flight rules.

"IFR over-the-top," with respect to the operation of aircraft, means the operation of an aircraft over-the-top on an IFR flight plan when cleared by air traffic control to maintain "VFR conditions" or "VFR conditions on top."

"Indicated airspeed" means the speed of an aircraft as shown on its pitot static airspeed indicator calibrated to reflect standard atmosphere adiabatic compressible flow at sea level uncorrected for airspeed system errors.

"Instrument" means a device using an internal mechanism to show visually or aurally the attitude, altitude, or operation of an aircraft or aircraft part. It includes electronic devices for automatically controlling an aircraft in flight.

"Interstate air commerce" means the carriage by aircraft of persons or property for compensation or hire, or the carriage of mail by aircraft, or the operation or navigation of aircraft in the conduct or furtherance of a business or vocation, in commerce between a place in any State of the United States, or the District of Columbia, and a place in any other State of the United States, or the District of Columbia; or between places in the same State of the United States through the airspace over any place outside thereof; or between places in the same territory or possession of the United States, or the District of Columbia.

"Intrastate air transportation" means the carriage of persons or property as a common carrier for compensation or hire, by turbojet-powered aircraft capable of carrying thirty or more persons, wholly within the same State of the United States.

"Interstate air transportation" means the carriage by aircraft of persons or property as a common carrier for compensation or hire, or the carriage of mail by aircraft, in commerce —

(1) Between a place in a State or the District of Columbia and another place in another State or the District of Columbia;

(2) Between places in the same State through the airspace of any place outside that State; or

(3) Between places in the same possession of the United States; whether that commerce moves wholly by aircraft or partly by aircraft and partly by other forms of transportation.

"Kite" means a framework, covered with paper, cloth, metal, or other material, intended to be flown at the end of a rope or cable, and having as its only support the force of the wind moving past its surfaces.

"Landing gear extended speed" means the maximum speed at which an aircraft can be safely flown with the landing gear extended.

"Landing gear operating speed" means the maximum speed at which the landing gear can be safely extended or retracted.

"Large aircraft" means aircraft of more than 12,500 pounds, maximum certificated takeoff weight.

"Lighter-than-air aircraft" means aircraft that can rise and remain suspended by using contained gas weighing less than the air that is displaced by the gas.

"Load factor" means the ratio of a specified load to the total weight of the aircraft. The specified load is expressed in terms of any of the following: aerodynamic forces, inertia forces, or ground or water reactions.

"Mach number" means the ratio of true airspeed to the speed of sound.

"Main rotor" means the rotor that supplies the principal lift to a rotorcraft.

"Maintenance" means inspection, overhaul, repair, preservation, and the replacement of parts, but excludes preventive maintenance.

"Major alteration" means an alteration not listed in the aircraft, aircraft engine, or propeller specifications —

(1) That might appreciably affect weight, balance, structural strength, performance, powerplant operation, flight characteristics, or other qualities affecting airworthiness; or

(2) That is not done according to accepted practices or cannot be done by elementary operations.

"Major repair" means a repair —

(1) That, if improperly done, might appreciably affect weight, balance, structural strength, performance, powerplant operation, flight characteristics, or other qualities affecting airworthiness; or

(2) That is not done according to accepted practices or cannot be done by elementary operations.

"Manifold pressure" means absolute pressure as measured at the appropriate point in the induction system and usually expressed in inches of mercury.

"Medical certificate" means acceptable evidence of physical fitness on a form prescribed by the Administrator.

"Minimum descent altitude" means the lowest altitude, expressed in feet above mean sea level, to which descent is authorized on final approach or during circle-to-land maneuvering in execution of a standard instrument approach procedure, where no electronic glide slope is provided.

"Minor alteration" means an alteration other than a major alteration.

"Minor repair" means a repair other than a major repair.

"Navigable airspace" means airspace at and above the minimum flight altitudes prescribed by or under this chapter, including airspace needed for safe takeoff and landing.

"Night" means the time between the end of evening civil twilight and the beginning of morning civil twilight, as published in the American Air Almanac, converted to local time.

"Nonprecision approach procedure" means a standard instrument approach procedure in which no electronic glide slope is provided.

"Operate," with respect to aircraft, means use, cause to use or authorize to use aircraft, for the purpose (except as provided in §91.13 of this chapter) of air navigation including the piloting of aircraft, with or without the right of legal control (as owner, lessee, or otherwise).

"Operational control," with respect to a flight, means the exercise of authority over initiating, conducting, or terminating a flight.

"Overseas air commerce" means the carriage by aircraft of persons or property for compensation or hire, or the carriage of mail by aircraft, or the operation or navigation of aircraft in the conduct of furtherance of a business or vocation, in commerce between a place in any State of the United States, or the District of Columbia, and any place in a territory or possession of the United States; or between a place in a territory or possession of the United States, and a place in any other territory or possession of the United States.

"Overseas air transportation" means the carriage by aircraft of persons or property as a common carrier for compensation or hire, or the carriage of mail by aircraft, in commerce —

(1) Between a place in a State or the District of Columbia and a place in a possession of the United States; or

(2) Between a place in a possession of the United States and a place in another possession of the United States;

whether that commerce moves wholly by aircraft or partly by aircraft and partly by other forms of transportation.

"Over-the-top" means above the layer of clouds or other obscuring phenomena forming the ceiling.

"Parachute" means a device used or intended to be used to retard the fall of a body or object through the air.

"Person" means an individual, firm, partnership, corporation, company, association, joint-stock association, or governmental entity. It includes a trustee, receiver, assignee, or similar representative of any of them.

"Pilotage" means navigation by visual reference to landmarks.

"Pilot in command" means the pilot responsible for the operation and safety of an aircraft during flight time.

"Pitch setting" means the propeller blade setting as determined by the blade angle measured in a manner, and at a radius, specified by the instruction manual for the propeller.

"Positive control" means control of all air traffic, within designated airspace, by air traffic control.

"Precision approach procedure" means a standard instrument approach procedure in which an electronic glide slope is provided, such as ILS and PAR.

"Preventive maintenance" means simple or minor preservation operations and the replacement of small standard parts not involving complex assembly operations.

"Prohibited area" means designated airspace within which the flight of aircraft is prohibited.

"Propeller" means a device for propelling an aircraft that has blades on an engine- driven shaft and that, when rotated, produces by its action on the air, a thrust approximately perpendicular to its plane of rotation. It includes control components normally supplied by its manufacturer, but does not include main and auxiliary rotors or rotating airfoils of engines.

"Public aircraft" means aircraft used only in the service of a government, or a political subdivision. It does not include any government-owned aircraft engaged in carrying persons or property for commercial purposes.

"Rated continuous OEI power," with respect to rotorcraft turbine engines, means the approved brake horsepower developed under static conditions at specified altitudes and temperatures within the operating limitations established for the engine under *Part 33 of this chapter, and limited in use to the time required to complete the flight after the failure of one engine of a multiengine rotorcraft.

"Rated maximum continuous augmented thrust," with respect to turbojet engine type certification, means the approved jet thrust that is developed statically or in flight, in standard atmosphere at a specified altitude, with fluid injection or with the burning of fuel in a separate combustion chamber, within the engine operating limitations established under *Part 33, and approved for unrestricted periods of use.

"Rated maximum continuous power," with respect to reciprocating, turbopropeller, and turboshaft engines, means the approved brake horsepower that is developed statically or in flight, in standard atmosphere at a specified altitude, within the engine operating limitations established under *Part 33, and approved for unrestricted periods of use.

"Rated maximum continuous thrust," with respect to turbojet engine type certification, means the approved jet thrust that is developed statically or in flight, in standard atmosphere at a specified altitude, without fluid injection and without the burning of fuel in a separate combustion chamber, within the engine operating limitations established under *Part 33 of this chapter, and approved for unrestricted periods of use.

"Rated takeoff augmented thrust," with respect to turbojet engine type certification, means the approved jet thrust that is developed statically under standard sea level conditions, with fluid injection or with the burning of fuel in a separate combustion chamber, within the engine operating limitations established under *Part 33 of this chapter, and limited in use to periods of not over 5 minutes for takeoff operation.

"Rated takeoff power," with respect to reciprocating, turbopropeller, and turboshaft engine type certification, means the approved brake horsepower that is developed statically under standard sea level conditions, within the engine operating limitations established under *Part 33, and limited in use to periods of not over 5 minutes for takeoff operation.

"Rated takeoff thrust," with respect to turbojet engine type certification, means the approved jet thrust that is developed statically under standard sea level conditions, without fluid injection and without the burning of fuel in a separate combustion chamber, within the engine operating limitations established under *Part 33 of this chapter, and limited in use to periods of not over 5 minutes for takeoff operation.

"Rated 30-minute OEI power", with respect to rotorcraft turbine engines, means the approved brake horsepower developed under static conditions at specified altitudes and temperatures within the operating limitations established for the engine under *Part 33 of this chapter, and limited in use to a period of not more than 30 minutes after the failure of one engine of a multiengine rotorcraft.

"Rated 21/2-minute OEI power", with respect to rotorcraft turbine engines, means the brake horsepower developed under static conditions at specified altitudes and temperatures within the operating limitations established for the engine under *Part 33 of this chapter, and limited in use to a period of not more than 21/2 minutes after the failure of one engine of a multiengine rotorcraft.

"Rating" means a statement that, as a part of a certificate, sets forth special conditions, privileges, or limitations.

"Reporting point" means a geographical location in relation to which the position of an aircraft is reported.

"Restricted area" means airspace designated under *Part 73 of this chapter within which the flight of aircraft, while not wholly prohibited, is subject to restriction.

"RNAV waypoint (W/P)" means a predetermined geographical position used for route or instrument approach definition or progress reporting purposes that is defined relative to a VORTAC station position.

"Rocket" means an aircraft propelled by ejected expanding gases generated in the engine from self-contained propellants and not dependent on the intake of outside substances. It includes any part which becomes separated during the operation.

"Rotorcraft" means a heavier-than-air aircraft that depends principally for its support in flight on the lift generated by one or more rotors.

"Rotorcraft-load combination" means the combination of a rotorcraft and an external load, including the external load attaching means. Rotorcraft-load combinations are designated as Class A, Class B, Class C, and Class D, as follows:

(1) "Class A rotorcraft-load combination" means one in which the external load cannot move freely, cannot be jettisoned, and does not extend below the landing gear.
(2) "Class B rotorcraft-load combination" means one in which the external load is jettisonable and is lifted free of land or water during the rotorcraft operations.
(3) "Class C rotorcraft-load combination" means one in which the external load is jettisonable and remains in contact with land or water during the rotorcraft operation.
(4) "Class D rotorcraft-load combination" means one in which the external- load is other than a Class A, B, or C and has been specifically approved by the Administrator for that operation.

"Route segment" means a part of a route. Each end of that part is identified by —

(1) a continental or insular geographical location; or
(2) a point at which a definite radio fix can be estabished.

"Sea level engine" means a reciprocating aircraft engine having a rated takeoff power that is producible only at sea level.

"Second in command" means a pilot who is designated to be second in command of an aircraft during flight time.

"Show," unless the context otherwise requires, means to show to the satisfaction of the Administrator.

"Small aircraft" means aircraft of 12,500 pounds or less, maximum certificated takeoff weight.

"Special VFR conditions" means meteorological conditions that are less than those required for basic VFR fight in controlled airspace and in which some aircraft are permitted flight under visual flight rules.

"Special VFR operations" means aircraft operating in accordance with clearances within controlled airspace in meteorological conditions less than the basic VFR weather minima. Such operations must be requested by the pilot and approved by ATC.

"Standard atmosphere" means the atmosphere defined in *U.S. Standard Atmosphere, 1962* (Geopotential altitude tables).

"Stopway" means an area beyond the takeoff runway, no less wide than the runway and centered upon the extended centerline of the runway, able to support the airplane during an aborted takeoff, without causing structural damage to the airplane, and designated by the airport authorities for use in decelerating the airplane during an aborted takeoff.

"Takeoff power" —

(1) With respect to reciprocating engines, means the brake horsepower that is developed under standard sea level conditions, and under the maximum conditions of crankshaft rotational speed and engine manifold pressure approved for the normal takeoff, and limited in continuous use to the period of time shown in the approved engine specification; and

(2) With respect to turbine engines, means the brake horsepower that is developed under static conditions at a specified altitude and atmospheric temperature, and under the maximum conditions of rotorshaft rotational speed and gas temperature approved for the normal takeoff, and limited in continuous use to the period of time shown in the approved engine specification.

"Takeoff safety speed" means a referenced airspeed obtained after lift-off at which the required one-engine-inoperative climb performance can be achieved.

"Takeoff thrust," with respect to turbine engines, means the jet thrust that is developed under static conditions at a specific altitude and atmospheric temperature under the maximum conditions of rotorshaft rotational speed and gas temperature approved for the normal takeoff, and limited in continuous use to the period of time shown in the approved engine specification.

"Tandem wing configuration" means a configuration having two wings of similar span, mounted in tandem.

"TCAS I" means a TCAS that utilizes interrogations of, and replies from, airborne radar beacon transponders and provides traffic advisories to the pilot.

"TCAS II" means a TCAS that utilizes interrogations of, and replies from airborne radar beacon transponders and provides traffic advisories and resolution advisories in the vertical plane.

"TCAS III" means a TCAS that utilizes interrogation of, and replies from, airborne radar beacon transponders and provides traffic advisories and resolution advisories in the vertical and horizontal planes to the pilot.

"Time in service," with respect to maintenance time records, means the time from the moment an aircraft leaves the surface of the earth until it touches it at the next point of landing.

"Traffic pattern" means the traffic flow that is prescribed for aircraft landing at, taxiing on, or taking off from, an airport.

"True airspeed" means the airspeed of an aircraft relative to undisturbed air. True airspeed is equal to equivalent airspeed multiplied by $(\rho o/\rho)^{1/2}$.

"Type" —

(1) As used with respect to the certification, ratings, privileges, and limitations of airmen, means a specific make and basic model of aircraft, including modifications thereto that do not change its handling or flight characteristics. Examples include: DC-7, 1049, and F-27; and

(2) As used with respect to the certification of aircraft, means those aircraft which are similar in design. Examples include: DC-7 and DC-7C; 1049G and 1049H; and F-27 and F-27F.

(3) As used with respect to the certification of aircraft engines, means those engines which are similar in design. For example, JT8D and JT8D-7 are engines of the same type, and JT9D-3A and JT9D-7 are engines of the same type.

"United States," in a geographical sense, means (1) the States, the District of Columbia, Puerto Rico, and the possessions, including the territorial waters, and (2) the airspace of those areas.

"United States air carrier" means a citizen of the United States who undertakes directly by lease, or other arrangement, to engage in air transportation.

"VFR over-the-top," with respect to the operation of aircraft, means the operation of an aircraft over-the-top under VFR when it is not being operated on an IFR flight plan.

"Winglet or tip fin" means an out-of-plane surface extending from a lifting surface. The surface may or may not have control surfaces.

1.2 ABBREVIATIONS AND SYMBOLS

In Subchapters A through K of this chapter:

AGL means above ground level.
ALS means approach light system.
ASR means airport surveillance radar.
ATC means air traffic control.
CAS means calibrated airspeed.
CAT II means Category II.
CONSOL or CONSOLAN means a kind of low or medium frequency long range navigational aid.
DH means decision height.
DME means distance measuring equipment compatible with TACAN.
EAS means equivalent airspeed.
FAA means Federal Aviation Administration.
FM means fan marker.
GS means glide slope.
HIRL means high-intensity runway light system.
IAS means indicated airspeed.
ICAO means International Civil Aviation Organization.
IFR means instrument flight rules.
ILS means instrument landing system.
IM means ILS inner marker.
INT means intersection.
LDA means localizer-type directional aid.
LFR means low-frequency radio range.
LMM means compass locator at middle marker.
LOC means ILS localizer.
LOM means compass locator at outer marker.
M means mach number.
MAA means maximum authorized IFR altitude.
MALS means medium intensity approach light system.
MALSR means medium intensity approach light system with runway alignment indicator lights.
MCA means minimum crossing altitude.
MDA means minimum descent altitude.
MEA means minimum enroute IFR altitude.
MM means ILS middle marker.
MOCA means minimum obstruction clearance altitude.

MRA means minimum reception altitude.
MSL means mean sea level.
NDB(ADF) means nondirectional beacon (automatic direction finder).
NOPT means no procedure turn required.
OEI means one engine inoperative.
OM means ILS outer marker.
PAR means precision approach radar.
RAIL means runway alignment indicator light system.
RBN means radio beacon.
RCLM means runway centerline marking.
RCLS means runway centerline light system.
REIL means runway end identification lights.
RR means low or medium frequency radio range station.
RVR means runway visual range as measured in the touchdown zone area.
SALS means short approach light system.
SSALS means simplified short approach light system.
SSALSR means simplified short approach light system with runway alignment indicator lights.
TACAN means ultra-high frequency tactical air navigational aid.
TAS means true airspeed.
TCAS means a traffic alert and collision avoidance system.
TDZL means touchdown zone lights.
TVOR means very high frequency terminal omnirange station.
V_A means design maneuvering speed.
V_B means design speed for maximum gust intensity.
V_C means design cruising speed.
V_D means design diving speed.
V_{DF}/M_{DF} means demonstrated flight diving speed.
V_F means design flap speed.
V_{FC}/M_{FC} means maximum speed for stability characteristics.
V_{FE} means maximum flap extended speed.
V_H means maximum speed in level flight with maximum continuous power.
V_{LE} means maximum landing gear extended speed.
V_{LO} means maximum landing gear operating speed.
V_{LOF} means lift-off speed.
V_{MC} means minimum control speed with the critical engine inoperative.
V_{MO}/M_{MO} means maximum operating limit speed.
V_{MU} means minimum unstick speed.
V_{NE} means never-exceed speed.
V_{NO} means maximum structural cruising speed.
V_R means rotation speed.

V_S	means the stalling speed or the minimum steady flight speed at which the airplane is controllable.
V_{S_0}	means the stalling speed or the minimum steady flight speed in the landing configuration.
V_{S_1}	means the stalling speed or the minimum steady flight speed obtained in a specified configuration.
V_{TOSS}	means takeoff safety speed for Category A rotorcraft.
V_X	means speed for best angle of climb.
V_Y	means speed for best rate of climb.
V_1	means takeoff decision speed (formerly denoted as critical engine failure speed).
V_2	means takeoff safety speed.
$V_{2\,min}$	means minimum takeoff safety speed.
VFR	means visual flight rules.
VHF	means very high frequency.
VOR	means very high frequency omnirange station.
VORTAC	means collocated VOR and TACAN.

1.3 RULES OF CONSTRUCTION

(a) In Subchapter A through K of this chapter, unless the context requires otherwise:
  (1) Words importing the singular include the plural;
  (2) Words importing the plural include the singular; and
  (3) Words importing the masculine gender include the feminine.
(b) In Subchapters A through K of this chapter, the word:
  (1) "Shall" is used in an imperative sense:
  (2) "May" is used in a permissive sense to state authority or permission to do the act prescribed, and the words "no person may . . ." or "a person may not . . ." mean that no person is required, authorized, or permitted to do the act prescribed; and
  (3) "includes" means "includes but is not limited to."

FEDERAL AVIATION REGULATIONS

PART 135 AIR TAXI OPERATORS AND COMMERCIAL OPERATORS

TABLE OF CONTENTS

SUBPART A — GENERAL

TABLE OF CONTENTS

SUBPART B — FLIGHT OPERATIONS

TABLE OF CONTENTS

SUBPART B — FLIGHT OPERATIONS (cont)

SUBPART C — AIRCRAFT AND EQUIPMENT

TABLE OF CONTENTS

SUBPART C — AIRCRAFT AND EQUIPMENT (Cont)

SUBPART D — VFR/IFR OPERATING LIMITATIONS AND WEATHER REQUIREMENTS

TABLE OF CONTENTS

SUBPART E — FLIGHT CREWMEMBER REQUIREMENTS

SUBPART F — FLIGHT CREWMEMBER FLIGHT TIME LIMITATIONS AND REST REQUIREMENTS

SUBPART G — CREWMEMBER TESTING REQUIREMENTS

TABLE OF CONTENTS

SUBPART H — TRAINING

SUBPART I — AIRPLANE PERFORMANCE OPERATING LIMITATIONS

TABLE OF CONTENTS

SUBPART I — AIRPLANE PERFORMANCE OPERATING LIMITATIONS (cont)

TABLE OF CONTENTS

SUBPART J — MAINTENANCE, PREVENTIVE MAINTENANCE, AND ALTERATIONS

SUBPART A — GENERAL

135.1 APPLICABILITY

(a) Except as provided in paragraph (b) of this section, this part prescribes rules governing —
  (1) Air taxi operations conducted under the exemption authority of Part 298 of this title;
  (2) The transportation of mail by aircraft conducted under a postal service contract awarded under §5402c of Title 39, United States Code;
  (3) The carriage in air commerce of persons or property for compensation or hire as a commercial operator (not an air carrier) in aircraft having a maximum seating capacity of less than 20 passengers or a maximum payload capacity of less than 6,000 pounds, or the carriage in air commerce of persons or property in common carriage operations solely between points entirely within any state of the United States in aircraft having a maximum seating capacity of 30 seats or less or a maximum payload capacity of 7,500 pounds or less; and
  (4) Each person who applies for provisional approval of an Advanced Qualification Program curriculum, curriculum segment, or portion of a curriculum segment under SFAR No. 58 and each person employed or used by an air carrier or commercial operator under this part to perform training, qualification, or evaluation functions under an Advanced Qualification Program under SFAR No. 58; and
  (5) Each person who is on board an aircraft being operated under this part.

(b) Except as provided in paragraph (c) of this section, this part does not apply to —
  (1) Student instruction;
  (2) Nonstop sightseeing flights that begin and end at the same airport, and are conducted within a 25 statute mile radius of that airport;
  (3) Ferry or training flights;
  (4) Aerial work operations, including —
    (i) Crop dusting, seeding, spraying, and bird chasing;
    (ii) Banner towing;
    (iii) Aerial photography or survey;
    (iv) Fire fighting;
    (v) Helicopter operations in construction or repair work (but not including transportation to and from the site of operations); and
    (vi) Powerline or pipeline patrol, or similar types of patrol approved by the Administrator;
  (5) Sightseeing flights conducted in hot air balloons;
  (6) Nonstop flights conducted within a 25 statute mile radius of the airport of takeoff carrying persons for the purpose of intentional parachute jumps;

(7) Helicopter flights conducted within a 25 statute mile radius of the airport of takeoff, if —
   (i) Not more than two passengers are carried in the helicopter in addition to the required flight crew;
   (ii) Each flight is made under VFR during the day;
   (iii) The helicopter used is certificated in the standard category and complies with the 100-hour inspection requirements of Part 91 of this chapter;
   (iv) The operator notifies the FAA Flight Standards District Office responsible for the geographic area concerned at least 72 hours before each flight and furnishes any essential information that the office requests;
   (v) The number of flights does not exceed a total of six in any calendar year;
   (vi) Each flight has been approved by the Administrator; and
   (vii) Cargo is not carried in or on the helicopter;
(8) Operations conducted under Part 133 or 375 of this title;
(9) Emergency mail service conducted under §405(h) of the Federal Aviation Act of 1958; or
(10) The Part does not apply to operations conducted under the provisions of §91.321.

(c) For the purpose of §§135.249, 135.251, 135.253, 135.255, and 135.353, *operator* means any person or entity conducting non-stop sightseeing flights for compensation or hire in an airplane or rotorcraft that begin and end at the same airport and are conducted within a 25 statute mile radius of that airport.

(d) Notwithstanding the provisions of this Part and Appendices I and J to Part 121 of this chapter, an operator who does not hold a Part 121 or Part 135 certificate is permitted to use a person who is otherwise authorized to perform aircraft maintenance or preventive maintenance duties and who is not subject to FAA-approved anti-drug and alcohol misuse prevention programs to perform —
(1) Aircraft maintenance or preventive maintenance on the operator's aircraft if the operator would otherwise be required to transport the aircraft more than 50 nautical miles further than the repair point closest to operator's principal place of operation to obtain these services; or
(2) Emergency repairs on the operator's aircraft if the aircraft cannot be safely operated to a location where an employee subject to FAA-approved programs can perform the repairs.

EXPLANATION

Selling a Part 135 Operation: the FAA takes the position that a certificate issued under Part 135 is not the certificate holder's asset. The certificate alone cannot be sold. Thus, if a certificate holder decides to sell all of its assets, the purchaser, if desiring to continue to operate under Part 135, must apply for a new certificate. However, if the entity that holds the certificate is a corporation which remains intact and there is a transfer of the ownership of the stock only, recertification is not required because of the stock transfer. In other words, you can sell the whole charter corporation, but not the charter certificate. However, the Federal Aviation Administration should be advised of such a stock sale.

§135.1(b): §91.501 outlines several types of "for hire" operations which may not constitute "common carriage" and do not require a certificate under Part 135 or Part 121. Any arrangement in which airplane **and** crew are provided by a single entity for any type of reimbursement should be carefully reviewed.

§135.1(b)(7) applies to special helicopter flights, such as Santa Claus flights. Insofar as sightseeing flights by a helicopter, 135(b)(2) applies to all sightseeing flights.

All operations listed in §135.1(b), while not requiring a certificate under Part 135, may, in fact, be flights for compensation or hire. Accordingly, there may be insurance or tax ramifications. Discuss your plans with your insurance agent/broker and attorney or other tax consultant.

Operators of nonstop sightseeing flights for compensation or hire in an airplane or rotorcraft that begin and end at the same airport and are conducted within a 25-mile radius of that airport are subject to the provisions of the Anti-Drug and Alcohol Misuse Prevention Programs, except as provided for in §135.1(d)(1) & (2).

Although a person applying for provisional approval of an Advanced Qualification Program (AQP) curriculum, curriculum segment, or portion of a curriculum segment under SFAR No. 58 and each person employed or used by a certificate holder to perform the functions required by an AQP are subject to the provisions of Part 135, they are not considered as certificate holders and hold the same status as a maintenance facility that provides service to a Part 135 certificate holder.

If operations are to be conducted outside the United States, familiarity with the pertinent annexes of the International Civil Aviation Organization (ICAO) and the aviation regulations, customs laws, etc., of the concerned country is essential. Information on ICAO publications can be obtained by writing to Public Information Office, International Civil Aviation Organization, 1000 Sherbrooke Street West, Suite 400, Montreal, Quebec, Canada H3A, 2R2.

Part 135 operators conducting interstate common carriage will be issued air carrier certificates, while those conducting intrastate common carriage or interstate or intrastate private carriage will be issued operating certificates.

Common carriage means any operation for compensation or hire in which the operator holds itself out, by advertising or any other means, as willing to furnish transportation for any member of the public who seeks the service the operator is offering. Private carriage does not involve offering or holding out by the operator through advertising or any other means. (See: Advisory Circular 120-12A, Private Carriage Versus Common Carriage of Persons or Property (4-24-86).)

Dead bodies are considered "property." Therefore, the transportation of corpses for compensation or hire requires that the operator hold an appropriate Part 135 certificate.

Prior to obtaining a certificate, an applicant for a Part 135 certificate should use caution in entering into contracts that call for commencement of the flights on a specific date. Should the certification process take longer than anticipated, the applicant will not be able to meet its obligations by providing the service at no cost since the economic advantage, retaining the customer, of conducting such flights will bring them under Part 135.

Applicants for Part 135 certificates desiring to operate on a small scale (single pilot, single pilot-in-command, or Basic Part 135) are not required to comply with all the requirements for manuals, training programs, and management positions.

It must be understood that the test referred to in the definition of "commercial operator," i.e. "whether the carriage by air is merely incidental to the person's other business or is, in itself, a major enterprise for profit," comes into play only if there is some doubt that the operation is for "compensation or hire." If there is clear evidence that "compensation or hire" is involved, this test is not necessary and, accordingly, is not applied, unless the operation is conducted under §91.501 or a §135.1(b) exception.

Air ambulance operations (previously known as "emergency medical services"), both helicopter and airplane, are presently conducted under Part 135. Such operators are issued Operations Specifications unique to their operations. Air ambulance operators must comply with all the requirements of the regulations under which they are certified.

CROSS REFERENCES

91.501, Applicability; 135.2(b), Air Taxi Operations with Large Aircraft; 135.3, Rules Applicable to Operations Subject to this Part; 135.5, Certificate and Operations Specifications Required; 135.87(c), Carriage of Cargo Including Carry-on Baggage; 135.91, Oxygen for Medical Use by Passengers; 135.249, Use of Prohibited Drugs; 135.251, Testing for Prohibited Drugs; 135.253, Misuse of Alcohol; 135.255, Testing for Alcohol; 135.271, Helicopter Hospital Emergency Medical Evacuation Service (HEMES); 135.327, Training Program: Curriculum; 135.353, Prohibited Drugs; 135.423, Maintenance, Preventive Maintenance, and Alteration Organization; 135.425, Maintenance, Preventive Maintenance, and Alteration Programs; 135.437, Authority to Perform and Approve Maintenance, Preventive Maintenance and Alterations.

Part 133, Rotorcraft External-Load Operations; 49 U.S.C. 405(h); Part 298, Exemptions for Air Taxi and Commuter Air Carrier Operations (DOT); 39 U.S.C. 5402(c); Special Federal Aviation Regulation (SFAR) No. 38-2, Certificate and Operating Requirements; Special Federal Aviation Regulation (SFAR) No. 58, Advanced Qualification Program; ICAO ANNEX 2; ICAO ANNEX 6; Appendix I, Part 121, Drug Testing Program; Appendix J, Part 121, Alcohol Misuse Prevention Program.

"Air Ambulance Guidelines" published by U.S. Department of Transportation, National Highway Traffic Safety Administration and American Medical Association Commission on Emergency Medical Services.

ADVISORY CIRCULARS

AC 120-12A *Private Carriage Versus Common Carriage of Persons or Property* (1986).

AC 120-49 *Certification of Air Carriers* (1988).

AC 135-13A *List of Air Carriers Certificated by FAR Part 135* (1992).

AC 135-14A *Emergency Medical Services/Helicopter (EMS/H)* (1991).

AC 135-15 *Emergency Medical Services/Airplane (EMS/A)* (1990).

Information Packet on How to Become a Certificated Air Carrier
(Published by FAA and available at Flight Standards District Offices)

NTSB DECISIONS

Board held that, even assuming respondent did not realize a profit from the flights (or even assuming he operated them at a loss), it is well-established that intangible benefits, such as good will or the expectation of future economic benefits, can render a flight one for "compensation or hire." *Administrator v. Platt,* EA-4012 (11-17-93).

Obtaining of both a flight crew and an airplane from the same source (a wet lease) is usually considered conclusive evidence of carriage for compensation or hire. *Administrator v. Poirier,* 5 NTSB 1928 (1987); *Administrator v. Cason and H & H Air Services, Inc. d/b/a Cal-Todd Aviation,* 5 NTSB 741 (1985); *Administrator v. Platt,* EA-4012 (1993).

Where operator, on reaching destination and finding weather below Part 135 landing minimums, offered to refund the fares paid by the passenger and conduct a "look see" approach and land or execute a missed approach, the Board held that conversion to Part 91 could not be made where sole purpose was to avoid the instrument landing minimums applicable to Part 135. The Board also stated that expectancy of future business alone may be sufficient to make a flight for which there was no direct compensation subject to Part 135. *Administrator v. Cunningham,* 5 NTSB 516 (1985).

The Board has consistently held that a flight can be for compensation or hire even though a profit is not made and, in fact, a loss is incurred. See e.g. *Administrator v. Reimer*, 3 NTSB 2306 (1980); *Administrator v. Plowman*, 5 NTSB 957, Footnote (1986).

The Board found that the flight was conducted under a contract between respondent's employer (Advanced Aviation Services) and Purolater, Inc., and that even though no actual payment was made for the flight, it was for compensation or hire (and therefore governed by Part 135) because of the effect on future operations under the contract. *Administrator v. Rasmussen*, 5 NTSB 1680 (1987).

An operator had a contract to transport checks and other documents. It acquired an aircraft to accomplish the work under the contract, but, by reason of problems encountered in adding the aircraft to its operating certificate, the aircraft was not available on the start date of the contract. The operator fulfilled its obligations under the contract but made no charge for the services. The Board held that conduct of the flights ensured the continuation of the contract and, accordingly, was to the economic advantage of the operator. This was sufficient to make the flights ones for compensation or hire. *Administrator v. Blackburn,* 4 NTSB 409 (1982).

The Board has held that cadavers are "property" and their carriage for compensation is covered by Part 135. Also, it has held that an operation for compensation or hire need not involve a profit and "community service" is not an exception to the applicability of Part 135. *Administrator v. Ferguson,* 4 NTSB 488 (1982).

If a pilot knows prior to departure that, in addition to aerial photography, the passengers also desire a landing, the flight is not exempt from Part 135. However, where a pilot hired for aerial photography finds out only in the air that the passengers desire a landing, the aerial photography exception applied. *Administrator v. Southeast Air, et al.,* 4 NTSB 517 (1982); *Administrator v. Bryan*, 4 NTSB 1166 (1983); *Henderson v. Federal Aviation Administration*, et al., 7 F3d 875 (9th Cir. 1993).

FAA CHIEF COUNSEL OPINIONS

Where restaurant owner offers a package deal that includes transportation to and from the restaurant in the restaurant's helicopter and dinner, and the price for the package includes the cost of the transportation, the restaurant must hold a Part 135 operating certificate. (11-7-77).

A Part 135 passenger carrying operator who conducts operations solely within one state is not an air carrier as defined in the Federal Aviation Act. Consequently, such operator is not subject to the operating rules which are limited in applicability by the term "commuter air carrier." However, the conduct of flights between two points in the same state which go over areas beyond the 3-mile international boundary limit may result in a finding that the operator is engaging in interstate transportation. (11-27-79). [Editor's Note: The 3 miles would now be 12 miles. [See 91.1(b)]].

The "aerial photography or survey" exception of §135.1(b)(4)(iii) does not apply if the aircraft lands at a site other than its origin. A prudent operator should inquire before the commencement of the flight to determine what is contemplated by the passengers. Having so inquired, the operator can determine what rules apply. (4-7-89, 4-12-89, 4-28-90) [Editor's Note: If the landing is solely for the purpose of refueling and/or physiological reasons, it probably would not result in the flight being determined to be subject to the requirements of Part 135.]

In the case of the carriage of law enforcement personnel to provide aerial surveillance for a marijuana eradication program, if the sole purpose is to spot marijuana, it may come within the exception relating to "aerial survey" or "powerline or pipeline patrol, or similar types of patrol approved by the Administrator." However, if the operation includes transporting an individual to a meeting place to coordinate the search with others; or landing in a field to obtain samples; or landing to allow the officer on board to perform an investigatory function, then transportation, rather than surveillance, becomes the primary purpose of the flight and a Part 135 certificate is required. (6-26-89).

When an Emergency Medical Service helicopter is owned and operated by a hospital, which holds a Part 135 certificate, and all personnel, pilot and medical personnel, on board are employees of the hospital, operation without a patient on board could be conducted under Part 91. (6-7-90). [CAUTION: See §135.271 regarding relationship of such flights to flight and duty time limitations.]

When an aircraft is owned and operated by a Part 135 certificate holder under a contract to a hospital or hospitals and the pilots are employees of the certificate holder with the medical personnel being employees of the hospital, whether operation without a patient on board can be conducted under Part 91 depends on the status of the medical personnel. If the medical personnel meet the requirements of the definition of a crewmember as set forth in Part 1, "a person assigned to perform duty in an aircraft during flight time," then it could be conducted under Part 91. If they do not come within the definition, they would be considered passengers and, if the certificate holder is receiving any compensation or benefit from the carriage, it must be conducted under Part 135. (6-7-90). [CAUTION: See §135.271 regarding relationship of such flights to flight and duty time limitations.]

The Federal Aviation Administration takes the position that operations conducted for compensation or hire are conducted for commercial purposes requiring an appropriate certificate issued by the Administrator, regardless of what entity conducts the operations. (6-8-90).

Operation of the aircraft solely for the carriage of human remains and their disposal during flight is an aerial operation within the scope of §135.1(b)(4). (4-3-78).

Where a flight is a direct inducement for a raffle solicitation, the flight is a charter type flight. If the length of the flight removed it from the exemption provisions of §135.1(b)(2), an appropriate Part 135 certificate is required. (5-26-87).

135.2 AIR TAXI OPERATIONS WITH LARGE AIRCRAFT

(a) Except as provided in paragraph (d) of this section, no person may conduct air taxi operations in large aircraft under an individual exemption and authorization issued by the Civil Aeronautics Board or under the exemption authority of Part 298 of this title, unless that person —
   (1) Complies with the certification requirements for supplemental air carriers in Part 121 of this chapter, except that the person need not obtain, and that person is not eligible for, a certificate under that part; and
   (2) Conducts those operations under the rules of Part 121 of this chapter that apply to supplemental air carriers.
   However, the Administrator may issue Operations Specifications which require an operator to comply with the rules of Part 121 of this chapter that apply to domestic or flag air carriers, as appropriate, in place of the rules required by paragraph (a)(2) of this section, if the Administrator determines compliance with those rules is necessary to provide an appropriate level of safety for the operation.

(b) The holder of an operating certificate issued under this part who is required to comply with Subpart L of Part 121 of this chapter, under paragraph (a) of this section, may perform and approve maintenance, preventive maintenance, and alterations on aircraft having a maximum passenger seating configuration, excluding any pilot seat, of 30 seats or less and a maximum payload capacity of 7,500 pounds or less as provided in that subpart. The aircraft so maintained shall be identified by registration number in the Operations Specifications of the certificate holder using the aircraft.

(c) Operations that are subject to paragraph (a) of this section are not subject to §§135.21 through 135.43 of Subpart A and Subparts B through J of this part. Seaplanes used in operations that are subject to paragraph (a) of this section are not subject to §121.29(a) of this chapter.

(d) Operations conducted with aircraft having a maximum passenger seating configuration, excluding any pilot seat, of 30 seats or less, and a maximum payload capacity of 7,500 pounds or less shall be conducted under the rules of this part. However, a certificate holder who is conducting operations on December 1, 1978, in aircraft described in this paragraph may continue to operate under paragraph (a) of this section.

(e) For the purposes of this part —

(10) "Maximum payload capacity" means:

(i) For an aircraft for which a maximum zero fuel weight is prescribed in FAA technical specifications, the maximum zero fuel weight, less empty weight less all justifiable aircraft equipment, and less the operating load (consisting of minimum flight crew, foods and beverages and supplies and equipment related to foods and beverages, but not including disposable fuel or oil);

(ii) For all other aircraft, the maximum certificated takeoff weight of an aircraft, less the empty weight, less all justifiable aircraft equipment, and less the operating load (consisting of minimum fuel load, oil, and flight crew). The allowance for the weight of the crew, oil, and fuel is as follows:

(A) Crew — 200 pounds for each crewmember required under this chapter.

(B) Oil — 350 pounds.

(C) Fuel — the minimum weight of fuel required under this chapter for a flight between domestic points 174 nautical miles apart under VFR weather conditions that do not involve extended overwater operations.

(2) "Empty weight" means the weight of the airframe, engines, propellers, rotors, and fixed equipment. Empty weight excludes the weight of the crew and payload, but includes the weight of all fixed ballast, unusable fuel supply, undrainable oil, total quantity of engine coolant, and total quantity of hydraulic fluid.

(3) "Maximum zero fuel weight" means the maximum permissible weight of an aircraft with no disposable fuel or oil. The zero fuel weight figure may be found in either the aircraft type certificate data sheet or the approved Aircraft Flight Manual, or both.

(4) For the purposes of this paragraph, "justifiable aircraft equipment" means any equipment necessary for the operation of the aircraft. It does not include equipment or ballast specifically installed, permanently or otherwise, for the purpose of altering the empty weight of an aircraft to meet the maximum payload capacity specified in paragraph (d) of this section.

EXPLANATION

Definitions in this section are identical to those in SFAR 38-2 relating to certification and operating requirements.

The Department of Transportation now has the responsibility of issuing exemptions under 14 CFR Part 298.

Part 1 defines a "large aircraft" as an aircraft of more than 12,500 pounds, maximum certificated takeoff weight. This definition is governing insofar as the Federal Aviation Regulations, not the definition of "large aircraft" as set forth in 14 CFR Part 298.

CROSS REFERENCES

91.605, Transport Category Civil Airplane Weight Limitations; 135.5, Certificate and Operations Specifications Required; 135.11(b)(2)(iii) and (iv), Application and Issue of Certificate and Operations Specifications; 135.63, Recordkeeping Requirements; 135.71, Airworthiness Check; 135.73, Inspection and Tests; 135.149, Equipment Requirements: General; 135.169, Additional Airworthiness Requirements; 135.181, Performance Requirements: Aircraft Operated Over-the-Top or in IFR Conditions; 135.183, Performance Requirements: Land Aircraft Operated Over Water; 135.185, Empty Weight and Center of Gravity: Currency Requirement; 135.209, VFR: Fuel Supply; 135.365, Large Transport Category Airplanes: Reciprocating Engine Powered: Weight Limitations; 135.437, Authority to Perform and Approve Maintenance, Preventive Maintenance, and Alterations; Special Federal Aviation Regulation (SFAR) No. 38-2, Certification and Operating Requirements; Part 121, Certification and Operations: Domestic, Flag, and Supplemental Air Carriers and Commercial Operators of Large Aircraft; Part 205, Aircraft Accident Liability Insurance (DOT); Part 298, Exemptions For Air Taxi and Commuter Air Carrier Operations (DOT).

ADVISORY CIRCULARS

AC 91-56 *Supplemental Structural Inspection Program for Large Transport Category Airplanes* (1981).

AC 120-30 *Reporting Requirements of Air Carriers, Commercial Operators, Travel Clubs, and Air Traffic* (1976).

AC 120-33 *Operational Approval of Airborne Long-Range Navigation Systems for Flight Within the North Atlantic Minimum Navigation Performance Specifications Airspace* (1977).

AC 120-37 *Operational and Airworthiness Approval of Airborne Omega Radio Navigational Systems as a Sole Means of Long Range Navigation Outside the United States* (1978).

AC 120-55A *Air Carrier Operational Approval and Use of TCAS II* (1993).

AC 120-58 *Pilot Guide for Large Aircraft Ground Deicing* (1992).

AC 125-1 *Operations of Large Airplanes Subject to Federal Aviation Regulations Part* 125 (1981).

FAA CHIEF COUNSEL OPINIONS

A Part 121 certificate holder may not perform maintenance on a Part 135 operator's large aircraft that is required to be maintained in accordance with Subpart L of Part 121. Thus §121.379 does not apply to air taxi operators since they are not eligible for a certificate under Part 121. (4-10-75).

The provisions of §121.59 are applicable to a Part 135.2 operator operating aircraft having a maximum passenger seating configuration of more than 30 seats, excluding any pilot seat, and a maximum payload capacity of more than 7,500 pounds. Accordingly, a Director of Maintenance, who would be available "as needed" after 3:30PM each day and on his days off, would not be acceptable in view of the full time requirement of §121.59. (1-28-76).

[Editor's Note: Both of these opinions were issued before the rewrite of Part 135 in 1978, but they still appear to be valid.]

135.3 RULES APPLICABLE TO OPERATIONS SUBJECT TO THIS PART

Each person operating an aircraft in operations under this part shall —

(a) While operating inside the United States, comply with the applicable rules of this chapter; and

(b) While operating outside the United States, comply with Annex 2, Rules of the Air, to the Convention on International Civil Aviation or the regulations of any foreign country, whichever applies, and with any rules of Parts 61 and 91 of this chapter and this part that are more restrictive than that Annex or those regulations and that can be complied with without violating that Annex or those regulations. Annex 2 is incorporated by reference in §91.703(b) of this chapter.

EXPLANATION

The requirements of §135.3(b) emphasize the importance of proper preparation for flights conducted outside the United States.

Except where the regulation specifically exempts them, Part 135 operators must comply with all the Federal Aviation Regulations applicable to them, e.g. Parts 61 and 91.

This regulation is the basis for bringing enforcement action in the event of a violation of the regulations of another country while conducting a Part 135 operation.

CROSS REFERENCES

91.205, Powered Civil Aircraft with Standard Category U.S. Airworthiness Certificates: Instrument and Equipment Requirements; 91.703(b), Operations of Civil Aircraft of U.S. Registry Outside of the United States; 135.43, Crewmember Certificate: International Operations: Application and Issue.

International Flight Information Manual*; International Notices to Airmen*;
*(Can be purchased from Superintendent of Documents, P.O. Box 371954, Pittsburgh, PA 15250-7954)

Annex 2, Rules of the Air, to Convention on International Civil Aviation (can be purchased from: Public Information Office, ICAO, 1000 Sherbrooke Street West, Suite 400, Montreal, Quebec, Canada H3A 2R2).

AIRMAN'S INFORMATION MANUAL

International Civil Aviation Organization (ICAO) Terminal Forecasts (TAF), Para. 7-29.

135.5 CERTIFICATE AND OPERATIONS SPECIFICATIONS REQUIRED

No person may operate an aircraft under this part without, or in violation of, an air taxi/commercial operator (ATCO) operating certificate and appropriate Operations Specifications issued under this part, or, for operations with large aircraft having a maximum passenger seating configuration, excluding any pilot seat, of more than 30 seats, or a maximum payload capacity of more than 7,500 pounds, without, or in violation of, appropriate Operations Specifications issued under Part 121 of this chapter.

EXPLANATION

The provisions of a Part 135 certificate holder's Operations Specifications are made enforceable by this section.

This is the primary regulation charged when that person conducts an operation that requires a Part 135 certificate when they do not hold such a certificate.

Operations under §91.501 must be conducted in strict compliance with the requirements of that section or they may become subject to the provisions of Part 135.

If any economic advantage, including, but not limited to, good will, is obtained as the result of a flight carrying persons or property, the flight is one conducted for compensation or hire and subject to the provisions of Part 135, unless the operation falls under an exception in §135.1(b) or is conducted under §91.501.

CROSS REFERENCES

135.11, Application and Issue of Certificate and Operations Specifications; 135.143, General Requirements; 135.429, Required Inspection Personnel; 135.435, Certificate Requirements.

NTSB DECISIONS

Where a pilot asserted that payments he received were intended only to cover the cost of the aircraft rental, and that he provided a pilot (either himself or another pilot) for free, the Board stated that it has held that obtaining both a flightcrew and an airplane from the same source (a wet lease) is usually considered conclusive evidence of carriage for compensation or hire. *Administrator v. Platt*, EA-4012 (1993); *Administrator v. Poirier,* 5 NTSB 1928 (1987).

Aside from showing that respondent and pilots shared office space and facilities, the Board found no evidence that the pilots were subject to respondent's influence in any way concerning the flights they performed for a company. The relationship between the company and the respondent was essentially a rental agreement under which the respondent would make a plane available on a steady basis. When the company needed to transport parts or a mechanic, it would make its own arrangements for a pilot. Later, the pilot and the respondent would bill the company. Since there was no evidence of respondent having operational control over company's flight, a Part 135 certificate was not required. *Administrator v. Patterson,* EA-3762 (1992).

Where a company's Part 135 certificate had been revoked and it conducted three flights carrying passengers, the Board, in finding a violation of §135.5, stated that a violation was supported by (1) each of the passengers had been carried previously on charter flights by the company and each approached the flights in question with the same expectation and (2) on each flight, the plane and pilot were in effect supplied by the company. It found further that it can be reasonably concluded that, even though payment was not made as if the flights were chartered, and even if in fact a loss were incurred, it was in the economic interest of the company to conduct the flights in order to maintain customer good will and the effect that it might have on prospective business. *Administrator v. Muscatine Flying Service, Inc. and Anderson,* 5 NTSB 2132 (1987); *Administrator v. Plowman,* 5 NTSB 957 (1986).

Where certificate holder inadvertently used an aircraft not listed on its Operations Specifications, the Board held that such inadvertence did not excuse the violation of §135.5. *Administrator v. Muscatine Flying Service, Inc. and Letts,* 5 NTSB 1785 (1987).

Where ambulance company provided service consisting of both ground and air legs and on the billing indicated no charge for the air portion, the Board held that it was in fact an operation subject to Part 135. The Board held that, since the helicopter service was part of the commercial ambulance enterprise that the company held itself out to the public as being prepared and able to perform, any billing covering the provision of the service which utilized the aircraft must be deemed to reflect a charge for each and every element of the service provided. *Administrator v. Wrenke,* 4 NTSB 852 (1983).

§135.5 applies to the pilot of an aircraft on a flight subject to Part 135. Its application is not restricted to the business entity or entrepreneur responsible for the flight. *Administrator v. McLaren*, 4 NTSB 731 (1983).

The Board dismissed the charge of a violation of §135.5 stating that there was not evidence that respondent either knew or should have known the cargo being carried did not belong to the operator of the aircraft. Although any pilot might be wise to investigate an employer to ensure he is not operating illegally, that may not always be possible. *Administrator v. Fulop*, 6 NTSB 298 (1988).

In upholding the administrative law judge's dismissal of a §135.5 charge against an operator where it was alleged that the operator was conducting a scheduled operation instead of an on demand charter, the Board looked at whether the flights had been conducted in accordance with a published schedule that was either "openly advertised or otherwise made readily available to the general public." [See SFAR 38-2, §6(b)(4)]. While the FAA conceded that the flights were not "openly advertised," it maintained that they were nevertheless "readily available to the general public" because potential customers could learn of the schedule by visiting or calling one of respondent's offices. The Board went on to say that, since the FAA could have prohibited a charter operator from making a schedule available to the public under any circumstances, it would appear that by qualifying "available" with "readily" it did not intend to preclude an operator from doing no more than furnishing on request information concerning an unadvertised flight schedule. The Board found it reasonable to assume that the intent of the language was to forbid charter operators from using a schedule directly or indirectly to solicit customers. Since those calling or visiting the respondent to ask about its services would not know beforehand that it attempted to operate with any degree of regularity, they would not have been solicited by some reliance on a schedule. *Administrator v. Kingfisher Air Service, Inc. d/b/a Air Safari, Inc. d/b/a/ Lewis Airlines, Inc., and Bjarnarson,* 5 NTSB 945 (1986).

Where a private pilot flew the sick father of a friend to a hospital, the Board found a violation of 135.5. The basis of the finding were that the pilot charged for the total cost of the flight and the pilot and passenger did not have a common purpose insofar as the flight was concerned §61.118(b), "sharing the costs.") *Administrator v. Carter,* EA-3730 (1992).

FAA CHIEF COUNSEL OPINIONS

A commercially rated pilot offers to provide pilot services to various entities. He suggests that they rent an aircraft from a local fixed based operator and hire him to fly the rental aircraft. If the pilot is perceived as actually arranging the entire flight, and the entity who rents the aircraft acts as the agent of the pilot, it would amount to an impermissible avoidance of the certification requirements of FAR 135.5 and FAR 135.25. It is important, however, to distinguish the situation where there is a simple provision of pilot services, and the pilot has no part in the renting of the aircraft, where it is clear that the renter hires the pilot and has operational control over the airplane. The pilot must be the servant of the entity renting the aircraft, and the fewer the ties between pilot services and an operation conducted for hire. The pilot must be paid by the entity renting the aircraft and should not be involved in any way in the renting process. (4-8-91).

[See FAA Chief Counsel Opinions under §135.1.]

135.7 APPLICABILITY OF RULES TO UNAUTHORIZED OPERATORS

The rules in this part which apply to a person certificated under §135.5 also apply to a person who engages in any operation governed by this part without an appropriate certificate and Operations Specifications required by §135.5.

EXPLANATION

In the event a person is found to have conducted a flight that is subject to Part 135 when that person does not hold an appropriate certificate and Operations Specifications, the person is not just in violation of §135.5, but also every other section of Part 135 applicable to the flight conducted. This can result in a very substantial civil penalty action.

CROSS REFERENCES

135.5, Certificate and Operations Specifications Required.

135.9 DURATION OF CERTIFICATE

(a) An ATCO operating certificate is effective until surrendered, suspended or revoked. The holder of an ATCO operating certificate that is suspended or revoked shall return it to the Administrator.

(b) Except as provided in paragraphs (c) and (d) of this section, an ATCO operating certificate in effect on December 1, 1978, expires on February 1, 1979. The certificate holder must continue to conduct operations under Part 135 and the Operations Specifications in effect on November 30, 1978, until the certificate expires.

(c) If the certificate holder applies before February 1, 1979, for new Operations Specifications under this part, the operating certificate held continues in effect and the certificate holder must continue operations under Part 135 and Operations Specifications in effect on November 30, 1978, until the earliest of the following —

(1) The date on which new Operations Specifications are issued; or

(2) The date on which the Administrator notifies the certificate holder that the application is denied; or

(3) August 1, 1979.

If new Operations Specifications are issued under paragraph (c)(1) of this paragraph, the ATCO operating certificate continues in effect until surrendered, suspended or revoked under paragraph (a) of this section.

(d) A certificate holder may obtain an extension of the expiration date in paragraph (c) of this section, but not beyond December 1, 1979, from the Director, Flight Standards Service, if before July 1, 1979, the certificate holder —

(1) Shows that due to the circumstances beyond its control it cannot comply by the expiration date; and

(2) Submits a schedule for compliance, acceptable to the Director, indicating that compliance will be achieved at the earliest practicable date.

(e) The holder of an ATCO operating certificate that expires, under paragraphs (b), (c), or (d) of this section, shall return it to the Administrator.

EXPLANATION

135.9(a) is self-explanatory, however, it should be noted that, if the certificate is suspended or revoked, failure to return it to the Administrator can be the basis of a civil penalty action.

CROSS REFERENCES

135.15, Amendment of Certificate; 135.35, Termination of Operations; 135.435, Certificate Requirements.

135.10 COMPLIANCE DATES FOR CERTAIN RULES

After January 2, 1991, no certificate holder may use a person as a flight crewmember unless that person has completed the windshear ground training required by §§135.345(b)(6) and 135.351(b)(2) of this part.

EXPLANATION

This requirement does not apply to rotorcraft pilots.

CROSS REFERENCES

135.345(b)(6), Pilots: Initial, Transition, and Upgrade Ground Training; 135.351(b)(2), Recurrent Training.

ADVISORY CIRCULARS

AC 00-54 *Pilot Windshear Guide* (1988).

AC 120-41 *Criteria for Operational Approval of Airborne Wind Shear Alerting and Flight Guidance Systems* (1983).

AC 120-50 *Guidelines for Operational Approval of Windshear Training Programs* (1989).

AIRMAN'S INFORMATION MANUAL

Low Level Wind Shear Alert System (LLWAS), Para. 4-56;
Wind Shear Pireps, Para. 7-22;
Microbursts, Para. 7-24.

135.11 APPLICATION AND ISSUE OF CERTIFICATE AND OPERATIONS SPECIFICATIONS

(a) An application for an ATCO operating certificate and appropriate Operations Specifications is made on a form and in a manner prescribed by the Administrator and filed with the FAA Flight Standards District Office that has jurisdiction over the area in which the applicant's principal business office is located.

(b) An applicant who meets the requirements of this part is entitled to —

- (1) An ATCO operating certificate containing all business names under which the certificate holder may conduct operations and the address of each business office used by the certificate holder; and
- (2) Separate Operations Specifications, issued to the certificate holder, containing:
  - (i) The type and area of operations authorized.
  - (ii) The category and class of aircraft that may be used in those operations.
  - (iii) Registration numbers and types of aircraft that are subject to an airworthiness maintenance program required by §135.411(a)(2), including time limitations or standards for determining time limitations, for overhauls, inspections, and checks for airframes, aircraft engines, propellers, rotors, appliances, and emergency equipment.
  - (iv) Registration numbers of aircraft that are to be inspected under an approved aircraft inspection program under §135.419.
  - (v) Additional maintenance items required by the Administrator under §135.421.
  - (vi) Any authorized deviation from this part.
  - (vii) Any other items the Administrator may require or allow to meet any particular situation.

(c) No person holding Operations Specifications issued under this part may list on its Operations Specifications or on the current list of aircraft required by §135.63(a)(3) any airplane listed on Operations Specifications issued under Part 125.

EXPLANATION

The FAA Flight Standards District Offices have available a video tape and other information that is very helpful for someone considering certification under Part 135. If you are not familiar with Part 135, review the tape and other information before you make any firm commitments regarding such an undertaking, i.e. purchase of aircraft.

An applicant for a Part 135 certificate must be a citizen of the United States (§135.19(a)(1)). If your business is a partnership of which one member is a corporation, it does not meet the definition of "citizen of the United States" as set forth in §101(16) of the Federal Aviation Act of 1958, as amended [49 U.S.C. App. §1301(16)]. The definition of "citizen of the United States" as set forth in §135.19(a)(1) differs, but the definition in the Federal Aviation Act is the one that determines the status of a partnership.

Small, less complex operators who are required to comply with Part 135 may be eligible to use a modified certification process. While the FAA will proceed with the certification process, it will not issue a certificate until the applicant provides proof that appropriate DOT economic authority has been obtained. Accordingly, contact with the DOT should be made in a timely manner.

The FAA inspectors can furnish informal guidance and advice, but the production of acceptable documents and manuals rests solely on the applicant.

Purchase and use of the Airworthiness Inspector's Handbook, 8300.10 and Air Transportation Operations Inspector's Handbook, 8400.10 (with changes) is recommended. These publications can be helpful during and after the certification process. Both documents can be purchased from the Superintendent of Documents, P.O. Box 371954, Pittsburgh, PA 15250-7954.

In the case of operation of civil aircraft of U.S. registry outside of the United States, compliance with certain flight rules of Subpart B, Part 91, not already required by §91.703, is made mandatory by their incorporation into the Operations Specifications.

For fixed-wing airplane operations there are three kinds of operations that can be authorized: (1) commuter airplane; (2) on-demand airplane, and (3) on-demand cargo only airplane.

An operator can only be authorized for one kind of operation. However, an operator authorized for commuter airplane operations is automatically authorized to conduct on-demand (nonscheduled) operations. The FAA uses the same operations classifications for rotorcraft.

CROSS REFERENCES

135.27, Business Office and Operations Base; 135.29, Use of Business Names; 135.63(a)(3), Recordkeeping Requirements; 135.411(a)(2), Applicability; 135.419, Approved Aircraft Inspection Program; 135.421 Additional Maintenance Requirements.

§101(16) of the Federal Aviation Act of 1958, as amended [49 U.S.C.App. §1301 16)]; FAA Order 8400.10, Chapter 2. The Certification Process — Part 121 and Part 135, Air Transportation Operations Inspector's Handbook; FAA Order 8300.10, Airworthiness Inspector's Handbook; Part 125, Certification and Operations: Airplanes Having a Seating Capacity of 20 or More Passengers or a Maximum Payload Capacity of 6,000 Pounds or More.

ADVISORY CIRCULARS

AC 120-49 *Certification of Air Carriers* (1988).

AC 135-4A *Aviation Security: Air Taxi Commercial Operators (ATCO)* (1976).

AC 135-7 *FAR 135: Additional Maintenance Requirements for Aircraft Type Certificated for Nine or Less Passenger Seats* (1978).

135.13 ELIGIBILITY FOR CERTIFICATE AND OPERATIONS SPECIFICATIONS

(a) To be eligible for an ATCO operating certificate and appropriate Operations Specifications, a person must —

(1) Be a citizen of the United States, a partnership of which each member is a citizen of the United States, or a corporation or association created or organized under the laws of the United States or any state, territory, or possession of the United States, of which the president and two-thirds or more of the board of directors and other managing officers are citizens of the United States and in which at least 75 percent of the voting interest is owned or controlled by citizens of the United States or one of its possessions; and

(2) Show, to the satisfaction of the Administrator, that the person is able to conduct each kind of operation for which the person seeks authorization in compliance with applicable regulations; and

(3) Hold any economic authority that may be required by the Civil Aeronautics Board.

However, no person holding a commercial operator operating certificate issued under Part 121 of this chapter is eligible for an ATCO operating certificate unless the person shows to the satisfaction of the Administrator that the person's contract carriage business in large aircraft, having a maximum passenger seating configuration, excluding any pilot seat; of more than 30 seats or a maximum payload capacity of more than 7,500 pounds, will not result directly or indirectly from the person's air taxi business.

(b) The Administrator may deny any applicant a certificate under this part if the Administrator finds —

(1) That an air carrier or commercial operator operating certificate under Part 121 or an ATCO operating certificate previously issued to the applicant was revoked; or

(2) That a person who was employed in a position similar to general manager, director of operations, director of maintenance, chief pilot, or chief inspector, or who has exercised control with respect to any ATCO operating certificate holder, air carrier, or commercial operator, whose operating certificate has been revoked, will be employed in any of those positions or similar position, or will be in control of or have a substantial ownership interest in the applicant, and that the person's employment or control contributed materially to the reasons for revoking that certificate.

EXPLANATION

§101(16) of the Federal Aviation Act of 1958, as amended [49 U.S.C. §1301(16)], has been interpreted to say that, if a partnership includes a partner that is a corporation, the partnership is not considered a "citizen of the United States" under the Federal Aviation Act. Although §135.13(a)(1) reads differently, insofar as partnership is concerned, the statutory definition is the controlling definition.

Part 298 of the Department of Transportation (DOT) Regulations (14 C.F.R. Part 298) provides a grant of exemption from certain DOT economic certificate requirements and requires registration by each air carrier who intends to conduct air transportation with aircraft having a seating capacity of 60 seats or less, or a maximum payload capacity of 18,000 pounds or less.

An operator seeking DOT authority under Part 298 for scheduled passenger operations must (1) register with DOT; (2) apply for fitness determination; (3) submit information requested by DOT; and (4) submit proof of insurance. DOT conducts fitness determinations, issues a show cause order allowing interested parties to state why an operation should not be authorized, and issues the final order. If a final order is favorable to the applicant, the DOT issues registration.

An operator who wants to conduct nonscheduled operation under Part 298 must register with DOT and show proof of insurance. The DOT then issues registration.

DOT registrations are written evidence of official economic authority issued by DOT.

In the event the FAA denies the issuance of a certificate under Part 135, the applicant may seek a review of that denial under Part 13 of the Federal Aviation Regulations (§13.20 and Sub-part D of Part 13).

An applicant should carefully screen anyone that it proposes to put in positions described in §135.13(b)(2) regarding past employment with Part 121 or Part 135 operators.

The FAA's authority to deny issuance of a certificate, §135.13(b), is discretionary. The FAA may do so at any time before issuance of the certificate.

A corporation that meets the citizenship requirements except for the one relating to 75% of the voting stock being held by U.S. citizens may be able to qualify, "citizenship-wise," for a Part 135 certificate through a voting trust. However, before any other action is taken in regard to applying for certificate, the action should be submitted to appropriate FAA legal office for review.

The term "show" in §135.12(a)(2) means "to demonstrate."

The provisions of §135.13(a)(2) are continuing in nature. At any time the holder of a Part 135 certificate does not meet the requirements of §135.13(a)(2), the FAA may take action to suspend or revoke the certificate.

CROSS REFERENCES

Part 13, Subpart D, Rules of Practice for FAA Hearings; 13.20, Orders of Compliance, Cease and Desist Orders, Orders of Denial, and Other Orders; 135.5, Certificate and Operations Specifications Required.

FAA CHIEF COUNSEL OPINIONS

An applicant for a Part 135 certificate that is a partnership with a corporate member is not eligible for such a certificate since it is not a "citizen of the United States" as the same is defined in the Federal Aviation Act of 1958, as amended [49 U.S.C.App. §1301(16)].

135.15 AMENDMENT OF CERTIFICATE

(a) The Administrator may amend an ATCO operating certificate —
   (1) On the Administrator's own initiative, under §609 of the Federal Aviation Act of 1958 (49 U.S.C. 1429) and Part 13 of this chapter; or
   (2) Upon application by the holder of that certificate.

(b) The certificate holder must file an application to amend an ATCO operating certificate at least 15 days before the date proposed by the applicant for the amendment to become effective, unless a shorter filing period is approved. The application must be on a form and in a manner prescribed by the Administrator and must be submitted to the FAA Flight Standards District Office charged with the overall inspection of the certificate holder.

(c) The FAA Flight Standards District Office charged with the overall inspection of the certificate holder grants an amendment to the ATCO operating certificate if it is determined that safety in air commerce and the public interest allow that amendment.

(d) Within 30 days after receiving a refusal to amend the operating certificate, the certificate holder may petition the Director, Flight Standards Service, to reconsider the request.

EXPLANATION

An action by the Administrator to amend an ATCO operating certificate may be appealed to the National Transportation Safety Board (NTSB).

Where a certificate holder requests amendment and FAA denies request, there is no appeal to the NTSB. The only resource is to request a review by the Director, Flight Standards Service. From that office's decision, pursuant to §1006 of the Federal Aviation Act of 1958 as amended (49 U.S.C. §1486), the certificate holder may seek review of the decision order by the appropriate U.S. Court of Appeals.

CROSS REFERENCES

135.9, Duration of Certificate; 135.73, Inspections and Tests; Federal Aviation Act of 1958 (49 U.S.C. §1429); Part 13, Investigative and Enforcement Procedures; §609 of the Federal Aviation Act of 1958, as amended (49 U.S.C. App. §1429); §1006 of the Federal Aviation Act of 1958, as amended (49 U.S.C. App. §1429); 13.19, Certificate Action; 49 C.F.R. Part 821, Rules of Practice in Air Safety Proceedings (NTSB Regulations).

135.17 AMENDMENT OF OPERATIONS SPECIFICATIONS

(a) The FAA Flight Standards District Office charged with the overall inspection of the certificate holder may amend any Operations Specifications issued under this part if —
  (1) It determines that safety in air commerce requires that amendment; or
  (2) Upon application by the holder, that District Office determines that safety in air commerce allows that amendment.

(b) The certificate holder must file an application to amend Operations Specifications at least 15 days before the date proposed by the applicant for the amendment to become effective, unless a shorter filing period is approved. The application must be on a form and in a manner prescribed by the Administrator and be submitted to the FAA Flight Standards District Office charged with the overall inspection of the certificate holder.

(c) Within 30 days after a notice of refusal to approve a holder's application for amendment is received, the holder may petition the Director, Flight Standards Service for amendments pertaining to flight operations, to reconsider the refusal to amend.

(d) When the FAA Flight Standards District Office charged with the overall inspection of the certificate holder amends Operations Specifications, that District Office gives notice in writing to the holder of a proposed amendment to the Operations Specifications, fixing a period of not less than 7 days within which the holder may submit written information, views, and arguments concerning the proposed amendment. After consideration of all relevant matter presented, that Flight Standards District Office notifies the holder of any amendment adopted, or a recision of the notice. The amendment becomes effective not less than 30 days after the holder receives notice of the adoption of the amendment, unless the holder petitions the Director, Flight Standards Service for amendments pertaining to flight operations, for reconsideration of the amendment. In that case, the effective date of the amendment is stayed pending a decision by the Director. If the Director finds there is an emergency requiring immediate action as to safety in air commerce that makes the provisions of this paragraph impracticable or contrary to the public interest, the Director notifies the certificate holder that the amendment is effective on the date of receipt, without previous notice.

EXPLANATION

Any application to amend Operations Specifications should include supporting documentation with special emphasis on the effect on safety.

If the Director, Flight Standards Service denies certificate holder's appeal, the Federal Aviation Regulations do not provide any additional appeal rights.

CROSS REFERENCES

135.73, Inspections and Tests.

135.19 EMERGENCY OPERATIONS

(a) In an emergency involving the safety of persons or property, the certificate holder may deviate from the rules of this part relating to aircraft and equipment and weather minimums to the extent required to meet that emergency.
(b) In an emergency involving the safety of persons or property, the pilot in command may deviate from the rules of this part to the extent required to meet that emergency.
(c) Each person who, under the authority of this section, deviates from a rule of this part shall, within 10 days, excluding Saturdays, Sundays, and Federal holidays, after the deviation, send to the FAA Flight Standards District Office charged with the overall inspection of the certificate holder a complete report of the aircraft operation involved, including a description of the deviation and reasons for it.

EXPLANATION

The term "emergency operations" means an immediate but temporary action to prevent or reduce the loss of life or property when an unanticipated threat to life or property occurs, i.e. rescue, firefighting, security, etc.

"Emergency operations" under §135.19 are not related to the pilot-in-command emergency authority provided in §91.3.

Long term contracts to provide services in case of "emergency" situations cannot be described as an unanticipated, temporary action.

CROSS REFERENCES

91.3, Responsibility and Authority of the Pilot In Command; 91.155, Basic VFR Weather Minimums; 135.69, Restriction or Suspension of Operations: Continuation of Flight in an Emergency; 135.65(a), Reporting Mechanical Irregularities; 135.123(a), Emergency and Emergency Evacuation Duties; 135.129(d), Exit Seating; 135.150, Public Address and Crewmember Interphone Systems; 135.151(c), Cockpit Voice Recorders; 135.152(e), Flight Recorders; 135.155, Fire Extinguishers: Passenger-Carrying Aircraft; 91.157, Special VFR Weather Minimums; 135.167, Emergency Equipment: Extended Over Water Operations; 135.178, Additional Emergency Equipment; 135.177, Emergency Equipment Requirements for Aircraft Having a Passenger Seating Configuration of More Than 19 Passengers.

ADVISORY CIRCULARS

AC 120-30A *Reporting Requirements of Air Carriers, Commercial Operators, Travel Clubs, and Air Traffic* (1976).

AC 120-56 *Air Carrier Voluntary Disclosure Reporting Procedures* (1992).

AC 135-15 *Emergency Medical Service/Airplane* (EMS/A)(1990).

AC 139.49-1 *Programs for Training of Fire Fighting and Rescue Personnel* (1974).

AIRMAN'S INFORMATION MANUAL

Transponder Emergency Operations, Para. 6-2;
Emergency Locator Transmitters, Para. 6-14;
Search & Rescue, Para. 6-16;
Distress & Urgency Communications, Para. 6-20;
Obtaining Emergency Assistance, Para. 6-21;
Ditching Procedures, Para. 6-22;
Special Emergency (Air Piracy), Para. 6-23;
Fuel Dumping, Para. 6-24;
Two-way Radio Communications Failure, Para.6-30;
Transponder Operation During Two-Way Communications Failure, Para. 6-31;
Aircraft Accident & Incident Reporting, Para. 7-91;
Near Midair Collision Reporting, Para. 7-92.

FAA CHIEF COUNSEL OPINIONS

A "bona fide" emergency situation must have existed at the time of any deviation from the regulations. Upon receipt of the report required by §135.19(c), the Flight Standards District Office (FSDO) charged with the overall inspection of the certificate holder will then determine the validity of such emergency and whether the deviation was necessary to meet the emergency. The determination is dependent upon the specific facts. If upon review of the report required by §135.19(c), it is the FAA's opinion that the deviation was not justified, then enforcement action is possible. (11-23-90)

A pilot-in-command may deviate from the rest of the requirements of Part 135 to the extent necessary to provide transportation during a bona fide medical emergency. However, the pilot-in-command must provide the FAA with a complete report surrounding the deviation within 10 days. In appropriate situations §135.19 permits deviations from Part 135 rules regardless of whether the emergency developed in flight or at some other time and place. The provisions of §91.3(b) are specifically limited to and excuse only those emergency situation that develop in-flight. If the emergency did not develop in-flight, the pilot-in-command would be required to comply with all the applicable rules under Part 91, and whatever rules under Part 135 that could not be legitimately subject to a deviation due to the emergency situation. (4-16-93)

135.21 MANUAL REQUIREMENTS

(a) Each certificate holder, other than one who uses only one pilot in the certificate holder's operations, shall prepare and keep current a manual setting forth the certificate holder's procedures and policies acceptable to the Administrator. This manual must be used by the certificate holder's flight, ground, and maintenance personnel in conducting its operations. However, the Administrator may authorize a deviation from this paragraph if the Administrator finds that, because of the limited size of the operation, all or part of the manual is not necessary for guidance of flight, ground, or maintenance personnel.

(b) Each certificate holder shall maintain at least one copy of the manual at its principal operations base.

(c) The manual must not be contrary to any applicable Federal regulations, foreign regulation applicable to the certificate holder's operations in foreign countries, or the certificate holder's operating certificate or Operations Specifications.

(d) A copy of the manual, or appropriate portions of the manual (and changes and additions) shall be made available to maintenance and ground operations personnel by the certificate holder and furnished to —

(1) Its flight crewmembers; and

(2) Representatives of the Administrator assigned to the certificate holder.

(e) Each employee of the certificate holder to whom a manual or appropriate portions of it are furnished under paragraph (d)(1) of this section shall keep it up to date with the changes and additions furnished to them.

(f) Except as provided in paragraph (g) of this section, each certificate holder shall carry appropriate parts of the manual on each aircraft when away from the principal operations base. The appropriate parts must be available for use by ground or flight personnel.

(g) If a certificate holder conducts aircraft inspections or maintenance at specified stations where it keeps the approved inspection program manual, it is not required to carry the manual aboard the aircraft enroute to those stations.

EXPLANATION

"One pilot" operations include both single pilot operators and single pilot-in-command operators. A single pilot operator is a certificate holder using only one pilot for Part 135 operations. The pilot must be identified by name on the certificate holder's Operations Specifications. Such an operator cannot use "freelance" pilots or temporary pilot employees in place of the pilot named on the Operations Specifications. Single pilot-in-command operators use one pilot-in-command who is identified by name in the Operations Specifications. "Freelance" pilots or temporary pilot employees cannot be used in place of the named pilot. A certificate holder can use no more than three individuals as second-in-command and they shall be named in Operations Specifications and meet all Part 135 requirements for second-in-command. Also, certificate holders are not authorized to operate aircraft type certificated for more than nine passengers, conduct Category II or III operations or conduct operations outside the United States, Canada, Mexico, or the Caribbean.

Basic Part 135 operators may obtain authorized deviations from manual requirements. To qualify they must meet each of the following conditions and limitations: (1) No more than five pilots including seconds-in-command are used in the operations; (2) No more than five aircraft are used in the operation; (3) No more than three different types of aircraft are used in the operation; (4) For scheduled passenger (commuter) operations, initial operating experience (IOE) check airmen are the only check airmen authorized for use by the operator; (5) No aircraft type certificated for more than nine passenger seats is used in the operation; (6) No Category II or III operations are conducted; and (7) No operations are conducted outside the United States, Canada, Mexico, and the Caribbean.

This section only requires the operator to have one manual. However, a system of manuals is usually necessary even in the less complex operations.

If adapting a manual used by another Part 135 operator, be very careful. The other operators may have included limitations not required by the FAA.

When "approved" is used to describe a document, manual, or checklist, it means that a regulation requires FAA approval and that the FAA has evaluated and specifically approved the document, manual, or checklist.

"Accepted" is used to describe a document, manual, or checklist which does not have, or is not required to have, FAA approval. Operators submit the entire manual to the FAA for review. If the FAA finds that an accepted section of the manual is not in compliance, the FAA must formally notify the operator of the deficiency. The operator must take action to resolve the deficiency.

The preparation of the manual will necessarily involve extensive communications between the operator and the FAA certificating office regarding approval of portions of the manual. To avoid misunderstandings it is strongly recommended that the operator request FAA put all comments in writing in letter form. Using only informal notes or oral exchanges can cause serious problems.

Where an operator contracts out for services, such as fueling, it must ensure that the contractor has, and its employees are familiar with, the pertinent portions of the certificate holder's manual.

Preparing an acceptable manual is one of the most time consuming aspects of the certification process. Unless the applicant has adequate experienced personnel to prepare the manual, use of a consultant may expedite the certification process.

CROSS REFERENCES

135.81, Informing Personnel of Operational Information and Appropriate Changes; 135.293, Initial and Recurrent Pilot Testing Requirements; 135.299(c), Pilot In Command: Line Checks: Routes and Airports.

ADVISORY CIRCULARS

AC 121-1A *Standard Operations Specifications - Aircraft Maintenance Handbook* (1973).

AC 121-21B *Information Guide for Training Programs and Manual Requirement in the Air Transportation of Hazardous Materials* (1983).

NTSB DECISIONS

The Board held that §135.21(a) applies to the holders of operating certificates and not to individual employees of certificate holders. *Administrator v. Hughes,* 6 NTSB 827 (1988).

The regulations [135.21] impose on the certificate holders the responsibility to maintain and keep current in accessible form various manuals and documents. It does not excuse noncompliance during periods of office remodeling or for other circumstances fully within the certificate holder's control. *Administrator v. Eagle Commuter Airlines, Inc.,* 5 NTSB 1106 (1986).

FAA CHIEF COUNSEL OPINIONS

While a reading of §135.21(a) might be taken as an indication that it is enforceable against Part 135 employees, since it requires that the manual be used by Part 135 employees, the National Transportation Safety Board has held otherwise. (2-28-91).

135.23 MANUAL CONTENTS

Each manual shall have the date of the last revision on each revised page. The manual must include —

(a) The name of each management person required under §135.37(a) who is authorized to act for the certificate holder, the person's assigned area of responsibility, the person's duties, responsibilities, and authority, and the name and title of each person authorized to exercise operational control under §135.77;

(b) Procedures for ensuring compliance with aircraft weight and balance limitations and, for multi-engine aircraft, for determining compliance with §135.185;

(c) Copies of the certificate holder's Operations Specifications or appropriate extracted information, including area of operations authorized, category and class of aircraft authorized, crew complements, and types of operations authorized;

(d) Procedures for complying with accident notifications requirements;

(e) Procedures for ensuring that the pilot in command knows that required airworthiness inspections have been made and that the aircraft has been approved for return to service in compliance with applicable maintenance requirements;

(f) Procedures for reporting and recording mechanical irregularities that come to the attention of the pilot in command before, during, and after completion of a flight;

(g) Procedures to be followed by the pilot in command for determining that mechanical irregularities or defects reported for previous flights have been corrected or that correction has been deferred;

(h) Procedures to be followed by the pilot in command to obtain maintenance, preventive maintenance, and servicing of the aircraft at a place where previous arrangements have not been made by the operator, when the pilot is authorized to so act for the operator;

(i) Procedures under §135.179 for the release for, or continuation of, flight if any item of equipment required for the particular type of operation becomes inoperative or unserviceable enroute;

(j) Procedures for refueling aircraft, eliminating fuel contamination, protecting from fire (including electrostatic protection), and supervising and protecting passengers during refueling;

(k) Procedures to be followed by the pilot in command in the briefing under §135.117;

(l) Flight locating procedures, when applicable;

(m) Procedures for ensuring compliance with emergency procedures, including a list of the functions assigned each category of required crewmembers in connection with an emergency and emergency evacuation duties under §135.123;

(n) Enroute qualification procedures for pilots, when applicable;

(o) The approved aircraft inspection program, when applicable;

(p) Procedures and instructions to enable personnel to recognize hazardous materials, as defined in Title 49 CFR, and if these materials are to be carried, stored, or handled, procedures and instruction for —
   (1) Accepting shipment of hazardous material required by Title 49 CFR, to assure proper packaging, marking, labeling, shipping documents, compatibility of articles, and instructions on their loading, storage, and handling;
   (2) Notification and reporting hazardous material incidents as required by Title 49 CFR; and
   (3) Notification of the pilot in command when there are hazardous materials aboard, as required by Title 49 CFR;

(q) Procedures for the evacuation of persons who may need the assistance of another person to move expeditiously to an exit if an emergency occurs; and

(r) Other procedures and policy instructions regarding the certificate holder's operations, that are issued by the certificate holder.

EXPLANATION

In view of the turn-over rate at some of the smaller operators, care should be taken to ensure that the portion of the manual that refers to persons by name is kept current and the FAA is provided with the updates in a timely manner.

Rather than including copies of the applicable parts of the Operations Specifications in the manuals, it is considered better to extract the necessary information from the Operations Specifications and include it in the manual. This relieves personnel from the need of trying to interpret the terms of the Operations Specifications.

In regard to fueling, the manual should include a description of the procedures for reporting fuel spills, etc. to the appropriate local, state and Federal environmental agencies.

CROSS REFERENCES

135.37(a), Management Personnel Required; 135.65(a) and (b), Reporting Mechanical Irregularities; 135.77, Responsibility for Operational Control; 135.79, Flight Locating Requirements; 135.117, Briefing of Passengers Before Flight; 135.123, Emergency and Emergency Evacuation Duties; 135.179, Inoperable Instruments and Equipment; 135.185, Empty Weight and Center of Gravity: Currency Requirement; 49 C.F.R. Part 830, Rules Pertaining to the Notification and Reporting of Aircraft Accidents or Incidents and Overdue Aircraft and Preservation of Aircraft Wreckage, Mail, Cargo, and Records.

ADVISORY CIRCULARS

AC 120-48 *Communication and Coordination Between Flight Crewmembers and Flight Attendants* (1988).

AC 120-52 *Radiation Exposure of Air Carrier Crewmembers* (1990).

AC 121-1A *Standard Operations Specifications - Aircraft Maintenance Handbook* (1973).

AC 121-16 *Maintenance Certificate Procedures* (1970).

AC 121-21B *Information Guide for Training Programs and Manual Requirements in the Air Transportation of Hazardous Materials* (1983).

AC 129-4 *Maintenance Programs for U.S. Registered Aircraft Under FAR Part 129* (1988).

FAA CHIEF COUNSEL OPINIONS

The procedures and policy instructions issued by the certificate holder through the means of a station manual and operations safety memos relating to ground handling of aircraft would come within the purview of §135.23(r) and would be considered part of the certificate holder's manual. Accordingly, this material must be determined acceptable to the Administration and the requirements of §135.21 applied to this material. (4-17-84).

135.25 AIRCRAFT REQUIREMENTS

(a) Except as provided in paragraph (d) of this section, no certificate holder may operate an aircraft under this part unless that aircraft —
  (1) Is registered as a civil aircraft of the United States and carries an appropriate and current airworthiness certificate issued under this chapter; and
  (2) Is in an airworthy condition and meets the applicable airworthiness requirements of this chapter, including those relating to identification and equipment.

(b) Each certificate holder must have the exclusive use of at least one aircraft that meets the requirements for at least one kind of operation authorized in the certificate holder's Operations Specifications. In addition, for each kind of operation for which the certificate holder does not have the exclusive use of an aircraft, the certificate holder must have available for use under a written agreement (including arrangements for performing required maintenance) at least one aircraft that meets the requirements for that kind of operation. However, this paragraph does not prohibit the operator from using or authorizing the use of the aircraft for other than air taxi or commercial operations and does not require the certificate holder to have exclusive use of all aircraft that the certificate holder uses.

(c) For the purposes of paragraph (b) of this section, a person has exclusive use of an aircraft if that person has the sole possession, control, and use of it for flight, as owner, or has a written agreement (including arrangements for performing required maintenance), in effect when the aircraft is operated, giving the person that possession, control, and use for at least 6 consecutive months.

(d) A certificate holder may operate in common carriage, and for the carriage of mail, a civil aircraft which is leased or chartered to it without crew and is registered in a country which is a party to the Convention on International Civil Aviation if —

(1) The aircraft carries an appropriate airworthiness certificate issued by the country of registration and meets the registration and identification requirements of that country;

(2) The aircraft is of a type design which is approved under a U.S. type certificate and complies with all of the requirements of this chapter (14 CFR Chapter 1) that would be applicable to that aircraft were it registered in the United States, including the requirements which must be met for issuance of a U.S. standard airworthiness certificate (including type design conformity, condition for safe operation, and the noise, fuel venting, and engine emission requirements of this chapter), except that a U.S. registration certificate and a U.S. standard airworthiness certificate will not be issued for the aircraft;

(3) The aircraft is operated by a U.S. certificated airmen employed by the certificate holder; and

(4) The certificate holder files a copy of the aircraft lease or charter agreement with the FAA Aircraft Registry, Department of Transportation, 6400 South MacArthur Boulevard, Oklahoma City, Oklahoma (Mailing address: P.O. Box 25504, Oklahoma City, Oklahoma 73125).

EXPLANATION

The FAA does not make a predetermination that the minimum airworthiness requirements of the foreign country of registry meet the minimum U.S. airworthiness requirements. The certificate holder must provide documentation and records necessary to determine type certification conformity. In some cases it may be necessary to make alterations or obtain exemptions from the country of registry requirements in order to operate the aircraft in United States air carrier operations.

The aircraft must be leased or chartered without a crew and the country of registry must be a member country of the Convention of the International Civil Aviation Organization (ICAO).

Since some countries do not require compliance with U.S. airworthiness directives, when evaluating the use of a foreign owned and registered aircraft, consideration should be given to the cost of complying with all applicable airworthiness directives.

A certificate holder is required to have the exclusive use of at least one aircraft.

CROSS REFERENCES

91.23, Truth-in-Leasing Clause Requirement in Leases and Conditional Sales Contracts; 91.409, Inspections; 91.807, Phased Compliance Under Parts 121, 125, and 135: Subsonic Airplanes; 135.9, Duration of Certificate; 135.11, Application and Issue of Certificate and Operations Specifications; 135.71, Airworthiness Check; 135.73, Inspections and Tests; 135.419, Approved Aircraft Inspection Program; 135.87(c), Carriage of Cargo Including Carry-on Baggage; 135.143, General Requirements; 135.149, Equipment Requirements: General; 135.293, Initial and Recurrent Pilot Testing Requirements; 135.301, Crewmember: Tests and Checks, Grace Provisions, Training to Accepted Standards; 135.443, Airworthiness Release or Aircraft Maintenance Log Entry; Part 34, Fuel Venting and Exhaust Emission Requirements for Turbine Engine Powered Airplanes; Part 36, Noise Standards: Aircraft Type and Airworthiness Certification.

ADVISORY CIRCULARS

AC 120-27B *Aircraft Weight and Balance Control* (1990).

AC 120-46 *Use of Advanced Training Devices (Airplane Only)*(1987).

AC 135-13A *List of Air Carriers Certificated by FAR Part 135* (1992).

NTSB DECISIONS

The Board, in dismissing an appeal by the Administrator from a finding of the Administrative Law Judge of no violation of §135.25(a)(2) said that, while it is true that "the prohibition against operating an unairworthy aircraft applies whether or not the operator has had the discrepancies brought to its attention," the basic premises that the aircraft was unairworthy must first be established. *Administrator v. Lang Enterprises, Inc.*, EA-3569 (1992).

FAA CHIEF COUNSEL OPINIONS

Under the provisions of §135.25(c), a Part 135 certificate holder cannot allow other air taxi operators to have possession, use, and control of that operator's "exclusive use" aircraft when the operator does not have the aircraft scheduled for use. (1-5-90).

Where owner operates aircraft in the morning under Part 91 (exclusive of Subpart F) for business purposes and under Part 135 for compensation in the afternoon of same day, its ownership of the aircraft and its use in this manner meets the requirements of §135.31 (now 135.25) (9-12-75).

135.27 BUSINESS OFFICE AND OPERATIONS BASE

(a) Each certificate holder shall maintain a principal business office.

(b) Each certificate holder shall, before establishing or changing the location of any business office or operations base, except a temporary operations base, notify in writing the FAA Flight Standards District Office charged with the overall inspection of the certificate holder.

(c) No certificate holder who establishes or changes the location of any business office or operations base, except a temporary operations base, may operate an aircraft under this part unless the certificate holder complies with paragraph (b) of this section.

EXPLANATION

The "principal base of operations" means the primary operating location as designated by the Administrator. A certificate holder must maintain its certificate and a complete and separate set of its Operations Specifications at its principal base of operations.

It is acceptable to have main operations base and main maintenance base at separate locations.

The FAA will make the final decision on what FAA office will have responsibility for the certificate.

CROSS REFERENCES

135.11(a) and (b)(1), Application and Issue of Certificate and Operations Specifications; 135.13(a) and (b), Eligibility for Certificate and Operations Specifications; 135.21(b), Manual Requirements; 135.29, Use of Business Names; 135.63(a) and (b), Recordkeeping Requirements.

135.29 USE OF BUSINESS NAMES

No certificate holder may operate an aircraft under this part under a business name that is not on the certificate holder's operating certificate.

EXPLANATION

If there is a change in the name of the certificate holder, the change must appear not only on the certificate and in the operating specifications, but also the Department of Transportation must be advised so that Part 298 registration can be updated.

The certificate holder should ensure that state laws relating to the use of "doing business as (d/b/a)" are complied with fully.

CROSS REFERENCES

135.11, Application and Issue of Certificate and Operations Specifications; 135.25, Aircraft Requirements.

ADVISORY CIRCULARS

AC 135-13A *List of Air Carriers Certificated by FAR Part 135* (1992).

135.31 ADVERTISING

No certificate holder may advertise or otherwise offer to perform operations subject to this part that are not authorized by the certificate holder's operating certificate and Operations Specifications.

EXPLANATION

Certificate holders should ensure that advertising in telephone directories, etc. does not appear prior to actual certification of the operation by the FAA.

CROSS REFERENCES

135.11, Application and Issue of Certificate and Operations Specifications.

135.33 AREA LIMITATIONS ON OPERATIONS

(a) No person may operate an aircraft in a geographical area that is not specifically authorized by appropriate Operations Specifications issued under this part.
(b) No person may operate an aircraft in a foreign country unless that person is authorized to do so by that country.

EXPLANATION

To obtain information regarding the offices to contact in foreign countries for authority to operate therein, contact the local Flight Standards District Office or the Office of International Aviation, AIA-1, Federal Aviation Administration, 800 Independence Avenue, S.W., Washington, DC 20591, (202) 267-3213.

CROSS REFERENCES

135.5, Certificate and Operations Specifications Required; 135.11, Application and Issue of Certificate and Operations Specifications; 135.13, Eligibility for Certificate and Operations

Specifications; 135.21, Manual Requirements; 135.43, Crewmember Certificate: International Operations: Application and Issue.

ADVISORY CIRCULARS

AC 99-1C *Security Control of Air Traffic* (1989).

AC 120-26H *International Civil Aviation Organization Three-Letter and Radio Telephony Designators* (1991).

AC 129-3 *Foreign Air Carrier* (1982).

AIRMAN'S INFORMATION MANUAL

Prohibited Area, Para. 3-31;
Restricted Area, Para. 3-32;
Warning Area, Para. 3-33;
Military Operations Areas (MOA), Para. 3-34;
Alert Area, Para. 3-35;
Controlled Firing Areas, Para. 3-36;
Airport Advisory Area, Para. 3-40;
Military Training Routes (MTR), Para. 3-41;
Published VFR Routes, Para. 3-45;
Flights Outside the United States and U.S. territories, Para. 5-9;
Airways and Route Systems, Para. 5-33.

135.35 TERMINATION OF OPERATIONS

Within 30 days after a certificate holder terminates operations under this part, the operating certificate and Operations Specifications must be surrendered by the certificate holder to the FAA Flight Standards District Office charged with the overall inspection of the certificate holder.

EXPLANATION

If a certificate holder temporarily ceases operation with the intent of resuming at a time more than 30 days in the future, it should contact the FAA and see if some sort of arrangement can be made to allow resumption without a complete recertification process.

CROSS REFERENCES

135.9, Duration of Certificate; 135.37, Management Personnel Required.

135.37 MANAGEMENT PERSONNEL REQUIRED

(a) Each certificate holder, other than one who uses only one pilot in the certificate holder's operations, must have enough qualified management personnel in the following or equivalent positions to ensure safety in its operations:
  (1) Director of operations.
  (2) Chief pilot.
  (3) Director of maintenance.

(b) Upon application by the certificate holder, the Administrator may approve different positions or numbers of positions than those listed in paragraph (a) of this section for a particular operation if the certificate holder shows that it can perform its operations safely under the direction of fewer or different categories of management personnel.

(c) Each certificate holder shall —
  (1) Set forth the duties, responsibilities, and authority of the personnel required by this section in the manual required by §135.21;
  (2) List in the manual required by §135.21 the name of the person or persons assigned to those positions; and
  (3) Within 10 working days, notify the FAA Flight Standards District Office charged with the overall inspection of the certificate holder of any change made in the assignment of persons to the listed positions.

EXPLANATION

See explanation portion of §135.21 regarding the types of operators that may seek a deviation from the management personnel requirements of this section.

Deviations for a Basic Part 135 Operator who proposes to conduct on-demand passenger or cargo carrying operations, or only scheduled cargo carrying operations can be authorized by the Manager of the Flight Standards District Office assigned certification responsibilities. For Basic Part 135 Operators proposing to conduct scheduled passenger (commuter) operations, deviations must be approved by the Regional Flight Standards Division Manager.

Director of Maintenance serves as administrative controller with overall responsibility for separating inspections and maintenance functions.

Part 135 operators may use part-time personnel, but they must have the necessary qualifications to fulfill the responsibilities of the position and must be readily available to fulfill those responsibilities.

CROSS REFERENCES

135.21, Manual Requirements; 135.63(a)(4), Recordkeeping Requirements.

NTSB DECISIONS

In a case involving numerous other violations, the Board found a violation of §135.37(a)(1),(2),(3), and (c). The Board stated that although respondent exercised some efforts to fill these positions, and in fact submitted the names of several persons to be Director of Maintenance which were rejected by the FAA, the fact remained that respondent operated for extended periods of time during which these critical positions were vacant.

In a footnote, the Board commented that, although some reasonable "grace period" should be allowed in filling such vacancies, they could not find the periods involved herein (9 months for Director of Maintenance and Director of Operations and 3 months for Chief Pilot) acceptable. *Administrator v. Southeast Air, Inc.,* 5 NTSB 705 (1985).

135.39 MANAGEMENT PERSONNEL QUALIFICATIONS

(a) *Director of operations.* No person may serve as director of operations under §135.37(a) unless that person knows the contents of the manual required by §135.21, the Operations Specifications, the provisions of this part and other applicable regulations necessary for the proper performance of the person's duties and responsibilities and:
  (1) The director of operations for a certificate holder conducting any operations for which the pilot in command is required to hold an airline transport pilot certificate must —
    (i) Hold or have held an airline transport pilot certificate; and
    (ii) Have at least 3 years of experience as pilot in command of an aircraft operated under this part, Part 121 or Part 127 of this chapter; or
    (iii) Have at least 3 years of experience as director of operations with a certificate holder operating under this part, Part 121 or Part 127 of this chapter.
  (2) The director of operations for a certificate holder who is not conducting any operation for which the pilot in command is required to hold airline transport pilot certificate must —
    (i) Hold or have held a commercial pilot certificate; and
    (ii) Have at least 3 years of experience as a pilot in command of an aircraft operated under this part, Part 121 or Part 127 of this chapter; or
    (iii) Have at least 3 years of experience as director of operations with a certificate holder operating under this part, Part 121 or Part 127 of this chapter.

(b) *Chief pilot.* No person may serve as chief pilot under §135.37(a) unless that person knows the contents of the manual required by §135.21, the Operations Specifications, the provisions of this part and other applicable regulations necessary for the proper performance of the person's duties, and:
  (1) The chief pilot of a certificate holder conducting any operation for which the pilot in command is required to hold an airline transport pilot certificate must —

(i) Hold a current airline transport pilot certificate with appropriate ratings for at least one of the types of aircraft used; and

(ii) Have at least 3 years of experience as a pilot in command of an aircraft under this part, Part 121 or Part 127 of this chapter.

(2) The chief pilot of a certificate holder who is not conducting any operation for which the pilot in command is required to hold an airline transport pilot certificate must —

(i) Hold a current, commercial pilot certificate with an instrument rating. If an instrument rating is not required for the pilot in command under this part, the chief pilot must hold a current, commercial pilot certificate; and

(ii) Have at least 3 years of experience as a pilot in command of an aircraft under this part, Part 121 or Part 127 of this chapter.

(c) *Director of maintenance.* No person may serve as a director of maintenance under §135.37(a) unless that person knows the maintenance sections of the certificate holder's manual, the Operations Specifications, the provisions of this part and other applicable regulations necessary for the proper performance of the person's duties, and —

(1) Holds a mechanic certificate with both airframe and powerplant ratings; and

(2) Has at least 3 years of maintenance experience as a certificated mechanic on aircraft, including, at the time of appointment as director of maintenance, the recent experience requirements of §65.83 of this chapter in the same category and class of aircraft as used by the certificate holder, or at least 3 years of experience with a certificated airframe repair station, including 1 year in the capacity of approving aircraft for return to service.

(d) Deviation from this section may be authorized if the person has had equivalent aeronautical experience. The Flight Standards Division Manager in the region of the certificate holding district office may authorize a deviation for the director of operations, chief pilot, and the director of maintenance.

EXPLANATION

Deviations may be granted from the minimum experience requirements of this section; however, the appropriate certificates and ratings must be held.

The director of operations is not required to presently hold an airline transport pilot or commercial pilot certificate as appropriate. It is sufficient that he/she held one at some time. Chief Pilots must presently hold appropriate current airman certificates.

CROSS REFERENCES

65.83, Recent Experience Requirements; 135.17(a), (b) and (d), Amendment of Operations Specifications; 135.21, Manual Requirements; 135.37(a), Management Personnel Required; 135.243, Pilot-In-Command Qualification; 135.244, Operating Experience; 135.247, Pilot Qualifications: Recent Experience; 135.215, IFR: Operating Limitations; 135.427, Manual Requirements; 135.15(b) Amendment of Certificate.

ADVISORY CIRCULARS

AC 120-51A *Crew Resource Management Training* (1993).

AC 120-53 *Crew Qualification and Pilot Type Rating Requirements for Transport Category Aircraft Operated Under FAR Part 121* (1991).

135.41 CARRIAGE OF NARCOTIC DRUGS, MARIHUANA, AND DEPRESSANT OR STIMULANT DRUGS OR SUBSTANCES

If the holder of a certificate issued under this part allows any aircraft owned or leased by that holder to be engaged in any operation that the certificate holder knows to be in violation of §91.19(a) of this chapter, that operation is a basis for suspending or revoking the certificate.

EXPLANATION

If a certificate holder is the owner of the aircraft and is found to have violated this section, the registration certificate of the aircraft may be subject to revocation.

Aircraft found to be carrying controlled substances may be subject to seizure by Federal agencies, i.e. Drug Enforcement Agency (DEA).

CROSS REFERENCES

91.19(a), Carriage of Narcotic Drugs, Marijuana, and Depressant or Stimulant Drugs or Substances; 135.35, Termination of Operations; §501(e)(2) of the Federal Aviation Act of 1958, as amended (49 U.S.C.App. §1401(e)(2)).

ADVISORY CIRCULARS

AC 121-30 *Guidelines for Developing an Anti-Drug Plan for Aviation Personnel* (1989).

AIRMAN'S INFORMATION MANUAL

Interception Procedures, Para. 5-91.

NTSB DECISIONS

The Board sustained the administrative law judge's finding that the FAA had failed to prove that the aircraft carrying the narcotics was "owned or leased" by the Part 135 certificate holder and, therefore, there was no evidence of a violation of §135.41. *Administrator v. Golden Eagle Air Service, Inc.,* 4 NTSB 918 (1983).

135.43 CREWMEMBER CERTIFICATE: INTERNATIONAL OPERATIONS: APPLICATION AND ISSUE

(a) This section provides for the issuance of a crewmember certificate to United States citizens who are employed by certificate holders as crewmembers on United States registered aircraft engaged in international air commerce. The purpose of the certificate is to facilitate the entry and clearance of those crewmembers into ICAO contracting states. They are issued under Annex 9, as amended, to the Convention on International Civil Aviation.

(b) An application for a crewmember certificate is made on FAA Form 8060-6, "Application for Crewmember Certificate," to the FAA Flight Standards District Office charged with the overall inspection of the certificate holder by whom the applicant is employed. The certificate is issued on FAA Form 8060- 42, "Crewmember Certificate."

(c) The holder of a certificate issued under this section, or the certificate holder by whom the holder is employed, shall surrender the certificate for cancellation at the nearest FAA Flight Standards District Office or submit it for cancellation to the Airmen Certification Branch, AAC-260, P.O. Box 25082, Oklahoma City, Oklahoma 73125, at the termination of the holder's employment with that certificate holder.

EXPLANATION

Crewmember certificates are issued only to U.S. citizens. When making application for a certificate, an applicant must have proof of birth. Documents entitled "Notification of Birth Registration" or "Birth Announcement" are not acceptable. If an applicant does not have a birth certificate indicating that it was filed within one year after the date of birth, an applicant should contact the local Flight Standards District Office to determine what additional documentation will be required.

Temporary removal from international duty assignment with the intent to return to such duty with the same employer does not require surrender of the certificate.

CROSS REFERENCES

135.13, Eligibility for Certificate and Operations Specifications; 135.35, Termination of Operations; 135.63, Recordkeeping Requirements.

ADVISORY CIRCULARS

AC 120-35B *Line Operational Simulations: Line-Oriented Flight Training, Special Purpose Operational Training, Line Operational Evaluation* (1990).

AC 120-51A *Crew Resource Management Training* (1993).

AC 120-53 *Crew Qualification and Pilot Type Rating Requirements for Transport Category Aircraft Operated Under FAR Part 121* (1991).

AC 129-3 *Foreign Air Carrier* (1982).

AIRMAN'S INFORMATION MANUAL

Flights Outside the United States and U.S. Territories, Para. 5-9;
Airways and Route Systems, Para. 5-33.
International Civil Aviation Organization (ICAO) Terminal Forecasts (TAF), Para. 7-29;

SUBPART B — FLIGHT OPERATIONS

135.61 GENERAL

This subpart prescribes rules, in addition to those in Part 91 of this chapter, that apply to operations under this part.

EXPLANATION

Part 135 operators must also comply with the regulations in Part 91, except where Part 135 operations are expressly excepted.

135.63 RECORDKEEPING REQUIREMENTS

(a) Each certificate holder shall keep at its principal business office or at other places approved by the Administrator, and shall make available for inspection by the Administrator the following —
   (1) The certificate holder's operating certificate;
   (2) The certificate holder's Operations Specifications;
   (3) A current list of the aircraft used or available for use in operations under this part and the operations for which each is equipped; and
   (4) An individual record of each pilot used in operations under this part, including the following information:
      (i) The full name of the pilot.
      (ii) The pilot certificate (by type and number) and ratings that the pilot holds.
      (iii) The pilot's aeronautical experience in sufficient detail to determine the pilot's qualifications to pilot aircraft in operations under this part.
      (iv) The pilot's current duties and the date of the pilot's assignment to those duties.
      (v) The effective date and class of the medical certificate that the pilot holds.
      (vi) The date and result of each of the initial and recurrent competency tests and proficiency and route checks required by this part and the type of aircraft flown during that test or check.
      (vii) The pilot's flight time in sufficient detail to determine compliance with the flight time limitations of this part.
      (viii) The pilot's check pilot authorization, if any.
      (ix) Any action taken concerning the pilot's release from employment for physical or professional disqualification.
      (x) The date of the completion of the initial phase and each recurrent phase of the training required by this part.

(b) Each certificate holder shall keep each record required by paragraph (a)(3) of this section for at least 6 months, and each record required by paragraph (a)(4) of this section for at least 12 months, after it is made.

(c) For multi-engine aircraft, each certificate holder is responsible for the preparation and accuracy of a load manifest in duplicate containing information concerning the loading of the aircraft. The manifest must be prepared before each takeoff and must include —
   (1) The number of passengers;
   (2) The total weight of the loaded aircraft;
   (3) The maximum allowable takeoff weight for that flight;
   (4) The center of gravity limits;
   (5) The center of gravity of the loaded aircraft, except that the actual center of gravity need not be computed if the aircraft is loaded according to a loading schedule or other approved method that ensures that the center of gravity of the loaded aircraft is within approved limits. In those cases, an entry shall be made on the manifest indicating that the center of gravity is within limits according to a loading schedule or other approved method;
   (6) The registration number of the aircraft or flight number;
   (7) The origin and destination; and
   (8) Identification of crewmembers and their crew position assignments.

(d) The pilot in command of an aircraft for which a load manifest must be prepared shall carry a copy of the completed load manifest in the aircraft to its destination. The certificate holder shall keep copies of completed load manifests for at least 30 days at its principal operations base, or at another location used by it and approved by the Administrator.

EXPLANATION

"Paper violations" may seem unimportant, but Part 135 operators should take recordkeeping seriously. Records are the only way to prove compliance with the safety regulations. The FAA might assume that an operation that is careless about records is also careless about safety.

135.63(a)(4): Pilot records regarding flight time must reflect "other commercial flying" even if done for another employer. See §135.267(c)(2).

Part 121 requires that computer-based record-keeping systems be approved by the FAA. §135.63 does not specify the method by which the records are kept nor does it require approval of computer-based record systems for Part 135 operators.

135.63(b): Maintaining records beyond the time required by the regulations gives the FAA more to look at and greater chance for the discovery of discrepancies that may have occurred in the past.

However, operators may want to retain crewmember records beyond the required period. Remember that, in order to establish a crewmember's qualifications, evidence of certain training and testing (i.e. basic indoctrination, initial, transition, upgrade training, and one-time initial qualifications such as operating experience required by §135.244) must be available for the duration of the crewmember's employment. Recurrent training and qualification records which have been superseded by more recent records of the same type need not be retained more than 12 months (i.e., instrument checks or recency experience).

CROSS REFERENCES

135.2(e)(1)(i), Air Taxi Operations with Large Aircraft; 135.5, Certificate and Operations Specifications Required; 135.11(b)(2)(iii) and (iv), Application and Issue of Certificate and Operations Specifications; 135.13, Eligibility for Certificate and Operations Specifications; 135.23(b), Manual Contents; 135.27, Business Office and Operations Base; 135.185, Empty Weight and Center of Gravity: Currency Requirement; 135.243, Pilot In Command Qualifications; 135.244, Operating Experience; 135.245, Second In Command Qualifications; 135.247(a), Pilot Qualifications: Recent Experience; 135.293, Initial and Recurrent Pilot Testing Requirements; 135.337, Training Program: Check Airmen and Instructor Qualifications.

ADVISORY CIRCULARS

AC 120-53 *Crew Qualification and Pilot Type Rating Requirements for Transport Category Aircraft Operated Under Part 121* (1991).

NTSB DECISIONS

The Board held that, whether respondent calculated weight and balance aside from the load manifest, as he says he did, is not the issue. The absence of a load manifest is prima facie evidence that the requisite weight and balance calculations were not made. In any event, the allegation addressed only the matter of failure to prepare or carry a copy of the load manifest and even if respondent had, by some other means, computed weight and balance, the violation of §135.63(c) would still stand. *Administrator v. Hutt and Viking Aviation, Inc.*, 5 NTSB 2432 (1987).

In finding that the load manifests were incorrectly filled out, the Board held that the violations reflected, at best, extremely sloppy record-keeping and, at worst, the operation of aircraft outside of center of gravity limits. It went on to say that even if some of the aircraft only exceeded the limits slightly, the safety implications were obvious and significant. *Administrator v. Southeast Air, Inc.*, 5 NTSB 705 (1985).

In sustaining a violation of §135.63(d) the Board found that a copy of the load manifest carried by the pilot must be "completed". In this case, the manifests were incomplete in a number of significant respects. *Administrator v. Blackburn,* 4 NTSB 409 (1982).

FAA CHIEF COUNSEL OPINIONS

If a check pilot sitting in the jump seat has the requisite degree of control, authority, and responsibility regarding the safe operation of the flight, then the time so spent will count for purposes of flight time limitations. On the other hand, if the check pilot sitting in the jump seat is merely an observer/advisor with no control, authority, or responsibility regarding the safe operation of the flight, then the time so spent will not count for purposes of the flight time limitations and need not be recorded by the air carrier. (8-16-90).

§135.63(c) provides that load manifests must be prepared in duplicate. §135.63(d) requires that the pilot in command must carry a copy of the load manifest. There is no provision for the disposition of other copy or copies. The disposition of the copy or copies should be provided for in the operator's manual. (11-5-80).

135.65 REPORTING MECHANICAL IRREGULARITIES

(a) Each certificate holder shall provide an aircraft maintenance log to be carried on board each aircraft for recording or deferring mechanical irregularities and their correction.
(b) The pilot in command shall enter or have entered in the aircraft maintenance log each mechanical irregularity that comes to the pilot's attention during flight time. Before each flight, the pilot in command shall, if the pilot does not already know, determine the status of each irregularity entered in the maintenance log at the end of the preceding flight.
(c) Each person who takes corrective action or defers action concerning a reported or observed failure or malfunction of an airframe, powerplant, propeller, rotor, or appliance, shall record the action taken in the aircraft maintenance log under the applicable maintenance requirements of this chapter.
(d) Each certificate holder shall establish a procedure for keeping copies of the aircraft maintenance log required by this section in the aircraft for access by appropriate personnel and shall include that procedure in the manual required by §135.21.

EXPLANATION

A flight is considered to have departed when it moves under its own power (forward or backward) for purposes of flight.

"Mechanical irregularity" is not defined in the FAR. However, the NTSB has held that "any deviation from the normal functioning of an aircraft component **no matter how slight or momentary**," constitutes a mechanical irregularity.

Unlike §121.563, which requires that the mechanical irregularities be logged at the end of the flight time, §135.65(b) does not specify when it must be done. It is recommended that it be done at the end of the flight.

CROSS REFERENCES

135.21, Manual Requirements; 135.23(f), (g), (h), and (i), Manual Contents; 135.415, Mechanical Reliability Reports; 135.417(a) and (b), Mechanical Interruption Summary Report; 135.421(b), Additional Maintenance Requirements; 135.443, Airworthiness Release or Aircraft Maintenance Log Entry.

ADVISORY CIRCULARS

AC 120-30A *Reporting Requirements of Air Carriers, Commercial Operators, Travel Clubs, and Air Traffic* (1976).

AC 121-1A *Standard Operations Specifications-Aircraft Maintenance Handbook* (1978).

AC 129-4 *Maintenance Programs for U.S. Registered Aircraft Under FAR Part 129* (1988).

NTSB DECISIONS

The Board has held that "any deviation from the normal functioning of an aircraft component **no matter how slight or momentary**," constitutes a mechanical irregularity. The mechanical irregularity must be put directly onto the logbook's pages. The regulation is not complied with by the placing of a piece of paper with the discrepancies listed in the logbook. *Administrator v. Hardisson,* EA-3997 (1993).

The Board upheld an administrative law judge's finding of a violation of §135.65(b) where the judge, while noting that the regulation did not specify a time period in which the entry must be made, applied a reasonableness standard. The judge found that making the entry the next day, after the aircraft had been turned over to a mechanic, was not reasonable. *Administrator v. Chiplock,* EA-3556 (1992).

Where an operator used the sticker system for deferred items, the mere removal of the sticker at time of corrective action did not meet the requirements of this regulation. Corrective action must be logged. *Administrator v. Apollo Airways, Inc., d/b/a Pacific Coast Airlines, Inc.,* 5 NTSB 1284 (1986).

135.67 REPORTING POTENTIALLY HAZARDOUS METEOROLOGICAL CONDITIONS AND IRREGULARITIES OF COMMUNICATIONS OR NAVIGATION FACILITIES

Whenever a pilot encounters a potentially hazardous meteorological condition or an irregularity in a ground communications or navigational facility in flight, the knowledge of which the pilot considers essential to the safety of other flights, the pilot shall notify an appropriate ground radio station as soon as practicable.

EXPLANATION

Unlike §91.183, which applies only while an aircraft is being operated under IFR in controlled airspace, §135.67 applies to all flights in any airspace. Describing the problem in a NASA form is not required, but would help other pilots.

CROSS REFERENCES

91.25, Aviation Safety Reporting Program; 91.183, IFR Radio Communications; 121.561, Reporting Potentially Hazardous Meteorological Conditions and Irregularities of Ground and Navigation Facilities.

ADVISORY CIRCULARS

AC 00-46C *Aviation Safety Reporting Program* (1985).

AIRMAN'S INFORMATIONAL MANUAL

Pilot Weather Reports (PIREPS), Para. 7-19;
PIREPS Relating to Airframe Icing, Para. 7-20;
PIREPS Relating to Turbulence, Para. 7-21;
Wind Shear PIREPS, Para. 7-22;
Clear Air Turbulence (CAT) PIREPS, Para. 7-23.

135.69 RESTRICTION OR SUSPENSION OF OPERATIONS: CONTINUATION OF FLIGHT IN AN EMERGENCY

(a) During operations under this part, if a certificate holder or pilot in command knows of conditions, including airport and runway conditions, that are a hazard to safe operations, the certificate holder or pilot in command, as the case may be, shall restrict or suspend operations as necessary until those conditions are corrected.

(b) No pilot in command may allow a flight to continue toward any airport of intended landing under the conditions set forth in paragraph (a) of this section, unless in the opinion of the pilot in command, the conditions that are a hazard to safe operations may reasonably be expected to be corrected by the estimated time of arrival or, unless there is no safer procedure. In the latter event, the continuation toward that airport is an emergency situation under §135.19.

EXPLANATION

While Part 135 does not require operators to prepare a formal release authorizing a specific flight, use of such a system by a Part 135 certificate holder can give it the control necessary to ensure that there is compliance with §135.69.

The Notice To Airman (NOTAM) System is the best source for current airport information.

CROSS REFERENCES

135.19, Emergency Operations.

AIRMAN'S INFORMATION MANUAL

Notice To Airman (NOTAM) System, Para. 5-3;
Pilot Responsibility and Authority, Para. 6-1;
Distress and Urgency Communications, Para. 6-20;
Obtaining Emergency Assistance, Para. 6-21;
Special Emergency (Air Piracy), Para. 6-23.

135.71 AIRWORTHINESS CHECK

The pilot in command may not begin a flight unless the pilot determines that the airworthiness inspections required by §91.409 of this chapter, or §135.419, whichever is applicable, have been made.

CROSS REFERENCES

91.409, Inspections; 135.23(e), Manual Contents; 135.419, Approved Aircraft Inspection Program.

ADVISORY CIRCULARS

AC 91-60 *The Continued Airworthiness of Older Airplanes* (1983).

AC 120-16C *Continuous Airworthiness Maintenance Programs* (1980).

135.73 INSPECTIONS AND TESTS

Each certificate holder and each person employed by the certificate holder shall allow the Administrator, at any time or place, to make inspections or test (including enroute inspections) to determine the holder's compliance with the Federal Aviation Act of 1958, applicable regulations, and the certificate holder's operating certificate, and Operations Specifications.

EXPLANATION

The statutory basis for this regulation is §313(a) of the Federal Aviation Act of 1958, as amended [49 U.S.C.App. §1354(a)].

CROSS REFERENCES

135.5, Certificate and Operations Specifications Required; 135.75 Inspectors Credentials: Admission to Pilots' Compartment: Forward Observer's Seat.

135.75 INSPECTORS CREDENTIALS: ADMISSIONS TO PILOT'S COMPARTMENT: FORWARD OBSERVER'S SEAT

(a) Whenever, in performing the duties of conducting an inspection, an FAA inspector presents an Aviation Safety Inspector credential, FAA Form 110A, to the pilot in command of an aircraft operated by the certificate holder, the inspector must be given free and uninterrupted access to the pilot's compartment of that aircraft. However, this paragraph does not limit the emergency authority of the pilot in command to exclude any person from the pilot's compartment in the interest of safety.

(b) A forward observer's seat on the flight deck, or forward passenger seat with headset or speaker must be provided for use by the Administrator while conducting enroute inspections. The suitability of the location of the seat and the headset or speaker for use in conducting enroute inspections is determined by the Administrator.

EXPLANATION

All the certificate holder's personnel should be aware of the FAA inspector's priority in being provided with the jump seat or a forward passenger seat for the conduct of an enroute or other type of inspection.

While the FAA inspector must be provided with either a headset or a speaker to monitor crew communications, there is no requirement to provide a microphone.

CROSS REFERENCES

135.19(b), Emergency Operations; 135.73, Inspections and Tests.

FAA CHIEF COUNSEL OPINIONS

In response to an inquiry whether a certificate holder must offload a revenue passenger to accommodate an FAA inspector conducting an inspection and, if offloaded, what obligations does it owe to the passenger, the FAA stated that it is the FAA's policy to minimize any disruption of the certificate holder's operation caused by an inspection. Therefore, the inspector will usually inform the certificate holder in advance of the inspection. If there is a conflict, the planned inspection will be rescheduled in all but the most unusual cases. However, if the inspection must be conducted on that flight, the passenger must be offloaded. The certificate holder's obligations to the passenger would be governed by the provisions of its contract of carriage, local law, and any applicable economic regulations of the Department of Transportation.

If an operator has substituted a smaller aircraft due to passenger load on a flight that an FAA inspector has scheduled an inspection, the FAA has said that generally an FAA inspector would not require the certificate holder to use the larger aircraft.

Although §135.75 provides nearly unlimited access to a certificate holder's aircraft by FAA inspectors, cooperation between the certificate holder and its assigned FAA inspectors should minimize, and perhaps eliminate, problems such as those described. (2-13-87).

135.77 RESPONSIBILITY FOR OPERATIONAL CONTROL

Each certificate holder is responsible for operational control and shall list, in the manual required by §135.21, the name and title of each person authorized by it to exercise operational control.

EXPLANATION

"Operational control," with respect to a flight, means the exercise of authority over initiating, conducting, or terminating a flight. [14 CFR §1.1]

While the certificate holder may delegate the authority to exercise operational control to another person, such delegation does not relieve the certificate holder of the responsibility for operational control. Paragraph A8 of a certificate holder's Operations Specifications (ops specs) must define operational control.

Part 135 operators may contract for equipment, facilities, and the services of operational control personnel. However, the Part 135 operator is responsible for ensuring that contractor personnel are properly trained and qualified, perform their duties diligently, and that there is full compliance with its manual. The operator's manual must contain the names and titles of contract personnel to whom the exercise of operational control is delegated.

Even in an air ambulance service flight, the pilot in command must exercise final authority to initiate, conduct, or terminate a flight.

CROSS REFERENCES

135.21, Manual Requirements.

ADVISORY CIRCULARS

AC 121.445-1D *Pilot-In-Command Qualifications for Special Areas/Routes* and *Airports* (1990).

AIRMAN'S INFORMATION MANUAL

Pilot Responsibility and Authority, Para. 6-1;
Judgment Aspects of Collision Avoidance, Para. 8-8.

135.79 FLIGHT LOCATING REQUIREMENTS

(a) Each certificate holder must have procedures established for locating each flight, for which an FAA flight plan is not filed, that —
  (1) Provide the certificate holder with at least the information required to be included in a VFR flight plan;
  (2) Provide for timely notification of an FAA facility or search and rescue facility, if an aircraft is overdue or missing; and
  (3) Provide the certificate holder with the location, date, and estimated time for reestablishing radio or telephone communications, if the flight will operate in an area where communications cannot be maintained.

(b) Flight locating information shall be retained at the certificate holder's principal place of business, or at other places designated by the certificate holder in the flight locating procedures, until the completion of the flight.

(c) Each certificate holder shall furnish the representative of the Administrator assigned to it with a copy of its flight locating procedures and any changes or additions, unless those procedures are included in a manual required under this part.

EXPLANATION

An operator's general operations manual must prohibit the pilot-in-command from operating without an activated flight plan until arrival at the destination airport. Therefore, satisfying §135.79 by filing FAA flight plans may preclude certain types of operations. For example, a pilot cannot cancel an IFR flight plan at the last navigational fix and proceed to the destination VFR, because there will be a period of time when the flight is not under an active flight plan as the pilot switches to the FSS frequency to activate the VFR flight plan. **Air Traffic Control does not accept composite IFR/VFR flight plans and normally will not activate a VFR flight plan on an air traffic control frequency.**

A pilot who cancels IFR and then changes to a flight watch frequency to activate a VFR flight plan is not in compliance with §135.79.

CROSS REFERENCES

91.153, VFR Flight Plan: Information Required; 135.23(1) Manual Contents; 135.27, Business Office and Operations Base.

AIRMAN'S INFORMATION MANUAL

Preflight Preparation, Para. 5-1;
Flight Plan-VFR Flights, Para. 5-4;
Composite Flight Plan (VFR/IFR Flights), Para. 5-6;
Closing VFR/DVFR Flight Plans, Para. 5-12;
Search and Rescue, Para. 6-16.

135.81 INFORMING PERSONNEL OF OPERATIONAL INFORMATION AND APPROPRIATE CHANGES

Each certificate holder shall inform each person in its employment of the Operations Specifications that apply to that person's duties and responsibilities and shall make available to each pilot in the certificate holder's employ the following materials in current form:
(a) Airman's Information Manual (Alaska Supplement in Alaska and Pacific Chart Supplement in Pacific-Asia Regions) or a commercial publication that contains the same information.
(b) This part and Part 91 of this chapter.
(c) Aircraft Equipment Manuals, and Aircraft Flight Manual or equivalent.
(d) For foreign operations, the International Flight Information Manual or a commercial publication that contains the same information concerning the pertinent operational and entry requirements of the foreign country or countries involved.

EXPLANATION

A flight manual is any manual approved by the FAA that an operator uses to comply with this section. A flight manual may be an approved Airplane Flight Manual (AFM), an approved Rotorcraft Flight Manual (RFM), or an approved Company Flight Manual (CFM). If there is a CFM on board, an operator is not required to also have on board an AFM.

CROSS REFERENCES

135.21(d)(1), Manual Requirements; 135.43, Crewmember Certificate: International Operations: Application and Issue.

ADVISORY CIRCULARS

AC 120-51A *Crew Resource Management Training* (1993).

NTSB DECISIONS

The NTSB, in sustaining a finding of numerous violations, including one of §135.81(a) for failure to provide a current Airman's Information Manual, stated that this regulation does not excuse noncompliance during periods of office remodeling, as the operator appears to argue, or for other circumstances fully within the certificate holder's control. *Administrator v. Eagle Commuter Airlines, Inc.,* 5 NTSB 1106 (1986).

135.83 OPERATING INFORMATION REQUIRED

(a) The operator of an aircraft must provide the following materials, in current and appropriate form, accessible to the pilot at the pilot station, and the pilot shall use them:
   (1) A cockpit checklist.
   (2) For multi-engine aircraft or for aircraft with retractable landing gear, an emergency cockpit checklist containing the procedures required by paragraph (c) of this section, as appropriate.
   (3) Pertinent aeronautical charts.
   (4) For IFR operations, each pertinent navigational enroute, terminal area, and approach and letdown chart.
   (5) For multi-engine aircraft, one-engine-inoperative climb performance data and if the aircraft s approved for use in IFR or over-the-top operations, that data must be sufficient to enable the pilot to determine compliance with §135.181(a)(2).

(b) Each cockpit checklist required by paragraph (a)(1) of this section must contain the following procedures:
   (1) Before starting engines;
   (2) Before takeoff;
   (3) Cruise;
   (4) Before landing;
   (5) After landing;
   (6) Stopping engines.

(c) Each emergency cockpit checklist required by paragraph (a)(2) of this section must contain the following procedures, as appropriate:
   (1) Emergency operation of fuel, hydraulic, electrical, and mechanical systems.
   (2) Emergency operation of instruments and controls.
   (3) Engine inoperative procedures.
   (4) Any other emergency procedures necessary for safety.

EXPLANATION

Certificate holders should establish procedures to make sure that these materials are updated as required, and that the pilots use these materials.

CROSS REFERENCES

135.123, Emergency and Emergency Evacuation Duties; 135.181(a)(2), Performance Requirements: Aircraft Operated Over-the-Top or In IFR Conditions; 135.219, IFR: Destination Airport Weather Minimums.

AIRMAN'S INFORMATION MANUAL

Obtaining Civil Aeronautical Charts, Para. 9-2;
Related Publications, Para. 9-5.

NTSB DECISIONS

Where pilot conducted a VFR flight using only Jeppesen IFR charts for navigational assistance and argued, when charged with a violation of §135.83(a)(3), that, while he did not disagree that sectional and Terminal Area Charts are pertinent to VFR operations, that the Jeppesen charts were sufficient or "pertinent" to his flight since he had extensive experience flying this route, the Board sustained the finding of violation. The Board said that, while the Jeppesen IFR charts may furnish data suitable for radio navigation, they did not appear to contain sufficient information for VFR pilotage in the event of a radio equipment malfunction or other emergency necessitating visual reference to landmarks on the ground. In such circumstances, even a pilot with extensive VFR flight experience on a certain route may be required to alter his usual flight path and enter airspace with which he is not wholly familiar. Unable to use his customary visual guideposts, he would need to refer to sectional and/or Terminal Area Charts to safely plot an alternate course. *Administrator v. Murray,* EA-3988 (1993).

[See §135.81, NTSB Decisions: *Administrator v. Eagle Commuter Airlines, Inc.,* 5 NTSB 1106 (1986).]

135.85 CARRIAGE OF PERSONS WITHOUT COMPLIANCE WITH THE PASSENGER-CARRYING PROVISIONS OF THIS PART

The following persons may be carried aboard an aircraft without complying with the passenger-carrying requirements of this part:
(a) A crewmember or other employee of the certificate holder.
(b) A person necessary for the safe handling of animals on the aircraft.
(c) A person necessary for the safe handling of hazardous materials (as defined in Subchapter C of Title 49 CFR).
(d) A person performing duty as a security or honor guard accompanying a shipment made by or under the authority of the U.S. Government.
(e) A military courier or a military route supervisor carried by a military cargo contract air carrier or commercial operator in operations under a military cargo contract, if that carriage is specifically authorized by the appropriate military service.
(f) An authorized representative of the Administrator conducting an enroute inspection.
(g) A person, authorized by the Administrator, who is performing a duty connected with a cargo operation of the certificate holder.

CROSS REFERENCES

135.73, Inspections and Tests; 135.75, Inspectors Credentials: Admissions to Pilots' Compartment: Forward Observer's Seat; 135.333, Training Requirements: Handling and Carriage of Hazardous Materials.

135.87 CARRIAGE OF CARGO INCLUDING CARRY-ON BAGGAGE

No person may carry cargo, including carry-on baggage, in or on any aircraft unless —

(a) It is carried in an approved cargo rack, bin, or compartment installed in or on the aircraft;

(b) It is secured by an approved means; or

(c) It is carried in accordance with each of the following:

  (1) For cargo, it is properly secured by a safety belt of other tie-down having enough strength to eliminate the possibility of shifting under all normally anticipated flight and ground conditions, or for carry-on baggage, it is restrained so as to prevent its movement during air turbulence.

  (2) It is packaged or covered to avoid possible injury to occupants.

  (3) It does not impose any load on seats or on the floor structure that exceeds the load limitation for those components.

  (4) It is not located in a position that obstructs the access to, or use of, any required emergency or regular exit, or the use of the aisle between the crew and the passenger compartment, or located in a position that obscures any passenger's view of the "seat belt" sign, "no smoking" sign, or any required exit sign, unless an auxiliary sign or other approved means for proper notification of the passengers is provided.

  (5) It is not carried directly above seated occupants.

  (6) It is stowed in compliance with this section for takeoff and landing.

  (7) For cargo only operation, paragraph (c)(4) of this section does not apply if the cargo is loaded so that at least one emergency or regular exit is available to provide all occupants of the aircraft a means of unobstructed exit from the aircraft if an emergency occurs.

(d) Each passenger seat under which baggage is stowed shall be fitted with a means to prevent articles of baggage stowed under it from sliding under crash impacts severe enough to induce the ultimate inertia forces specified in the emergency landing condition regulations under which the aircraft was type certificated.

(e) When cargo is carried in cargo compartments that are designed to require the physical entry of a crewmember to extinguish any fire that may occur during flight, the cargo must be loaded so as to allow a crewmember to effectively reach all parts of the compartment with the contents of a hand fire extinguisher.

EXPLANATION

Part 135 does not require use of the under-seat area for stowing carry-on baggage, but it is allowed if the stated conditions are met.

CROSS REFERENCES

23.561- 23.562, Emergency Landing Conditions; 23.787, Baggage and Cargo Compartments; 25.561-25.563, Emergency Landing Conditions; 25.787, Stowage Compartments; 91.525, Carriage of Cargo; 135.127(f), Passenger Information; 135.129(a)(1), Exit Seating; 135.155(c), Fire Extinguishers: Passenger-Carrying Aircraft; 135.169(d), Additional Airworthiness Requirements; 135.178(f)(1), (2), (3), and (4) Additional Emergency Equipment.

ADVISORY CIRCULARS

AC 121-29 *Carry On Baggage* (1987).

NTSB DECISIONS

Mail bags are not personal baggage, but freight, and can not be secured under a passenger seat as provided by §137.87(c)(1). *Administrator v. Prout*, EA-3062 (1990).

The Board held that neither the possibility that the cargo net was inadequate for securing the cargo nor the fact that it may not have been respondent's duty to ensure that the aircraft was fitted with cargo restraints capable of easily accommodating different size loads relieve him of his responsibility to see that the cargo, whether he or someone else placed it aboard, was secured before operating the flight. *Administrator v. Shields*, 6 NTSB 294 (1988).

135.89 PILOT REQUIREMENTS: USE OF OXYGEN

(a) *Unpressurized aircraft.* Each pilot of an unpressurized aircraft shall use oxygen continuously when flying —
   (1) At altitudes above 10,000 feet through 12,000 feet MSL for that part of the flight at those altitudes that is of more than 30 minutes duration; and
   (2) Above 12,000 feet MSL.

(b) *Pressurized aircraft.*
   (1) Whenever a pressurized aircraft is operated with the cabin pressure altitude more than 10,000 feet MSL, each pilot shall comply with paragraph (a) of this section.
   (2) Whenever a pressurized aircraft is operated at altitudes above 25,000 feet through 35,000 feet MSL, unless each pilot has an approved quick- donning type oxygen mask —
      (i) At least one pilot at the controls shall wear, secured and sealed, an oxygen mask that either supplies oxygen at all times or automatically supplies oxygen whenever the cabin pressure altitude exceeds 12,000 feet MSL; and
      (ii) During that flight, each other pilot on flight deck duty shall have an oxygen mask, connected to an oxygen supply, located so as to allow immediate placing of the mask on the pilot's face sealed and secured for use.

(3) Whenever a pressurized aircraft is operated at altitudes above 35,000 feet MSL, at least one pilot at the controls shall wear, secured and sealed, an oxygen mask required by paragraph (2)(i) of this paragraph.

(4) If one pilot leaves a pilot duty station of an aircraft when operating at altitudes above 25,000 feet MSL, the remaining pilot at the controls shall put on and use an approved oxygen mask until the other pilot returns to the pilot duty station of the aircraft.

CROSS REFERENCES

91.211, Supplemental Oxygen.

ADVISORY CIRCULARS

AC 23.841-1 *Cabin Pressurization Systems In Small Airplanes* (1986).

AC 120-43 *The Influence of Beards on Oxygen Mask Efficiency* (1987).

AC 135-5B *Maintenance Program Approval for Carry-On Oxygen Equipment for Medical Purposes* (1983).

AIRMAN'S INFORMATION MANUAL

Effects of Altitude, Para. 8-2;
Vision in Flight, Para. 8-6.

135.91 OXYGEN FOR MEDICAL USE BY PASSENGERS

(a) Except as provided in paragraphs (d) and (e) of this section, no certificate holder may allow the carriage or operation of equipment for the storage, generation or dispensing of medical oxygen unless the unit to be carried is constructed so that all valves, fittings, and gauges are protected from damage during that carriage or operation and unless the following conditions are met —

(1) The equipment must be —

(i) Of an approved type or in conformity with the manufacturing, packaging, marking, labeling, and maintenance requirements of Title 49 CFR Parts 171, 172, and 173, except §173.24(a)(1);

(ii) When owned by the certificate holder, maintained under the certificate holders approved maintenance program;

(iii) Free of flammable contaminants on all exterior surfaces; and

(iv) Appropriately secured.

(2) When the oxygen is stored in the form of a liquid, the equipment must have been under the certificate holder's approved maintenance program since its purchase new or since the storage container was last purged.

(3) When the oxygen is stored in the form of a compressed gas as defined in Title 49 CFR §173.300(a) —

(i) When owned by the certificate holder, it must be maintained under its approved maintenance program; and

(ii) The pressure in any oxygen cylinder must not exceed the rated cylinder pressure.

(4) The pilot in command must be advised when the equipment is on board, and when it is intended to be used.

(5) The equipment must be stowed, and each person using the equipment must be seated, so as not to restrict access to or use of any required emergency or regular exit, or of the aisle in the passenger compartment.

(b) No person may smoke and no certificate holder may allow any person to smoke within 10 feet of oxygen storage and dispensing equipment carried under paragraph (a) of this section.

(c) No certificate holder may allow any person other than a person trained in the use of medical oxygen equipment to connect or disconnect oxygen bottles or any other ancillary component while any passenger is aboard the aircraft.

(d) Paragraph (a)(1)(i) of this section does not apply when that equipment is furnished by a professional or medical emergency service for use on board an aircraft in a medical emergency when no other practical means of transportation (including any other properly equipped certificate holder) is reasonably available and the person carried under the medical emergency is accompanied by a person trained in the use of medical oxygen.

(e) Each certificate holder who, under the authority of paragraph (d) of this section, deviates from paragraph (a)(1)(i) if this section under a medical emergency shall, within 10 days, excluding Saturdays, Sundays, and Federal holidays, after the deviation, send to the FAA Flight Standards District Office charged with the overall inspection of the certificate holder a complete report of the operation involved, including a description of the deviation and the reasons for it.

EXPLANATION

§135.91(a)(1)(i) allows some flexibility since the certificate holder may get FAA approval for the equipment or meet the applicable requirements of 49 C.F.R. Parts 171, 172, and 173.

CROSS REFERENCES

135.157, Oxygen Equipment Requirements; 135.178(f)(1), (2), (3), and (4), Additional Emergency Equipment; 135.425, Maintenance, Preventive Maintenance, and Alteration Programs.

ADVISORY CIRCULARS

AC 67-1 *Medical Information for Air Ambulance Operators* (1974).

AC 135-5B *Maintenance Program Approval for Carry-On Oxygen Equipment for Medical Purposes* (1983).

AC 135-14A *Emergency Medical Services/-Helicopter (EMS/H)* (1991).

AC 135-15 *Emergency Medical Services/-Airplane (EMS/A)* (1990).

AIRMAN'S INFORMATION MANUAL

Effects of Altitude, Para. 8-2.

135.93 AUTOPILOT: MINIMUM ALTITUDES FOR USE

(a) Except as provided in paragraphs (b), (c), and (d) of this section, no person may use an autopilot at an altitude above the terrain which is less than 500 feet or less than twice the maximum altitude loss specified in the approved Aircraft Flight Manual or equivalent for a malfunction of the autopilot, whichever is higher.

(b) When using an instrument approach facility other than ILS, no person may use an autopilot at an altitude above the terrain that is less than 50 feet below the approved minimum descent altitude for that procedure, or less than twice the maximum loss specified in the approved Airplane Flight Manual or equivalent for a malfunction of the autopilot under approach conditions, whichever is higher.

(c) For ILS approaches, when reported weather conditions are less than the basic weather conditions in §91.155 of this chapter, no person may use an autopilot with an approach coupler at an altitude above the terrain that is less than 50 feet above the terrain, or the maximum altitude loss specified in the approved Airplane Flight Manual or equivalent for the malfunction of the autopilot with approach coupler, whichever is higher.

(d) Without regard to paragraphs (a), (b), or (c) of this section, the Administrator may issue Operations Specifications to allow the use, to touchdown, of an approved flight control guidance system with automatic capability, if —

   (1) The system does not contain any altitude loss (above zero) specified in the approved Aircraft Flight Manual or equivalent for malfunction of the autopilot with approach coupler; and

   (2) The Administrator finds that the use of the system to touchdown will not otherwise adversely affect the safety standards of this section.

(e) This section does not apply to operations conducted in rotorcraft.

EXPLANATION

The term "Aircraft Flight Manual or equivalent" was included to recognize that some aircraft with autopilots do not have, and are not required to have, an airplane flight manual.

Use of automatic landing systems (Autoland) to touch down must be specifically authorized in the operator's Operations Specifications.

CROSS REFERENCES

91.155, Basic VFR Weather Minimums; 91.157, Special VFR Weather Minimums.

ADVISORY CIRCULARS

AC 20-57A *Automatic Landing Systems (ALS)* (1971).

AC 23.1329-2 *Automatic Pilot System Installation in Part 23 Airplanes* (1991).

AC 25.1329-1A *Automatic Pilot Systems Approval* (1968).

135.95 AIRMEN: LIMITATIONS ON USE OF SERVICES

No certificate holder may use the services of any person as an airman unless the person performing those services —

(a) Holds an appropriate and current airman certificate; and

(b) Is qualified, under this chapter, for the operation for which the person is to be used.

CROSS REFERENCES

61.3, Requirement for Certificates, Rating, and Authorizations; 61.65, Instrument Rating Requirements; 61.123, Eligibility Requirements: General (Subpart E — Commercial Pilots); 61.131, Rotorcraft Ratings: Aeronautical Experience (Subpart E — Commercial Pilots); 61.151, Eligibility Requirements: General (Subpart F — Airline Transport Pilots); 61.161, Rotorcraft Rating: Aeronautical Experience (Subpart F — Airline Transport Pilots); 135.243, Pilot-In-Command Qualifications; 135.245 Second-In Command Qualifications; Part 135, Subpart G, Crewmember Testing Requirements; Part 135, Subpart H, Training.

NTSB DECISIONS

In a situation where a violation of §135.95 was found to have occurred as a result of the use of an unqualified second in command, the Board sustained a finding of no violation against the operator. The situation involved use by the operator of a satellite base of operation through another company. The Board held that the other company's employees acted beyond the scope of their employment (through violation of explicit directions, either deliberately or mistakenly) and that the respondent was not negligent or even lax in its oversight responsibilities. *Administrator v. Orco Aviation, Inc. d/b/a Riverside Air Service*, EA-3579 (1992).

FAA CHIEF COUNSEL OPINIONS

A company employee may ride in the right front seat of an aircraft, having a passenger seating configuration, excluding any pilot seat, of less than 9 seats, during a cargo flight not requiring a second in command, if the person is not designated, nor does the person act, as a pilot and does not manipulate the airplane controls. On the other hand, even if it is assumed that a second in command is not required in the flights, if the employee were used as a second in command, it would be necessary that there be compliance with various requirements, including §§135.95, 135.245 and 135.293. (4-10-79).

135.97 AIRCRAFT AND FACILITIES FOR RECENT FLIGHT EXPERIENCE

Each certificate holder shall provide aircraft and facilities to enable each of its pilots to maintain and demonstrate the pilot's ability to conduct all operations for which the pilot is authorized.

CROSS REFERENCES

135.323(a)(2), Training Program: General.

ADVISORY CIRCULARS

AC 61.66 *Annual Pilot In Command Proficiency Checks* (1973).

AC 120-53 *Crew Qualification and Pilot Type Rating Requirements for Transport Category Aircraft Operated Under FAR Part 121* (1991).

FAA CHIEF COUNSEL OPINIONS

If the type of operations a pilot is authorized to fly by the pilot's certificate holder require a commercial pilot certificate, the operator is required under FAR 135.97 to provide the pilot with aircraft and facilities to maintain and demonstrate a pilot's ability to conduct those operations. The certificate holder is **not** required by 135.97 to provide a pilot with aircraft and facilities to maintain that pilot's currency and proficiency for certificates other than those that the pilot is authorized to fly. (12-8-92).

135.99 COMPOSITION OF FLIGHT CREW

(a) No certificate holder may operate an aircraft with less than the minimum flight crew specified in the aircraft operating limitations or the Aircraft Flight Manual for that aircraft and required by this part for the kind of operation being conducted.
(b) No certificate holder may operate an aircraft without a second in command if that aircraft has a passenger seating configuration, excluding any pilot seat, of ten seats or more.

CROSS REFERENCES

135.101, Second In Command Required in IFR Conditions; 135.103, Exception to Second In Command Requirement: IFR Operations; 135.105, Exception to Second In Command Requirement: Approval for Use of Autopilot System; 135.109, Pilot In Command or Second In Command: Designation Required; 135.111, Second In Command Required in Category II Operations; 135.245, Second-In-Command Qualifications.

135.100 FLIGHT CREWMEMBER DUTIES

(a) No certificate holder shall require, nor may any flight crewmember perform, any duties during a critical phase of flight except those duties required for the safe operation of the aircraft. Duties such as company required calls made for such nonsafety related purposes as ordering galley supplies and confirming passenger connections, announcements made to passengers promoting the air carrier or pointing out sights of interest, and filling out company payroll and related records are not required for the safe operation of the aircraft.
(b) No flight crewmember may engage in, nor may any pilot in command permit, any activity during a critical phase of flight which could distract any flight crewmember from the performance of his or her duties or which could interfere in any way with the proper conduct of those duties. Activities such as eating meals, engaging in nonessential conversations within the cockpit and nonessential communications between the cabin and cockpit crews, and reading publications not related to the proper conduct of the flight are not required for the safe operation of the aircraft.

(c) For the purposes of this section, critical phases of flight includes all ground operations involving taxi, takeoff and landing, and all other flight operations conducted below 10,000 feet, except cruise flight.

CROSS REFERENCES

91.123, Compliance with ATC Clearances and Instructions; 135.79, Flight Locating Requirements.

ADVISORY CIRCULARS

AC 25.1523-1 *Minimum Flightcrew* (1993).

AC 120-35B *Line Operational Simulations: Line-Oriented Flight Training, Special Purpose Operational Training, Line Operational Evaluation* (1990).

AIRMAN'S INFORMATION MANUAL

Taxiing, Para. 4-67.

NTSB DECISIONS

Where pilot in command, while aircraft was being taxied to ramp after landing, turned the aircraft over to the second in command dropped his trousers and "mooned" some persons on the airport. The Board ruled that pilot had violated §135.100(b) and §91.9 [now 91.13(a)]. The Board held that the pilot clearly engaged in an activity "which could distract any flight crewmember from his or her duties," in violation of §135.100(b). Also, it held that the pilot placed himself in a position where, albeit for only a brief period, he could perform no duties whatsoever and he also, in the process, distracted his co-pilot who had taken over the taxiing of the aircraft. *Administration v. Uppstrom*, 5 NTSB 1390 (1986).

FAA CHIEF COUNSEL OPINIONS

Calls made for the purpose of operational control and flight locating are permitted by §135.100 in compliance with the requirements of §135.79. (6-29-92).

135.101 SECOND IN COMMAND REQUIRED IN IFR CONDITIONS

Except as provided in §§135.103 and 135.105, no person may operate an aircraft carrying passengers in IFR conditions, unless there is a second in command in the aircraft.

EXPLANATION

If an aircraft is operated in IFR conditions, unless the conditions of either §§135.103 or 135.105 are met, the operator and/or pilot of the aircraft are in violation of §135.101. Since this section is specifically limited to operations in "IFR conditions," it appears operation under "IFR" in "VFR" conditions does not require a second in command.

CROSS REFERENCES

135.99(b), Composition of Flight Crew; 135.103 Exception to Second In Command Requirement: IFR Operations; 135.105, Exception to Second In Command Requirement: Approval for Use of Autopilot System; 135.215, IFR: Operating Limitations; 135.245, Second In Command Qualifications.

ADVISORY CIRCULARS

AC 25.1523-1 *Minimum Flightcrew* (1993).

NTSB DECISIONS

In a case where a pilot argued that he did not violate §135.101 because the reason he exceeded 15 minutes of operation in IFR conditions during departures was only because of vectors given him by ATC, the Board, in finding a violation, said that a reasonable and prudent pilot who had obtained the proper updates of weather should have foreseen that he likely would not have been able to clear IFR conditions within 15 minutes of takeoff. *Administrator v. Mikesell*, 6 NTSB 602 (1988).

135.103 EXCEPTION TO SECOND IN COMMAND REQUIREMENT: IFR OPERATIONS

The pilot in command of an aircraft carrying passengers may conduct IFR operations without a second in command under the following conditions:

(a) A takeoff may be conducted under IFR conditions if the weather reports or forecasts, or any combination of them, indicate that the weather along the planned route of flight allows flight under VFR within 15 minute flying time, at normal cruise speed, from the takeoff airport.

(b) Enroute IFR may be conducted if unforecast weather conditions below the VFR minimums of this chapter are encountered on a flight that was planned to be conducted under VFR.

(c) An IFR approach may be conducted if, upon arrival at the destination airport, unforecast weather conditions do not allow an approach to be completed under VFR.

(d) When IFR operations are conducted under this section:
   (1) The aircraft must be properly equipped for IFR operations under this part.
   (2) The pilot must be authorized to conduct IFR operations under this part.
   (3) The flight must be conducted in accordance with an ATC IFR clearance.

IFR operations without a second in command may not be conducted under this section in an aircraft requiring a second in command under §135.99.

EXPLANATION

Although violations of §135.103 are cited in some NTSB decisions, it is questionable whether this regulation can be violated. It merely states under what conditions operation in IFR conditions can be conducted without complying with §135.101.

CROSS REFERENCES

91.151, Special VFR Weather Minimums; 91.155, Basic VFR Weather Minimums; 135.99, Composition of Flight Crew; 135.163, Equipment Requirements: Aircraft Carrying Passengers Under IFR; 135.205, VFR: Visibility Requirements; 135.213, Weather Reports and Forecasts; 135.215, IFR: Operating Limitations; 135.245, Second In Command Qualifications; 135.293(a)(5), Initial and Recurrent Pilot Testing Requirements; 135.297(b) and (g)(1), Pilot In Command: Instrument Proficiency Check Requirements.

AIRMAN'S INFORMATION MANUAL

IFR Requirements, Para. 3-22;
Clearance, Para. 4-80.

NTSB DECISIONS

[See §135.101, NTSB Decisions: *Administrator v. Mikesell*, 6 NTSB 602 (1988).]

135.105 EXCEPTION TO SECOND IN COMMAND REQUIREMENT: APPROVAL FOR USE OF AUTOPILOT SYSTEM

(a) Except as provided in §§135.99 and 135.111, unless two pilots are required by this chapter for operations under VFR, a person may operate an aircraft without a second in command, if it is equipped with an operative approved autopilot system and the use of that system is authorized by appropriate Operations Specifications.
No certificate holder may use any person, nor may any person serve, as a pilot in command under this section of an aircraft operated by a Commuter Air Carrier (as defined in §298.2 of this title) in passenger-carrying operations unless that person has at least 100 hours pilot in command flight time in the make and model of aircraft to be flown and has met all other applicable requirements of this part.

(b) The certificate holder may apply for an amendment of its Operations Specifications to authorize the use of an autopilot system in place of a second in command.

(c) The Administrator issues an amendment to the Operations Specifications authorizing the use of an autopilot system, in place of a second in command, if —
   (1) The autopilot is capable of operating the aircraft controls to maintain flight and maneuver it about the three axes; and
   (2) The certificate holder shows, to the satisfaction of the Administrator, that operations using the autopilot system can be conducted safely and in compliance with this part.

The amendment contains any conditions or limitations on the use of the autopilot system that the Administrator determines are needed in the interest of safety.

EXPLANATION

This section alone is not authorization to operate under IFR without a second in command if the aircraft is equipped with an operative approved autopilot system. The Operations Specifications must be amended to allow such operations.

Because intrastate scheduled operations would be identical to a Commuter Air Carrier operation, the FAA applies §135.105(a) to pilots conducting intrastate scheduled operations by adding the requirement to their Operations Specifications. The FAA has the authority to do this under §135.11(b)(2)(vii).

CROSS REFERENCES

1.1, Definitions; 135.11, Application and Issue of Certificate and Operations Specifications; 135.17, Amendment of Operations Specifications; 135.93, Autopilot: Minimum Altitudes for Use; 135.99, Composition of Flight Crew; 135.111 Second In Command Required in Category II Operations; 135.245, Second In Command Qualifications; 298.2, Exemptions for Air Taxi and Commuter Air Carrier Operations.

135.107 FLIGHT ATTENDANT CREWMEMBER REQUIREMENT

No certificate holder may operate an aircraft that has a passenger seating configuration, excluding any pilot seat, of more than 19 unless there is a flight attendant crewmember on board the aircraft.

EXPLANATION

[Editor's Note: On March 31, 1993, the FAA issued a Notice of Proposed Rulemaking that would add §135.273, Duty Period Limitations and Rest Time Requirement, that would be applicable to flight attendants. While this will not increase the number of flight attendants on the aircraft, it may increase the number the operator must have available for duty.]

CROSS REFERENCES

91.533, Flight Attendant Requirements.

ADVISORY CIRCULARS

AC 25.785-1 *Flight Attendant Seat Requirements* (1981).

AC 120-48 *Communication and Coordination Between Flight Crewmembers and Flight Attendants* (1988).

AC 120-51A *Crew Resource Management Training* (1993).

135.109 PILOT IN COMMAND OR SECOND IN COMMAND: DESIGNATION REQUIRED

(a) Each certificate holder shall designate a —
  (1) Pilot in command for each flight; and
  (2) Second in command for each flight requiring two pilots.
(b) The pilot in command, as designated by the certificate holder, shall remain the pilot in command at all times during that flight.

EXPLANATION

A second in command may not be required by the type certificate, Aircraft Flight Manual, the nature of the operations, or the regulations. However, if one is designated, that person must meet all the regulatory requirements for a second in command.

CROSS REFERENCES

135.77, Responsibility for Operational Control; 135.243, Pilot In Command Qualifications; 135.245, Second In Command Qualifications.

ADVISORY CIRCULARS

AC 121.445-1D *Pilot In Command Qualifications for Special Areas/Routes and Airports Under FAR §121.445* (1990).

135.111 SECOND IN COMMAND REQUIRED IN CATEGORY II OPERATIONS

No person may operate an aircraft in a Category II operation unless there is a second in command of the aircraft.

CROSS REFERENCES

135.245, Second In Command Qualifications.

ADVISORY CIRCULARS

AC 91-16 *Category II Operations General Aviation Airplanes* (1967).

135.113 PASSENGER OCCUPANCY OF PILOT SEAT

No certificate holder may operate an aircraft type certificated after October 15, 1971, that has a passenger seating configuration, excluding any pilot seat, of more than eight seats if any person other than the pilot in command, a second in command, a company check airman, or an authorized representative of the Administrator, the National Transportation Safety Board, or the United States Postal Service occupies a pilot seat.

EXPLANATION

This regulation is very specific about who may occupy a pilot seat, i.e. a company employee, other than the pilot in command or second in command, can not occupy pilot seat.

"Type certificated" refers to date of type certificate, not necessarily the date the aircraft rolled out of the factory.

CROSS REFERENCES

135.243, Pilot In Command Qualifications; 135.245, Second In Command Qualifications.

135.115 MANIPULATION OF CONTROLS

No pilot in command may allow any person to manipulate the flight controls of an aircraft during flight conducted under this part, nor may any person manipulate the controls during such flight unless that person is —

(a) A pilot employed by the certificate holder and qualified in the aircraft; or

(b) An authorized safety representative of the Administrator who has the permission of the pilot in command, is qualified in the aircraft, and is checking flight operations.

EXPLANATION

The pilot in command should make any reasonable inquiries which are deemed necessary to determine the pilot qualifications of any authorized safety representative of the Administrator seeking to manipulate the controls of the aircraft.

A person is "qualified in the aircraft" if that person holds a pilot certificate with the appropriate category, class, and type rating for the aircraft operated and also meets the recency of experience for the aircraft.

135.115(a): "employed by the certificate holder" has not been interpreted by the FAA, although an opinion has been requested. Many certificate holders "employ" pilots on a part-time basis. The practice is widespread and has continued long enough that the FAA has implicitly authorized it.

ADVISORY CIRCULARS

AC 20-133 *Cockpit Noise and Speech Interference Between Crewmembers* (1989).

AC 120-51A *Crew Resource Management Training* (1993).

AIRMAN'S INFORMATION MANUAL

Pilot Responsibility and Authority, Para. 6-1.

NTSB DECISIONS

A pilot was found in violation of §135.115 when he allowed another pilot to manipulate the controls of the multi-engine aircraft. The other pilot was not employed by the operator of the flights; did not hold a multi-engine rating; and received flight instruction, which was logged and signed off, on several of the flights. *Administrator v. Graf*, 5 NTSB 2106 (1987).

The Board upheld a finding of a violation of §135.115(a) where the evidence showed that the pilot had given flight instruction on a Part 135 cargo flight. The person being given instruction was a line boy for the operator. *Administrator v. Johnson*, 5 NTSB 909 (1986).

135.117 BRIEFING OF PASSENGERS BEFORE FLIGHT

(a) Before each takeoff each pilot in command of an aircraft carrying passengers shall ensure that all passengers have been orally briefed on —

(1) *Smoking.* Each passenger shall be briefed on when, where, and under what conditions smoking is prohibited (including, but not limited to, any applicable requirements of part 252, of this title). This briefing shall include a statement that the Federal Aviation Regulations require passenger compliance with the lighted passenger information signs (if such signs are required), posted placards, areas designated for safety purposes as no smoking areas, and crewmember instructions with regard to these items. The briefing shall also include a statement (if the aircraft is equipped with a lavatory) that Federal law prohibits: tampering with, disabling, or destroying any smoke detector installed in an aircraft lavatory; smoking in lavatories; and, when applicable, smoking in passenger compartments.

(2) The use of safety belts, including instructions on how to fasten and unfasten the safety belts. Each passenger shall be briefed on when, where, and under what conditions the safety belt must be fastened about that passenger. This briefing shall include a statement that the Federal Aviation Regulations require passenger compliance with lighted passenger information signs and crewmember instructions concerning the use of safety belts.

(3) The placement of seat backs in an upright position before takeoff and landing;

(4) Location and means for opening the passenger entry door and emergency exits;

(5) Location of survival equipment;

(6) If the flight involves extended overwater operation, ditching procedures and the use of required flotation equipment;

(7) If the flight involves operations above 12,000 feet MSL, the normal and emergency use of oxygen; and

(8) Location and operation of fire extinguishers.

(b) Before each takeoff the pilot in command shall ensure that each person who may need the assistance of another person to move expeditiously to an exit if an emergency occurs and that person's attendant, if any, has received a briefing as to the procedures to be followed if an evacuation occurs. This paragraph does not apply to a person who has been given a briefing before a previous leg of a flight in the same aircraft.

(c) The oral briefing required by paragraph (a) of this section shall be given by the pilot in command or a crewmember.

(d) Notwithstanding the provisions of paragraph (c) of this section, for aircraft certificated to carry 19 passengers or less, the oral briefing required by paragraph (a) of this section shall be given by the pilot in command, a crewmember, or other qualified person designated by the certificate holder and approved by the Administrator.

(e) The oral briefing required by paragraph (a) shall be supplemented by printed cards which must be carried in the aircraft in locations convenient for the use of each passenger. The cards must —
   (1) Be appropriate for the aircraft on which they are to be used;
   (2) Contain a diagram of, and method of operating, the emergency exits; and
   (3) Contain other instructions necessary for the use of emergency equipment on board the aircraft.

(f) The briefing required by paragraph (a) may be delivered by means of an approved recording playback device that is audible to each passenger under normal noise levels.

EXPLANATION

An oral briefing ensures that passengers are adequately informed of basic information essential to their safety.

The general operations manual or flight attendant user manual must contain the briefing to be given.

Passenger briefing cards are also required for air ambulance operations.

If movies or video tape is used to conduct safety briefings, the certificate holder must make sure the screen does not protrude into the aisle.

CROSS REFERENCES

135.23(k), Manual Content; 135.127, Passenger Information; 135.128, Use of Safety Belts and Child Restraint Systems; 135.129, Exit Seating; 135.157, Oxygen Equipment Requirements; 135.167, Emergency Equipment: Extended Overwater Operations; 135.178, Additional Emergency Equipment; 135.349, Flight Attendants: Initial and Transition Ground Training; Part 252, Smoking Aboard Aircraft; §404(d) of the Federal Aviation Act of 1958, as amended [49 U.S.C. App. §1374(d)], Rates for Carriage of Persons and Property, Prohibition Against Smoking on Scheduled Flights and Tampering with Smoke Alarm Devices.

ADVISORY CIRCULARS

AC 121-24A *Passenger Safety Information Briefing and Briefing Cards* (1989).

AC 135-12A *Passenger Safety Information Briefing and Briefing Cards (FAR Part 135)* (1991).

NTSB DECISIONS

The Board, in sustaining a finding of a violation of §135.117(a), refused to overturn the administrative law judge's finding that "there was either an attempt at a briefing or a briefing which was not clearly heard — or a briefing which included only a limited number of items — but there was no explanation as to how any of this was to be used." *Administrator v. Kittelson*, EA-4068 (1994).

135.119 PROHIBITION AGAINST CARRIAGE OF WEAPONS

No person may, while on board an aircraft being operated by a certificate holder, carry on or about that person a deadly or dangerous weapon, either concealed or unconcealed. This section does not apply to —

(a) Officials or employees of a municipality or a State, or of the United States, who are authorized to carry arms; or

(b) Crewmembers and other persons authorized by the certificate holder to carry arms.

EXPLANATION

A person violating this section is subject to a civil penalty not to exceed $10,000 and possibly criminal action.

CROSS REFERENCES

135.125, Airplane Security; §315(a) of the Federal Aviation Act of 1958, as amended [49 U.S.C.App. §1356(a)], Screening of Passengers, Procedures and Facilities; §901(d) of the Federal Aviation Act of 1958, as amended [49 U.S.C.App. §1471(d)], Civil Penalties, Concealed Weapons; §902(l) of the Federal Aviation Act of 1958, as amended [49 U.S.C.App. §1472(l)], Criminal Penalties, Carrying Weapons or Explosives Aboard Aircraft; §1111 of the Federal Aviation Act of 1958, as amended [49 U.S.C.App. §1511], Authority to Refuse Transportation; Part 108, Airplane Operator Security.

ADVISORY CIRCULARS

AC 108-2 *Security Rules — Carriage of Weapons and Escorted Persons* (1981).

AIRMAN'S INFORMATION MANUAL

FAA Sponsored Explosives Detection (Dog/Handler Team) Locations, Para. 6-15.

135.121 ALCOHOLIC BEVERAGES

(a) No person may drink any alcoholic beverage aboard an aircraft unless the certificate holder operating the aircraft has served that beverage.
(b) No certificate holder may serve any alcoholic beverage to any person aboard its aircraft if that person appears to be intoxicated.
(c) No certificate holder may allow any person to board any of its aircraft if that person appears to be intoxicated.

EXPLANATION

This regulation does not prohibit a person from bringing his own alcoholic beverage on board, but the liquor must be given to operator's personnel who will serve it.

CROSS REFERENCES

91.17(b), Alcohol or Drugs.

AIRMAN'S INFORMATION MANUAL

Fitness for Flight, Para. 8-1.

FAA CHIEF COUNSEL OPINIONS

A pilot briefing to the passengers concerning alcohol consumption and pilot monitoring of the passengers, who serve their own alcoholic beverages, does not satisfy the requirement in FAR 135.121(a) which states that the certificate holder must serve all alcoholic beverages. (12-22-89).

A Part 135 certificate holder may place a nonrequired crewmember or employee on board a flight whose sole function is to serve food and beverages and provide other services to the passengers without training that person as a required crewmember. (12-22-89).

[Editor's Note: Since the person put on board the aircraft is not a required crewmember, that person must be considered a passenger and all regulations relating to passengers must be complied with fully.]

135.122 STOWAGE OF FOOD, BEVERAGE, AND PASSENGER SERVICE EQUIPMENT DURING AIRCRAFT MOVEMENT ON THE SURFACE, TAKEOFF, AND LANDING

(a) No certificate holder may move an aircraft on the surface, take off, or land when any food, beverage, or tableware furnished by the certificate holder is located at any passenger seat.
(b) No certificate holder may move an aircraft on the surface, take off, or land unless each food and beverage tray and seat back tray table is secured in its stowed position.
(c) No certificate holder may permit an aircraft to move on the surface, take off, or land unless each passenger serving cart is secured in its stowed position.
(d) Each passenger shall comply with instructions given by a crewmember with regard to compliance with this section.

EXPLANATION

The certificate holder should ensure there is an established procedure by which the flight crewmember can ensure that trays, seat back tray tables, and serving carts are secured in their stowed position so that the aircraft may move.

Operators of small aircraft that do not have galleys may comply with the regulation by stowing all food and beverage service items in other secured positions. Such items may be stowed in a passenger seat if items are secured in accordance with current cargo-carrying requirements in §135.87 provided they are stowed securely to prevent them from falling into the aisle and impeding passenger egress in case of an emergency.

CROSS REFERENCES

135.87, Carriage of Cargo Including Carry-On Baggage; 135.117(a)(3), Briefing of Passengers Before Flight.

135.123 EMERGENCY AND EMERGENCY EVACUATION DUTIES

(a) Each certificate holder shall assign to each required crewmember for each type of aircraft as appropriate, the necessary functions to be performed in an emergency or in a situation requiring emergency evacuation. The certificate holder shall ensure that those functions can be practicably accomplished, and will meet any reasonably anticipated emergency including incapacitation of individual crewmembers or their inability to reach the passenger cabin because of shifting cargo in combination cargo-passenger aircraft.
(b) The certificate holder shall describe in the manual required under §135.21 the functions of each category of required crewmembers assigned under paragraph (a) of this section.

CROSS REFERENCES

135.19(c), Emergency Operations; 135.21, Manual Requirements; 135.23(m), Manual Contents; 135.83(c), Operating Information Required; 135.87(c)(1), Carriage of Cargo Including Carry-On Baggage; 135.129, Exit Seating; 135.177, Emergency Equipment Requirements for Aircraft Having a Passenger Seating Configuration of More Than 19 Passengers; 135.329(a)(3), Crewmember Training Requirements; 135.331(c)(1), Crewmember Emergency Training; 135.341, Pilot and Flight Attendant Crewmember Training Programs; 135.349, Flight Attendants: Initial and Transition Ground Training.

ADVISORY CIRCULARS

AC 20-60 *Accessibility to Excess Emergency Exits* (1968).

AC 20-118A *Emergency Evacuation Demonstration* (1987).

AC 23.807-3 *Emergency Exits Openable From Outside for Small Airplanes* (1984).

AC 25.803-1 *Emergency Evacuation Demonstrations* (1989).

AC 25.807-1 *Uniform Distribution of Exits* (1990).

AC 25.812-1A *Floor Proximity Emergency Escape Path Marking* (1989).

AIRMAN'S INFORMATION MANUAL

Emergency Condition — Request Assistance Immediately, Para. 6-2;
Search and Rescue, Para. 6-16;
Ditching Procedures, Para. 6-22.

135.125 AIRPLANE SECURITY

Certificate holders conducting operations under this part shall comply with applicable security requirements in Part 108 of this chapter.

EXPLANATION

Operators utilizing airplanes for scheduled or public charter operations having a seating configuration of more than 60 seats must have a full security program under Part 108. Operators that use airplanes having a passenger seating configuration of more than 30 but less than 61 seats are not required to have a full security program.

A full security program is required for operations, no matter what the passenger seat configuration of the airplanes used, that provide deplaned passengers access to a sterile area at the next landing when the access is not controlled by another airplane operator's security program. Unscreened passengers may have access to a sterile area where the discharging operator has made a prior arrangement with another FAA certificate holder or a foreign air carrier, or in some cases the airport operator, having responsibility for the sterile area, for escort of the deplaning passengers into, through, and out of the sterile area or for the screening of those passengers before entry. Implementation of a full security program requires

(1) 100 percent screening of passengers and their accessible items be completed before last departure;
(2) the airplane be protected; and
(3) procedures be used to prevent or deter the introduction of explosives and incendiaries into checked baggage and cargo for those flights.

CROSS REFERENCES

135.119, Prohibition Against Carriage of Weapons; §316, of the Federal Aviation Act of 1958, as amended [49 U.S.C.App. §1357], Air Transportation Security.

ADVISORY CIRCULARS

AC 107-1 *Aviation Security — Airports* (1972).

AC 108-1 *Air Carrier Security* (1981).

AC 109-1 *Aviation Security — Acceptance and Handling Procedures Indirect Air Carrier Security* (1982).

135.127 PASSENGER INFORMATION

(a) No person may conduct a scheduled flight segment on which smoking is prohibited unless the "No Smoking" passenger information signs are lighted during the entire flight segment, or one or more "No Smoking" placards meeting the requirements of §25.1541 are posted during the entire flight segment. If both the lighted signs and the placards are used, the signs must remain lighted during the entire flight segment. Smoking is prohibited on scheduled flight segments:
  (1) Between any two points within Puerto Rico, the United States Virgin Islands, the District of Columbia, or any State of the United States (other than Alaska or Hawaii) or between any two points in any one of the above-mentioned jurisdictions (other than Alaska or Hawaii);
  (2) Within the State of Alaska or within the State of Hawaii; or

(3) Scheduled in the current Worldwide or North American Edition of the *Official Airline Guide* or 6 hours or less in duration and between any point listed in paragraph (a)(1) of this section and any point in Alaska or Hawaii, or between any point in Alaska and any point in Hawaii.

(b) No person may smoke while a "No Smoking" sign is lighted or while "No Smoking" placards are posted, except that the pilot in command may authorize smoking on the flight deck (if it is physically separated from the passenger compartment) except during any movement of an aircraft on the surface, takeoff, and landing.

(c) No person may smoke in any aircraft lavatory.

(d) After December 31, 1988, no person may operate an aircraft with a lavatory equipped with a smoke detector unless there is in that lavatory a sign or placard which reads: "Federal law provides for a penalty of up to $2,000 for tampering with the smoke detector installed in this lavatory."

(e) No person may tamper with, disable, or destroy any smoke detector installed in any aircraft lavatory.

(f) On flight segments other than those described in paragraph (a) of this section, the "No Smoking" sign required by §135.177(a)(3) of this part must be turned on during any movement of the aircraft on the surface, for each takeoff or landing, and at any other time considered necessary by the pilot in command.

(g) The passenger information requirements prescribed in §91.517(b) and (d) of this chapter are in addition to the requirements prescribed in this section.

(h) Each passenger shall comply with instructions given him or her by crewmembers regarding compliance with paragraphs (b), (c), and (e) of this section.

EXPLANATION

The certificate holder should establish methods for reporting cases where passengers have violated the smoking prohibition or tampered with a smoke detector. The regulations of the Office of the Secretary of Transportation also require air carriers to enforce the smoking prohibition.

The purpose of prohibiting smoking in the cabin is, in part, to protect the cabin air quality for passengers. Therefore, before smoking is allowed on the flight deck, the physical separation must be such that the smoke will not affect air quality in the passenger compartment.

CROSS REFERENCES

135.117, Briefing of Passengers Before Flight; 135.177, Emergency Equipment Requirements for Aircraft Having a Passenger Seating Configuration of More Than 19 Passengers; §404(d) of the Federal Aviation Act of 1958, as amended [49 U.S.C.App. §1374(d)], Rates for Carriage of Persons and Property, Prohibition Against Smoking on Scheduled Flights and Tampering with Smoke Alarm Devices; Part 252, Smoking Aboard Aircraft.

ADVISORY CIRCULARS

AC 135-12A *Passenger Safety Information Briefing and Briefing Cards (FAR Part 135)* (1991).

135.128 USE OF SAFETY BELTS AND CHILD RESTRAINT SYSTEMS

(a) Except as provided in this paragraph, each person on board an aircraft operated under this part shall occupy an approved seat or berth with a separate safety belt properly secured about him or her during movement on the surface, takeoff, and landing. For seaplane and float equipped rotorcraft operations during movement on the surface, the person pushing off the seaplane or rotorcraft from the dock and the person mooring the seaplane or rotorcraft at the dock are excepted from the preceding seating and safety belt requirements. A safety belt provided for the occupant of a seat may not be used by more than one person who has reached his or her second birthday. Notwithstanding the preceding requirements, a child may:

(1) Be held by an adult who is occupying an approved seat or berth if that child has not reached his or her second birthday; or

(2) Notwithstanding any other requirement of this chapter, occupy an approved child restraint system furnished by the certificate holder or one of the persons described in paragraph (a)(2)(i) of this section, provided:

(i) The child is accompanied by a parent, guardian, or attendant designated by the child's parent or guardian to attend to the safety of the child during the flight;

(ii) The approved child restraint system bears one or more labels as follows:

(A) Seats manufactured to U.S. standards between January 1, 1981, and February 25, 1985, must bear the label: "This child restraint system conforms to all applicable Federal motor vehicle safety standards." Vest- and harness-type child restraint systems manufactured before February 26, 1985, bearing such a label are not approved for the purposes of this section;

(B) Seats manufactured to U.S. standards on or after February 26, 1985, must bear two labels:

(1) "This child restraint system conforms to all applicable Federal motor vehicle safety standards"; and

(2) "THIS RESTRAINT IS CERTIFIED FOR USE IN MOTOR VEHICLES AND AIRCRAFT" in red lettering;

(C) Seats that do not qualify under paragraphs (a)(2)(ii)(A) and (a)(2)(ii)(B) of this section must bear either a label showing approval of a foreign government or a label showing that the seat was manufactured under the standards of the United Nations; and

(iii) The certificate holder complies with the following requirements:

(A) The restraint system must be properly secured to an approved forward-facing seat or berth;

(B) The child must be properly secured in the restraint system and must not exceed the specified weight limit for the restraint system; and

(C) The restraint system must bear the appropriate label(s).

(b) No certificate holder may prohibit a child, if requested by the child's parent, guardian, or designated attendant from occupying a child restraint system furnished by the child's parent, guardian, or designated attendant, provided the child holds a ticket for an approved seat or berth, or such seat or berth is otherwise made available by the certificate holder for the child's use, and the requirements contained in paragraphs (a)(2)(i) through (a)(2)(iii) of this section are met. This section does not prohibit the certificate holder from providing child restraint systems or, consistent with safe operating practices, determining the most appropriate passenger seat location for the child restraint system.

EXPLANATION

A certificate holder should consider making available to its concerned employees a list of acceptable child restraint systems identified by manufacturer and model number. This would not only expedite determining the acceptability of the particular system, but would help prevent errors that could result in enforcement action.

Children having reached their second birthday must be in a separate passenger seat. The weight limit on a child in a child restraint system is the one set for the particular restraint system.

The operator or certificate holder has the responsibility to ensure that a child restraint system is properly secured to a forward-facing seat, the child is properly secured and does not exceed the weight limit for the restraint system, and the child restraint is properly labeled. When the parent or guardian provides the child restraint system, it is the responsibility of the parent or guardian to ensure that the child restraint system to be used is free of any obvious defects and functions properly.

CROSS REFERENCES

135.117(2), Briefing of Passengers Before Flight.

ADVISORY CIRCULARS

AC 23-4 *Static Strength Substantiation of Attachment Points for Occupant Restraint System Installations* (1986).

AC 23.562-1 *Dynamic Testing of Part 23 Airplane Seat/Restraint Systems and Occupant Protection* (1989).

AC 91-62A *Use of Child Seats In Aircraft* (1992).

AC 91-65 *Use of Shoulder Harness In Passenger Seats* (1986).

135.129 EXIT SEATING

(a) Except for on-demand air taxis with nine or fewer passenger seats, each certificate holder shall determine, to the extent necessary to perform the applicable functions of paragraph (d) of this section, the suitability of each person it permits to occupy a seat in a row of seats that provides the most direct access to an exit (including all of the seats in the row from the fuselage to the first aisle inboard of the exit or, in cases where there is no aisle, in the closest row or in any seat that has direct access to an exit, hereafter referred to as exit row seats), in accordance with this section. These determinations shall be made in a non-discriminatory manner consistent with the requirements of this section, by the pilot in command, in those described in §135.21(a), when an operations manual is not required, or by persons designated in the certificate holder's manual if it is required by that section.

(1) Except for on-demand operations with aircraft having nine or fewer passenger seats, each certificate holder shall determine, to the extent necessary to perform the applicable functions of paragraph (d) of this section, the suitability of each person it permits to occupy an exit seat, in accordance with this section. For the purpose of this section —

(i) *Exit seat* means —

(A) Each seat having direct access to an exit; and,

(B) Each seat in a row of seats through which passengers would have to pass to gain access to an exit, from the first seat inboard of the exit to the first aisle inboard of the exit.

(ii) A passenger seat having "direct access" means a seat from which a passenger can proceed directly to the exit without entering an aisle or passing around an obstruction.

(2) Each certificate holder shall make the passenger exit seating determinations required by this paragraph in a non-discriminatory manner consistent with the requirements of this section, by persons designated in the certificate holder's required operations manual.
(3) Each certificate holder shall designate the exit seats for each passenger seating configuration in its fleet in accordance with the definitions in this paragraph and submit those designations for approval as part of the procedures required to be submitted for approval under paragraphs (n) and (p) of this section.

(b) No certificate holder may seat a person in a seat affected by this section if the certificate holder determines that it is likely that the person would be unable to perform one or more of the applicable functions listed in paragraph (d) of this section because —
(1) The person lacks sufficient mobility, strength, or dexterity in both arms and hands, and both legs:
(i) To reach upward, sideways, and downward to the location of emergency exit and exit-slide operating mechanisms;
(ii) To grasp and push, pull, turn, or otherwise manipulate those mechanisms;
(iii) To push, shove, pull, or otherwise open emergency exits;
(iv) To lift out, hold, deposit on nearby seats, or maneuver over the seatbacks to the next row objects the size and weight of over-wing window exit doors;
(v) To remove obstructions of size and weight similar over-wing exit doors;
(vi) To reach the emergency exit expeditiously;
(vii) To maintain balance while removing obstructions;
(viii) To exit expeditiously;
(ix) To stabilize an escape slide after deployment; or
(x) To assist others in getting off an escape slide;
(2) The person is less than 15 years of age or lacks the capacity to perform one or more of the applicable functions listed in paragraph (d) of this section without the assistance of an adult companion, parent, or other relative;
(3) The person lacks the ability to read and understand instructions required by this section and related to emergency evacuation provided by the certificate holder in printed or graphic form or the ability to understand oral crew commands.
(4) The person lacks sufficient visual capacity to perform one or more of the applicable functions in paragraph (d) of this section without the assistance of visual aids beyond contact lenses or eyeglasses;
(5) The person lacks sufficient aural capacity to hear and understand instructions shouted by flight attendants, without assistance beyond a hearing aid;
(6) The person lacks the ability adequately to impart information orally to other passengers; or,
(7) The person has:
(i) A condition or responsibilities, such as caring for small children, that might prevent the person from performing one or more of the applicable functions listed in paragraph (d) of this section; or
(ii) A condition that might cause the person harm if he or she performs one or more of the applicable functions listed in paragraph (d) of this section.

(c) Each passenger shall comply with instructions given by a crewmember or other authorized employee of the certificate holder implementing exit seating restrictions established in accordance with this section.

(d) Each certificate holder shall include on passenger information cards, presented in the language in which briefings and oral commands are given by the crew, at each exit seat affected by this section, information that, in the event of an emergency in which a crewmember is not available to assist, a passenger occupying an exit seat may use if called upon to perform the following functions:

(1) Locate the emergency exit;

(2) Recognize the emergency exit opening mechanism;

(3) Comprehend the instructions for operating the emergency exit;

(4) Operate the emergency exit;

(5) Assess whether opening the emergency exit will increase the hazards to which passengers may be exposed;

(6) Follow oral directions and hand signals given by a crewmember;

(7) Stow or secure the emergency exit door so that it will not impede use of the exit;

(8) Assess the condition of an escape slide, activate the slide, and stabilize the slide after deployment to assist others in getting off the slide;

(9) Pass expeditiously through the emergency exit; and

(10) Assess, select, and follow a safe path away from the emergency exit.

(e) Each certificate holder shall include on passenger information cards, at each exit seat —

(1) In the primary language in which emergency commands are given by the crew, the selection criteria set forth in paragraph (b) of this section, and a request that a passenger identify himself or herself to allow reseating if he or she —

(i) Cannot meet the selection criteria set forth in paragraph (b) of this section;

(ii) Has a nondiscernible condition that will prevent him or her from performing the applicable functions listed in paragraph (d) of this section;

(iii) May suffer bodily harm as the result of performing one or more of those functions; or

(iv) Does not wish to perform those functions; and,

(2) In each language used by the certificate holder for passenger information cards, a request that a passenger identify himself or herself to allow reseating if he or she lacks the ability to read, speak, or understand the language or the graphic form in which instructions required by this section and related to emergency evacuations are provided by the certificate holder, or the ability to understand the specified language in which crew commands will be given in an emergency;

(3) May suffer bodily harm as the result of performing one or more of those functions; or,

(4) Does not wish to perform those functions.

A certificate holder shall not require the passenger to disclose his or her reason for needing reseating.

(f) Each certificate holder shall make available for inspection by the public at all passenger loading gates and ticket counters at each airport where it conducts passenger operations, written procedures established for making determinations in regard to exit row seating.

(g) No certificate holder may allow taxi or pushback unless at least one required crewmember has verified that no exit seat is occupied by a person the crewmember determines is likely to be unable to perform the applicable functions listed in paragraph (d) of this section.

(h) Each certificate holder shall include in its passenger briefings a reference to the passenger information cards, required by paragraphs (d) and (e), the selection criteria set forth in paragraph (b), and the functions to be performed, set forth in paragraph (d) of this section.

(i) Each certificate holder shall include in its passenger briefings a request that a passenger identify himself or herself to allow reseating if he or she —

(1) Cannot meet the selection criteria set forth in paragraph (b) of this section;

(2) Has a nondiscernible condition that will prevent him or her from performing the applicable functions listed in paragraph (d) of this section;

(3) May suffer bodily harm as the result of performing one or more of those functions; or,

(4) Does not wish to perform those functions.

A certificate holder shall not require the passenger to disclose his or her reason for needing reseating.

(j) [Reserved]

(k) In the event a certificate holder determines in accordance with this section that it is likely that a passenger assigned to an exit seat would be unable to perform the functions listed in paragraph (d) of this section or a passenger requests a non-exit seat, the certificate holder shall expeditiously relocate the passenger to a non-exit seat.

(l) In the event of full booking in the non-exit seats and if necessary to accommodate a passenger being relocated from an exit seat, the certificate holder shall move a passenger who is willing and able to assume the evacuation functions that may be required, to an exit seat.

(m) A certificate holder may deny transportation to any passenger under this section only because —

(1) The passenger refuses to comply with instructions given by a crewmember or other authorized employee of the certificate holder implementing exit seating restrictions established in accordance with this section, or

(2) The only seat that will physically accommodate the person's handicap is an exit seat.

(n) In order to comply with this section certificate holders shall —
   (1) Establish procedures that address:
      (i) The criteria listed in paragraph (b) of this section;
      (ii) The functions listed in paragraph (d) of this section;
      (iii) The requirements for airport information, passenger information cards, crewmember verification of appropriate seating in exit seats, passenger briefings, seat assignments, and denial of transportation as set forth in this section;
      (iv) How to resolve disputes arising from implementation of this section, including identification of the certificate holder employee on the airport to whom complaints should be addressed for resolution; and,
   (2) Submit their procedures for preliminary review and approval to the principal operations inspectors assigned to them at the FAA Flight Standards District Offices that are charged with the overall inspection of their operations.

(o) Certificate holders shall assign seats prior to boarding consistent with the criteria listed in paragraph (b) and the functions listed in paragraph (d) of this section, to the maximum extent feasible.

(p) The procedures required by paragraph (n) of this section will not become effective until final approval is granted by the Director, Flight Standards Service, Washington, DC. Approval will be based solely upon the safety aspects of the certificate holder's procedures.

EXPLANATION

The verification that no unqualified person occupies an exit seat may be prior to, or after, the passenger entry doors are closed, but must be made prior to taxi or pushback of the aircraft.

CROSS REFERENCES

91.607, Emergency Exits for Airplanes Carrying Passengers for Hire; 135.19, Emergency Operations; 135.87, Carriage of Cargo Including Carry-On Baggage; 135.117, Briefing of Passengers Before Flight; 135.123, Emergency and Emergency Evacuation Duties.

ADVISORY CIRCULARS

AC 20-47 *Exterior Colored Band Around Exits on Transport Airplanes* (1966).

AC 20-118A *Emergency Evacuation Demonstration* (1987).

AC 25.803-1 *Emergency Evacuation Demonstrations* (1989).

AIRMAN'S INFORMATION MANUAL

Ditching Procedures, Para. 6-22.

SUBPART C — AIRCRAFT AND EQUIPMENT

135.141 APPLICABILITY

This subpart prescribes aircraft and equipment requirements for operations under this part. The requirements of this subpart are in addition to the aircraft and equipment requirements of Part 91 of this chapter. However, this part does not require the duplication of any equipment required by this chapter.

EXPLANATION

Where sections in this subpart provide that certain aircraft, because of seating configuration, do not require certain equipment, always check Part 91 since there may be a section requiring such equipment for all aircraft or under certain specific conditions (i.e., §§135.167 and 91.205(b)(11)).

CROSS REFERENCES

Part 91, Subpart C, Equipment, Instrument, and Certificate Requirements; 91.205, Powered Civil Aircraft with Standard Category U.S. Airworthiness Certificates: Instrument and Equipment Requirements; Part 91, Subpart G, Additional Equipment and Operating Requirements for Large and Transport Category Aircraft; 91.601, Applicability.

135.143 GENERAL REQUIREMENTS

(a) No person may operate an aircraft under this part unless that aircraft and its equipment meet the applicable regulations of this chapter.

(b) Except as provided in §135.179, no person may operate an aircraft under this part unless the required instruments and equipment in it have been approved and are in an operable condition.

(c) ATC transponder equipment installed within the time periods indicated below must meet the performance and environmental requirements of the following TSO's

(1) *Through January 1, 1992:*

(i) Any class of TSO-C74b or any class of TSO-C74c as appropriate, provided that the equipment was manufactured before January 1, 1990; or

(ii) The appropriate class of TSO-C112 (Mode S).

(2) *After January 1, 1992:* The appropriate class of TSO-C112 (Mode S). For purposes of paragraph (c)(2) of this section, "installation" does not include —
   (i) Temporary installation of TSO-C74b or TSO-C74c substitute equipment, as appropriate, during maintenance of the permanent equipment;
   (ii) Reinstallation of equipment after temporary removal for maintenance; or
   (iii) For fleet operations, installation of equipment in a fleet aircraft after removal of the equipment for maintenance from another aircraft in the same operator's fleet.

EXPLANATION

"Installed" does not include temporary substitutions, reinstallations, or swaps from another aircraft in operator's fleet for maintenance purposes.

"Operable condition" means that the instruments and equipment required to comply with the airworthiness requirements under which the airplane is type-certified shall be in a condition so as to operate efficiently and in the manner intended by the manufacturer. *U.S. v. Newman,* 331 F.Supp. 1240, 1244.

CROSS REFERENCES

91.207, Emergency Locator Transmitters; 91.413, ATC Transponder Tests and Inspections; Part 91, Subpart I, Operating Noise Limits; 135.25(a)(2), Aircraft Requirements; 135.161, Radio and Navigational Equipment: Carrying Passengers Under VFR at Night or Under VFR Over-The-Top; 135.165, Radio and Navigational Equipment: Extended Overwater or IFR Operations; 135.179, Inoperable Instruments and Equipment.

ADVISORY CIRCULARS

AC 20-41A *Substitute Technical Standard Order (TSO) Aircraft Equipment* (1977).

AC 43-6A *Automatic Pressure Altitude Encoding Systems and Transponders Maintenance and Inspection Practices* (1977).

AC 91-50 *Importance of Transponder Operation and Altitude Reporting* (1977).

AC 91-54 *Automatic Reporting Systems — Altimeter Setting and Other Operational Data* (1979).

AIRMAN'S INFORMATION MANUAL

Transponder Operation, Para. 4-19;
Transponder Emergency Operation, Para. 6-11.

NTSB DECISIONS

In this case an aircraft's right front seat was removed and a pedestal was placed in the tracks of the removed seat and bolted to the floor. One end of a stretcher then rested on the pedestal and was fastened by a harness, while the other end of the stretcher rested on the seat immediately aft to which it was fastened by the seatbelt. The patient was then held in the stretcher by two separate harnesses. The Board held that the installation altered the original type design (even if only in a minor respect) and that, while an STC may not have been required, at least FAA field approval, which is a less complex process, should have been obtained. *Administrator v. Muscatine Flying Service, Inc. and Letts*, 5 NTSB 1785 (1987).

FAA CHIEF COUNSEL OPINIONS

Life rafts on aircraft operating under Part 135 must be approved by the FAA. Approval by the FAA may be obtained in various ways, i.e. Parts Manufacturer Approval (PMA), Technical Standard Order (TSO). [Reference FAR §21.305]. (2-8-80).

135.145 AIRCRAFT PROVING TESTS

(a) No certificate holder may operate a turbojet airplane, or an aircraft for which two pilots are required by this chapter for operations under VFR, if it has not previously proved that aircraft or an aircraft of the same make and similar design in any operation under this part unless, in addition to the aircraft certification tests, at least 25 hours of proving tests acceptable to the Administrator have been flown by that certificate holder including —
  (1) Five hours of night time, if night flights are to be authorized;
  (2) Five instrument approach procedures under simulated or actual instrument weather conditions, if IFR flights are to be authorized; and
  (3) Entry into a representative number of enroute airports as determined by the Administrator.

(b) No certificate holder may carry passengers in an aircraft during proving tests, except those needed to make the tests and those designated by the Administrator to observe the tests. However, pilot flight training may be conducted during the proving tests.

(c) For the purposes of paragraph (a) of this section, an aircraft is not considered to be of similar design if an alteration includes —
  (1) The installation of powerplants other than those of a type similar to those with which it is certificated; or
  (2) Alterations to the aircraft or its components that materially affect flight characteristics.

(d) The Administrator may authorize deviations from this section if the Administrator finds that special circumstances make full compliance with this section unnecessary.

EXPLANATION

If an aircraft, previously proven by a certificate holder, is significantly altered in design, at least 25 hours of proving tests are required. "Significant alterations" are set forth in §135.145(c).

When seeking a deviation from the requirements of this section, the applicant must explain how it intends to demonstrate regulatory compliance with a reduced-hour program. The plan must include at least the total hours of operation; flight experience resume of crewmembers to be used (i.e., certificates, total flight time, any previous experience in the aircraft being tested, years of experience with the applicant being tested and any other experience in Part 135 operations, and other transport experience, such as military); justification statement and other information requested by FAA.

While carriage of revenue passengers on proving flights is prohibited, generally carriage of revenue cargo will be approved if applicant has appropriate Department of Transportation economic authority to carry revenue cargo.

Training flights may be credited toward proving test requirements, provided the training is according to the applicant's initially approved flight training curriculum. Line checks and operating experience may be accomplished on proving flights. To qualify, training flights must be observed by a qualified operations inspector.

Part 135 does not contain an authorization to use provisionally certificated aircraft for proving flights.

CROSS REFERENCES

1.1, General Definitions, "Night"; 91.421, Rebuilt Engine Maintenance Records; 135.205, VFR: Visibility Requirements; 135.215, IFR: Operating Limitations; 135.225, IFR: Takeoff, Approach and Landing Minimums; 135.425, Maintenance, Preventive Maintenance, and Alteration Programs; 135.437, Authority to Perform and Approve Maintenance, Preventive Maintenance, and Alterations.

ADVISORY CIRCULARS

AC 25.1523-1 *Minimum Flightcrew* (1993).

AC 61-66 *Annual Pilot in Command Proficiency Checks* (1973).

AC 61-98A *Currency and Additional Qualification Requirements for Certificated Pilots* (1991).

135.147 DUAL CONTROLS REQUIRED

No person may operate an aircraft in operations requiring two pilots unless it is equipped with functioning dual controls. However, if the aircraft type certification operating limitations do not require two pilots, a throwover control wheel may be used in place of two control wheels.

135.149 EQUIPMENT REQUIREMENTS: GENERAL

No person may operate an aircraft unless it is equipped with —
(a) A sensitive altimeter that is adjustable for barometric pressure;
(b) Heating or deicing equipment for each carburetor or, for a pressure carburetor, an alternate air source;
(c) For turbojet airplanes, in addition to two gyroscopic bank-and-pitch indicators (artificial horizons) for use at the pilot stations, a third indicator that is installed in accordance with the instrument requirements prescribed in §121.305(j) of this chapter.
  (1) Is powered from a source independent of the aircraft's electrical generating system;
  (2) Continues reliable operation for at least 30 minutes after total failure of the aircraft's electrical generating system;
  (3) Operates independently of any other attitude indicating system;
  (4) Is operative without selection after total failure of the aircraft's electrical generating system;
  (5) Is located on the instrument panel in a position that will make it plainly visible to, and usable by, any pilot at the pilot's station; and
  (6) Is appropriately lighted during all phases of operation;
(d) Reserved.
(e) For turbine powered aircraft, any other equipment as the Administrator may require.

EXPLANATION

The third gyroscopic bank and pitch indicator required by §135.149(c) must be electrically powered. However, the FAA has not specified how the requirement for an additional power source should be met as long as the power source for the indicator is independent from the electrical generating system.

CROSS REFERENCES

91.121, Altimeter Settings; 91.215(b), ATC Transponder and Altitude Reporting Equipment and Use; 121.305(j), Flight and Navigational Equipment; 135.2(e)(4), Air Taxi Operations with Large Aircraft; 135.25(a)(2), Aircraft Requirements; 135.63(a)(3), Recordkeeping Requirements; 135.163(e), Equipment Requirements: Aircraft Carrying Passengers Under IFR.

ADVISORY CIRCULARS

AC 23.1309-1A *Equipment, Systems, and Installations in Part 23 Airplanes* (1992).

AC 43-203B *Altimeter and Static System Tests and Inspections* (1979).

AC 91-46 *Gyroscopic Instruments--Good Operating Procedures* (1977).

AIRMAN'S INFORMATION MANUAL

Altimeter Errors, Para. 7-42.

FAA CHIEF COUNSEL OPINIONS

The airplane's battery could be used to power the third attitude gyro, provided the other specific requirements of §121.305(j) are met. (12-19-79).

135.150 PUBLIC ADDRESS AND CREWMEMBER INTERPHONE SYSTEMS

No person may operate an aircraft having a passenger seating configuration, excluding any pilot seat, of more than 19 unless it is equipped with —

(a) A public address system which —

(1) Is capable of operation independent of the crewmember interphone system required by paragraph (b) of this section, except for handsets, headsets, microphones, selector switches, and signaling devices;

(2) Is approved in accordance with §21.305 of this chapter;

(3) Is accessible for immediate use from each of two flight crewmember stations in the pilot compartment;

(4) For each required floor-level passenger emergency exit which has an adjacent flight attendant seat, has a microphone which is readily accessible to the seated flight attendant, except that one microphone may serve more than one exit, provided the proximity of the exits allows unassisted verbal communication between seated flight attendants;

(5) Is capable of operation within 10 seconds by a flight attendant at each of those stations in the passenger compartment from which its use is accessible;

(6) Is audible at all passenger seats, lavatories, and flight attendant seats and work stations; and

(7) For transport category airplanes manufactured on or after [insert a date one year after the effective date of this amendment], meets the requirements of §25.1423 of this chapter.

(b) A crewmember interphone system which —
  (1) Is capable of operation independent of the public address system required by paragraph (a) of this section, except for handsets, headsets, micro-phones, selector switches, and signaling devices;
  (2) Is approved in accordance with §21.305 of this chapter;
  (3) Provides a means of two-way communication between the pilot compartment and —
    (i) Each passenger compartment; and
    (ii) Each galley located on other than the main passenger deck level;
  (4) Is accessible for immediate use from each of two flight crewmember stations in the pilot compartment;
  (5) Is accessible for use from at least one normal flight attendant station in each passenger compartment;
  (6) Is capable of operation within 10 seconds by a flight attendant at each of those stations in each passenger compartment from which its use is accessible; and
  (7) For large turbojet-powered airplanes —
    (i) Is accessible for use at enough flight attendant stations so that all floor-level emergency exits (or entryways to those exits in the case of exits located within galleys) in each passenger compartment are observable from one or more of those stations so equipped;
    (ii) Has an alerting system incorporating aural or visual signals for use by flight crewmembers to alert flight attendants and for use by flight attendants to alert flight crewmembers;
    (iii) For the alerting system required by paragraph (b)(7)(ii) of this section, has a means for the recipient of a call to determine whether it is a normal call or an emergency call; and
    (iv) When the airplane is on the ground, provides a means of two-way communication between ground personnel and either of at least two flight crewmembers in the pilot compartment. The interphone system station for use by ground personnel must be so located that personnel using the system may avoid visible detection from within the airplane.

EXPLANATION

The requirements of this section are identical to those of §121.318 and related §121.319.

CROSS REFERENCES

21.305, Approval of Materials, Parts, Processes, and Appliances; 25.1423, Public Address System; 121.318, Public Address System; 121.319, Crewmember Interphone System; 135.349(b)(2), Flight Attendants: Initial and Transition Ground Training.

ADVISORY CIRCULARS

AC 120-48 *Communication and Coordination Between Flight Crewmembers and Flight Attendants* (1988).

AC 135-12A *Passenger Safety Information Briefing and Briefing Cards (FAR Part 135)* (1991).

135.151 COCKPIT VOICE RECORDERS

(a) After October 11, 1991, no person may operate a multi-engine, turbine-powered airplane or rotorcraft having a passenger seating configuration of six or more and for which two pilots are required by certification or operating rules unless it is equipped with an approved cockpit voice recorder that:
   (1) Is installed in compliance with §23.1457(a)(1) and (2), (b), (c), (d), (e), (f), and (g); §25.1457(a)(1) and (2), (b), (c), (d), (e), (f), and (g); §27.1457(a)(1) and (2), (b), (c), (d), (e), (f), and (g); §29.1457(a)(1) and (2), (b), (c), (d), (e), (f), and (g) of this chapter, as applicable; and
   (2) Is operated continuously from the use of the check list before the flight to completion of the final check list at the end of the flight.

(b) After October 11, 1991, no person may operate a multi-engine, turbine-powered airplane or rotorcraft having a passenger seating configuration of 20 or more seats unless it is equipped with an approved cockpit voice recorder that —
   (1) Is installed in compliance with §23.1457, §25.1457, §27.1457 or §29.1457 of this chapter, as applicable; and
   (2) Is operated continuously from the use of the check list before the flight to completion of the final check list at the end of the flight.

(c) In the event of an accident, or occurrence requiring immediate notification of the National Transportation Safety Board which results in termination of the flight, the certificate holder shall keep the recorded information for at least 60 days or, if requested by the Administrator or the Board, for a longer period. Information obtained from the record may be used to assist in determining the cause of accidents or occurrences in connection with investigations. The Administrator does not use the record in any civil penalty or certificate action.

(d) For those aircraft equipped to record the uninterrupted audio signals received by a boom or a mask microphone the flight crewmembers are required to use the boom microphone below 18,000 feet mean sea level. No person may operate a large turbine engine powered airplane manufactured after October 11, 1991, or on which a cockpit voice recorder has been installed after October 11, 1991, unless it is equipped to record the uninterrupted audio signal received by a boom or mask microphone in accordance with §25.1457(c)(5) of this chapter.

(e) In complying with this section, an approved cockpit voice recorder having an erasure feature may be used, so that during the operation of the recorder, information:
  (1) Recorded in accordance with paragraph (a) of this section and recorded more than 15 minutes earlier; or
  (2) Recorded in accordance with paragraph (b) of this section and recorded more than 30 minutes earlier; may be erased or otherwise obliterated.

EXPLANATION

While this section specifically states that the FAA does not use the record in any civil penalty or certificate action, the question of whether information obtained from the tapes can be used as a basis for reexamination of a pilot's competency under §609 of the Federal Aviation Act of 1958, as amended [49 U.S.C. App. §1429(a)] is not specifically addressed.

The release of cockpit voice recorder recordings and transcriptions to the public following an aircraft accident has been placed within the discretion of the National Transportation Safety Board. §306(c) of the Independent Safety Board Act of 1974, as amended [49 U.S.C. App. §1905(c)].

CROSS REFERENCES

23.1457(a)(1), and (2)(b),(c),(d),(e),(f), and (g), Cockpit Voice Recorders; 25.1457, Cockpit Voice Recorders; 27.1457, Cockpit Voice Recorders; 29.1457(a)(1) and (2)(b),(c),(d),(e),(f), and (g), Cockpit Voice Recorders; 91.609, Flight Recorders and Cockpit Voice Recorders; 135.83(b) and (c), Operating Information Required; 135.152, Flight Recorders.

ADVISORY CIRCULARS

AC 25.1457-1A *Cockpit Voice Recorder Installations* (1969).

135.152 FLIGHT RECORDERS

(a) No person may operate a multi-engine, turbine-powered airplane or rotorcraft having a passenger seating configuration, excluding any pilot seat, of 10 to 19 seats, that is brought onto the U.S. register after October 11, 1991, unless it is equipped with one or more approved flight recorders that utilize a digital method of recording and storing data, and a method of readily retrieving that data from the storage medium. The parameters specified in Appendix B or C, as applicable, of this part must be recorded within the range, accuracy, resolution, and recording intervals as specified. The recorder shall retain no less than 8 hours of aircraft operation.

(b) After October 11, 1991, no person may operate a multi-engine, turbine-powered airplane having a passenger seating configuration of 20 to 30 seats or a multi-engine, turbine-powered rotorcraft having a passenger seating configuration of 20 or more seats unless it is equipped with one or more approved flight recorders that utilize a digital method of recording and storing data, and a method of readily retrieving that data from the storage medium. The parameters in Appendix D or E of this part, as applicable, that are set forth below, must be recorded within the ranges, accuracies, resolutions, and sampling intervals as specified.

(1) Except as provided in paragraph (b)(3) of this section for aircraft type certificated before October 1, 1969, the following parameters must be recorded:
(i) Time;
(ii) Altitude;
(iii) Airspeed;
(iv) Vertical acceleration;
(v) Heading;
(vi) Time of each radio transmission to or from air traffic control;
(vii) Pitch attitude;
(viii) Roll attitude;
(ix) Longitudinal acceleration;
(x) Control column or pitch control surface position; and
(xi) Thrust of each engine.

(2) Except as provided in paragraph (b)(3) of this section for aircraft type certificated after September 30, 1969, the following parameters must be recorded:
(i) Time;
(ii) Altitude;
(iii) Airspeed;
(iv) Vertical acceleration;
(v) Heading;
(vi) Time of each radio transmission either to or from air traffic control;
(vii) Pitch attitude
(viii) Roll attitude;
(ix) Longitudinal acceleration;
(x) Pitch trim position;
(xi) Control column or pitch control surface position;
(xii) Control wheel or lateral control surface position;
(xiii) Rudder pedal or yaw control surface position;
(xiv) Thrust of each engine;
(xv) Position of each thrust reverser;
(xvi) Trailing edge flap or cockpit flap control position; and
(xvii) Leading edge flap or cockpit flap control position.

(3) For aircraft manufactured after October 11, 1991, all of the parameters listed in Appendix D or E of this part, as applicable, must be recorded.

(c) Whenever a flight recorder required by this section is installed, it must be operated continuously from the instant the airplane begins the takeoff roll or the rotorcraft begins the lift-off until the airplane has completed the landing roll or the rotorcraft has landed at its destination.

(d) Except as provided in paragraph (c) of this section, and except for recorded data erased as authorized in this paragraph, each certificate holder shall keep the recorded data prescribed in paragraph (a) of this section until the aircraft has been operating for at least 8 hours of the operating time specified in paragraph (c) of this section. In addition, each certificate holder shall keep the recorded data prescribed in paragraph (b) of this section for an airplane until the airplane has been operating for at least 25 hours, and for a rotorcraft until the rotorcraft has been operating for at least 10 hours, of the operating time specified in paragraph (c) of this section. A total of 1 hour of recorded data may be erased for the purpose of testing the flight recorder or the flight recorder system. Any erasure made in accordance with this paragraph must be of the oldest recorded data accumulated at the time of testing. Except as provided in paragraph (c) of this section, no record need be kept more than 60 days.

(e) In the event of an accident or occurrence that requires the immediate notification of the National Transportation Safety Board under 49 CFR Part 830 of its regulations and that results in termination of the flight, the certificate holder shall remove the recording media from the aircraft and keep the recorded data required by paragraphs (a) and (b) of this section for at least 60 days or for a longer period upon request of the Board or the Administrator.

(f) Each flight recorder required by this section must be installed in accordance with the requirements of §§23.1459, 25.1459, 27.1459, or 29.1459, as appropriate, of this chapter. The correlation required by paragraph (c) of §§23.1459, 25.1459, 27.1459, or 29.1459, as appropriate, of this chapter need be established only on one aircraft of a group of aircraft:

(1) That are of the same type:

(2) On which the flight recorder models and their installations are the same; and

(3) On which there are no differences in the type design with respect to the installation of the first pilot's instruments associated with the flight recorder. The most recent instrument calibration, including the recording medium from which this calibration is derived, and the recorder correlation must be retained by the certificate holder.

(g) Each flight recorder required by this section that records the data specified in paragraphs (a) and (b) of this section must have an approved device to assist in locating that recorder under water.

EXPLANATION

Flight recorder information, as opposed to cockpit voice recorder information, can be used as a basis for civil penalty or certificate action.

The references to "(c)" in the first sentence and last sentence of §135.152(d) should be to "(e)".

The retention period for aircraft subject to §135.152(a) is 8 hours of flight time, excluding the original recording time. In the case of aircraft subject to §135.152(b), the retention periods are, for airplanes, until the airplane has been operated for at least 25 hours, excluding the original recording time and, for rotorcraft, until the rotorcraft has been operated for at least 10 hours, excluding the original recording time.

CROSS REFERENCES

23.1459, Flight Recorders; 25.1459, Flight Recorders; 27.1459, Flight Recorders; 29.1459, Flight Recorders; 91.609, Flight Recorders and Cockpit Voice Recorders; 135.151, Cockpit Voice Recorders; 49 C.F.R. Part 830, Rules Pertaining to the Notification and Reporting of Aircraft Accidents or Incidents and Overdue Aircraft, and Preservation of Aircraft Wreckage, Mail, Cargo, and Records.

ADVISORY CIRCULARS

AC 91-54 *Automatic Reporting Systems — Altimeter Setting and Other Operational Data* (1979).

135.153 GROUND PROXIMITY WARNING SYSTEM

(a) Except as provided in paragraph (b) of this section after April 20, 1994, no person may operate a turbine-powered airplane having a passenger seating configuration, excluding any pilot seat, of 10 seats or more, unless it is equipped with an approved ground proximity warning system.

(b) Any airplane equipped before April 20, 1992, with an alternative system that conveys warnings of excessive closure rates with the terrain and any deviations below glide slope by visual and audible means may continue to be operated with that system until April 20, 1996, provided that —

- (1) The system must have been approved by the Administrator.
- (2) The system must have a means of alerting the pilot when a malfunction occurs in the system; and
- (3) Procedures must have been established by the certificate holder to ensure that the performance of the system can be appropriately monitored.

(c) For a system required by this section, the Airplane Flight Manual shall contain —

- (1) Appropriate procedures for —
  - (i) The use of the equipment;
  - (ii) Proper flight crew action with respect to the equipment; and
  - (iii) Deactivation for planned abnormal and emergency conditions; and
- (2) An outline of all input sources that must be operating.

(d) No person may deactivate a system required by this section except under procedures in the Airplane Flight Manual.

(e) Whenever a system required by this section is deactivated, an entry shall be made in the airplane maintenance record that includes the date and time of deactivation.

EXPLANATION

TSO-approved ground proximity warning systems (GPWS) have been shown to meet minimum performance specifications in all 5 modes of warning envelopes and provide a higher level of safety than advisory systems.

The inclusion in the Airplane Flight Manual of the items listed in §135.153(c) will necessitate training regarding the GPWS pursuant to §135.345(b)(11).

CROSS REFERENCES

135.443, Airworthiness Release or Aircraft Maintenance Log Entry.

ADVISORY CIRCULARS

AC 20-112 *Airworthiness and Operational Approval of Airborne Systems to be Used in Lieu of Ground Proximity Warning System (GWPS)* (1981).

AC 90-72B *Minimum Safe Altitude Warning (MSAW) En Route Safe Altitude Warning (E-MSAW)* (1991).

AC 91-22A *Altitude Alerting Devices/Systems* (1971).

AIRMAN'S INFORMATION MANUAL

Safety Alert, Para. 4-15.

135.155 FIRE EXTINGUISHERS: PASSENGER-CARRYING AIRCRAFT

No person may operate an aircraft carrying passengers unless it is equipped with hand fire extinguishers of an approved type for use in crew and passenger compartments as follows —

(a) The type and quantity of extinguishing agent must be suitable for all the kinds of fires likely to occur;

(b) At least one hand fire extinguisher must be provided and conveniently located on the flight deck for use by the flight crew; and

(c) At least one hand fire extinguisher must be conveniently located in the passenger compartment of each aircraft having a passenger seating configuration, excluding any pilot seat, of at least 10 seats but less than 31 seats.

EXPLANATION

The choice of extinguishing agent used is left to the operator. However, the FAA must approve the type of fire extinguisher used. Toxicity is one of the matters to be considered in the selection of the agent used.

CROSS REFERENCES

135.19, Emergency Operations; 135.87(e), Carriage of Cargo Including Carry-On Baggage; 135.117(a)(8), Briefing of Passengers Before Flight; 135.295(e), Initial and Recurrent Flight Attendant Crewmember Testing Requirements; 135.331(b)(2)(iii), Crewmember Emergency Training.

ADVISORY CIRCULARS

AC 20-42C *Hand Fire Extinguishers for Use in Aircraft* (1984).

AC 20-100 *General Guidelines for Measuring Fire-Extinguishing Agent Concentrations in Powerplant Compartments* (1977).

AC 25-16 *Electrical Fault and Fire Prevention and Protection* (1991).

AC 25-9 *Smoke Detection, Penetration, and Evacuation Tests and Related Flight Manual Emergency Procedures* (1986).

AC 150/5210-6C *Aircraft Fire and Rescue Facilities and Extinguishing Agents* (1985).

AC 150/5210-7B *Aircraft Fire and Rescue Communications* (1984).

135.157 OXYGEN EQUIPMENT REQUIREMENTS

(a) *Unpressurized aircraft.* No person may operate an unpressurized aircraft at altitudes prescribed in this section unless it is equipped with enough oxygen dispensers and oxygen to supply the pilots under §135.89(a) and to supply, when flying —
   (1) At altitudes above 10,000 feet through 15,000 feet MSL, oxygen to at least 10 percent of the occupants of the aircraft, other than the pilots, for that part of the flight at those altitudes that is of more than 30 minutes duration; and
   (2) Above 15,000 feet MSL, oxygen to each occupant of the aircraft other than the pilots.

(b) *Pressurized aircraft.* No person may operate a pressurized aircraft —
   (1) At altitudes above 25,000 feet MSL, unless at least a 10-minute supply of supplemental oxygen is available for each occupant of the aircraft, other than the pilots, for use when a descent is necessary due to loss of cabin pressurization; and
   (2) Unless it is equipped with enough oxygen dispensers and oxygen to comply with paragraph (a) of this section whenever the cabin pressure altitude exceeds 10,000 feet MSL and, if the cabin pressurization fails, to comply with §135.89(a) or to provide a 2-hour supply for each pilot, whichever is greater, and to supply when flying —
      (i) At altitudes above 10,000 feet through 15,000 feet MSL, oxygen to at least 10 percent of the occupants of the aircraft, other than the pilots, for that part of the flight at those altitudes that is of more than 30 minutes duration; and
      (ii) Above 15,000 feet MSL, oxygen to each occupant of the aircraft, other than the pilots, for one hour unless, at all times during flight above that altitude, the aircraft can safely descend to 15,000 feet MSL within four minutes, in which case only a 30-minute supply is required.

(c) The equipment required by this section must have a means —
   (1) To enable the pilots to readily determine, in flight, the amount of oxygen available in each source of supply and whether the oxygen is being delivered to the dispensing units; or
   (2) In the case of individual dispensing units, to enable each user to make those determinations with respect to that person's oxygen supply and delivery; and
   (3) To allow the pilots to use undiluted oxygen at their discretion at altitudes above 25,000 feet MSL.

CROSS REFERENCES

91.211, Supplemental Oxygen; 135.89(a), Pilot Requirements: Use of Oxygen.

ADVISORY CIRCULARS

AC 23.841-1 *Cabin Pressurization Systems in Small Airplanes* (1986).

AIRMAN'S INFORMATION MANUAL

Mountain Flying, Para. 7-84;
Effects of Altitude, Para. 8-2.

FAA CHIEF COUNSEL OPINIONS

The first part of the beginning sentence in §135.157(b)(2) states "Unless it is equipped with enough oxygen dispensers and oxygen to comply with paragraph (a) of this section whenever the cabin pressure altitude exceeds 10,000 feet MSL . . ." This language is a modification of the original language in Part 42a that provided, in pertinent part, "When a pressurized cabin aircraft is certificated to fly with cabin pressure altitude greater than 10,000 feet. . ." Since the drafters of the present language in Part 135 did not express a contrary intent, we are of the opinion that the drafter's intent remains unchanged and that the language refers to an aircraft with a pressurized cabin that is certificated to fly with a cabin pressure altitude greater than 10,000 feet. In this situation, those aircraft must meet the same oxygen supply requirements for passengers as unpressurized aircraft in paragraph "(a)" of §135.157 (Paragraph "(a)" also contains requirements to comply with the pilot oxygen requirements in §135.89(a)).

The remaining part of the beginning sentence in §135.157(b)(2) states that "**and**, if the cabin pressurization fails, to comply with §135.89(a) or to provide a 2-hour supply for each pilot, whichever is greater, and to supply when flying — . . ." the oxygen supply requirements in §135.157(b)(2)(i) or §135.157(b)(2)(ii). If the conjunction "and" is read literally, the result subjects an operator to both the requirements of §135.157(a) and the requirements in Sections 135.157(b)(2), including §135.157(b)(2)(i) or §135.157(b)(2)(ii). Because some of the oxygen supply requirements in §135.157(a) differ from some of the oxygen supply requirements in 135.157(b) (e.g., §135.157(a)(2) versus §135.157(b)(2)(ii)), an absurdity would result that makes the requirements inconsistent. A principle of statutory construction allows elimination or disregarding of a word where the inclusion of that word would lead to an absurdity, irrationality, or elimination is necessary to avoid inconsistences and harmonize the provisions of a regulation. Our opinion is that the language used in this part of the sentence establishes separate oxygen supply requirements in the event of a pressurization failure. Therefore, these requirements are separate and not in addition to the requirements in the beginning of this sentence concerning aircraft with a pressurized cabin that is certificated to fly with a cabin pressure altitude greater than 10,000 feet.

The words "when flying" are used at the end of the sentence in §135.157(b)(2). The oxygen supply requirements for a pressurized aircraft that is certificated to fly with a cabin pressure altitude no greater than 10,000 feet is based on the altitude that the aircraft descends to after a pressurization failure. Therefore, our opinion is that the oxygen supply requirements in §§135.157(b)(2)(i) and 135.157(b)(2)(ii) are applicable to an aircraft with a pressurized cabin that experiences a pressurization system failure and, after the pressurization failure, because of operational factors (e.g., terrain) must continue to fly above 10,000 feet MSL.

If an aircraft with a pressurized cabin is flying at an altitude of 25,000 feet MSL or below and the pressurization system fails and the flight continues to fly at an altitude "above 10,000 feet through 15,000 feet MSL, oxygen to **at least** 10 percent of the occupants of the aircraft, other than the pilots, for that part of the flight of more than 30 minutes duration" must be provided under §135.157(b)(2)(i). If an aircraft with a pressurized cabin is flying at an altitude of 25,000 feet MSL or below and the pressurization system fails and the flight continues to fly at an altitude "above 15,000 feet MSL, oxygen to each occupant of the aircraft, other than the pilots, for one hour unless, at all times during the flight above that altitude, the aircraft can safely descend to 15,000 feet MSL within four minutes, in which case only a 30-minute supply is required" under §135.157(b)(2)(ii).

If an aircraft with a pressurized cabin is flying at an altitude of 25,000 feet MSL or below and the pressurization system fails, neither §135.157(b)(2)(i) nor §135.157(b)(2)(ii) require a supply of oxygen for **passengers if** the aircraft descends to and continues to fly at 10,000 feet MSL or below. However, we must again consider the intent of the drafters which stated in the preamble language that "It will continue to be the primary responsibility of the air carrier to carry sufficient supply of oxygen for passenger safety and comfort at **any** altitude flown." Therefore, the air carrier must carry sufficient oxygen for passenger safety and comfort while descending from "25,000 feet MSL or below" to "10,000 feet MSL or below."

We emphasize the responsibility placed on the air carrier to carry sufficient oxygen and that oxygen amounts should be calculated based on "the assumption that a cabin pressurization failure will occur at that altitude or point of flight which is most critical from the standpoint of oxygen need." We point out that if an operator does not carry sufficient oxygen aboard a flight, such insufficient oxygen quantity "may endanger the life or property of others" and would constitute a violation of §91.13 of the FAR. §91.13(a) provides that "No person may operate an aircraft in a careless or reckless manner so as to endanger the life or property of another." Furthermore, the endangerment need not be actual, and a violation exists if the insufficient oxygen quantity subject life or property to potential endangerment.

Regarding calculating the time of the descent after a pressurization system failure, the intent of the drafters from the preamble language is to require the pilots of a pressurized aircraft that experiences a pressurization failure to descend in accordance with the emergency procedures specified in the Airplane Flight Manual without exceeding its operating limitations to a flight altitude that will permit successful termination of the flight. (10-31-91).

135.158 PITOT HEAT INDICATION SYSTEMS

(a) Except as provided in paragraph (b) of this section, after April 12, 1981, no person may operate a transport category airplane equipped with a flight instrument pitot heating system unless the airplane is also equipped with an operable pitot heat indication system that complies with §25.1326 of this chapter in effect on April 12, 1978.

(b) A certificate holder may obtain an extension of the April 12, 1981, compliance date specified in paragraph (a) of this section, but not beyond April 12, 1983, from the Director, Flight Standards Service if the certificate holder —

  (1) Shows that due to circumstances beyond its control it cannot comply by the specified compliance date; and

  (2) Submits by the specified compliance date a schedule for compliance, acceptable to the Director, indicating that compliance will be achieved at the earliest practicable date.

EXPLANATION

The indication system must provide an amber light that is in clear view of a flight crewmember and must alert the flight crew if either of the following conditions exist: (1) The pitot heating system is switched "off," and (2) The pitot heating system is switched "on" and any pitot tube heating element is inoperative.

CROSS REFERENCES

25.1326, Pitot Heat Indication Systems.

135.159 EQUIPMENT REQUIREMENTS: CARRYING PASSENGERS UNDER VFR AT NIGHT OR UNDER VFR OVER-THE-TOP CONDITIONS

No person may operate an aircraft carrying passengers under VFR at night or under VFR over-the-top, unless it is equipped with —

(a) A gyroscopic rate-of-turn indicator except on the following aircraft:

  (1) Airplanes with a third attitude instrument system usable through flight attitudes of 360 degrees of pitch-and-roll and installed in accordance with the instrument requirements prescribed in §121.305(j) of this chapter.

  (2) Helicopters with a third attitude instrument system usable through flight attitudes of ±80 degrees of pitch and ±120 degrees of roll and installed in accordance with §29.1303(g) of this chapter.

  (3) Helicopters with a maximum certificated takeoff weight of 6,000 pounds or less.

(b) A slip skid indicator.

(c) A gyroscopic bank-and-pitch indicator.

(d) A gyroscopic direction indicator.

(e) A generator or generators able to supply all probable combinations of continuous in-flight electrical loads for required equipment and for recharging the battery.

(f) For night flights —
   (1) An anticollision light system;
   (2) Instrument lights to make all instruments, switches, and gauges easily readable, the direct rays of which are shielded from the pilots' eyes; and
   (3) A flashlight having at least two size "D" cells or equivalent.

(g) For the purpose of paragraph (e) of this section, a continuous in-flight electrical load includes one that draws current continuously during flight, such as radio equipment and electrically driven instruments and lights, but does not include occasional intermittent loads.

(h) Notwithstanding provisions of paragraphs (b), (c), and (d), helicopters having a maximum certificated takeoff weight of 6,000 pounds or less may be operated until January 6, 1988, under visual flight rules at night without a slip skid indicator, a gyroscopic bank-and-pitch indicator, or a gyroscopic direction indicator.

EXPLANATION

This section permits Part 135 operations of any airplane with the installation of a third attitude instrument system instead of a gyroscopic rate-of-turn indicator, that is substantially the same as airplanes, similarly equipped, that are permitted in Part 121 operations.

CROSS REFERENCES

1.1, General Definitions, "Night," "Over-The-Top"; 91.157, Special VFR Weather Minimums; 91.155, Basic VFR Weather Minimums; 91.507, Equipment Requirements: Over-The-Top or Night VFR Operations; 121.305(j), Flight and Navigational Equipment; 135.205, VFR: Visibility Requirements; 135.211, VFR: Over-The-Top Carrying Passengers: Operating Limitations.

ADVISORY CIRCULARS

AC 20-74 *Aircraft Position and Anticollision Light Measurements* (1971).

AC 91-46 *Gyroscopic Instruments — Good Operating Practices* (1977).

135.161 RADIO AND NAVIGATIONAL EQUIPMENT: CARRYING PASSENGERS UNDER VFR AT NIGHT OR UNDER VFR OVER-THE-TOP

(a) No person may operate an aircraft carrying passengers under VFR at night, or under VFR over-the-top, unless it has two-way radio communications equipment able, at least in flight, to transmit to, and receive from, ground facilities 25 miles away.
(b) No person may operate an aircraft carrying passengers under VFR over-the-top unless it has radio navigational equipment able to receive radio signals from the ground facilities to be used.
(c) No person may operate an airplane carrying passengers under VFR at night unless it has radio navigational equipment able to receive radio signals from the ground facilities to be used.

EXPLANATION

A helicopter operating under VFR at night is not required to have radio navigational equipment. However, helicopter VFR over-the-top night operations require proper radio and navigational equipment.

The ground facilities and airborne equipment used must enable navigation to the degree of accuracy required for air traffic control.

CROSS REFERENCES

1.1, General Definitions, "Night," "Over-The-Top"; 91.155, Basic VFR Weather Minimums; 91.157, Special VFR Weather Minimums; 135.205, VFR: Visibility Requirements; 135.211, VFR: Over-The-Top Carrying Passengers: Operating Limitations.

AIRMAN'S INFORMATION MANUAL

Two-Way Radio Communications Failure, Para. 6-30.

FAA CHIEF COUNSEL OPINIONS

It is not required that the aircraft have frequencies capable of communicating with an air traffic control facility unless such air traffic control facility is within a 25-mile radius. Thus, the capability of the aircraft to communicate with a private ground facility within 25 miles of the aircraft would comply with the rule. (4-18-78).

135.163 EQUIPMENT REQUIREMENTS: AIRCRAFT CARRYING PASSENGERS UNDER IFR

No person may operate an aircraft under IFR, carrying passengers, unless it has —

(a) A vertical speed indicator
(b) A free-air temperature indicator;
(c) A heated pitot tube for each airspeed indicator;
(d) A power failure warning device or vacuum indicator to show the power available for gyroscopic instruments from each power source;
(e) An alternate source of static pressure for the altimeter and the airspeed and vertical speed indicators;
(f) For a single-engine aircraft, a generator or generators able to supply all probable combinations of continuous in-flight electrical loads for required equipment and for recharging the battery;
(g) For multi-engine aircraft, at least two generators each of which is on a separate engine, of which any combination of one-half of the total number are rated sufficiently to supply the electrical loads of all required instruments and equipment necessary for safe emergency operations of the aircraft except that for multi-engine helicopters, the two required generators may be mounted on the main rotor drive train; and
(h) Two independent sources of energy (with means of selecting either), of which at least one is an engine-driven pump or generator, each of which is able to drive all gyroscopic instruments and installed so that failure of one instrument or source does not interfere with the energy supply to the remaining instruments or the other energy source, unless, for single-engine aircraft, the rate-of-turn indicator has a source of energy separate from the bank and pitch and direction indicators. For the purpose of this paragraph, for multi-engine aircraft, each engine-driven source of energy must be on a different engine.
(i) For the purpose of paragraph (f) of this section, a continuous in-flight electrical load includes one that draws current continuously during flight such as radio equipment, electrically driven instruments, and lights, but does not include occasional intermittent loads.

EXPLANATION

For helicopters, the two required generators may be mounted on the main rotor drive train rather than on the engines.

Where a split panel is desired and the instrument panels have both electric and vacuum instruments, each engine must have both a generator and a vacuum pump.

CROSS REFERENCES

91.171, VOR Equipment Check for IFR Operations; 91.183, IFR Radio Communications; 91.185, IFR Operations: Two-Way Radio Communications Failure; 135.103(d)(1), Exception to Second-In-Command Requirement: IFR Operations; 135.158, Pitot Heat Indications Systems; 135.215, IFR: Operating Limitations.

135.165 RADIO AND NAVIGATIONAL EQUIPMENT: EXTENDED OVERWATER OR IFR OPERATIONS

(a) No person may operate a turbojet airplane having a passenger seating configuration, excluding any pilot seat, of 10 seats or more, or a multi-engine airplane carrying passengers as a "Commuter Air Carrier" as defined in Part 298 of this title, under IFR or in extended overwater operations unless it has at least the following radio communications and navigational equipment appropriate to the facilities to be used which are capable of transmitting to, and receiving from, at any place on the route to be flown, at least one ground facility:
(1) Two transmitters, (2)
(2) Two microphones,
(3) Two headsets or one headset and one speaker,
(4) A marker beacon receiver,
(5) Two independent receivers for navigation, and
(6) Two independent receivers for communications.

(b) No person may operate an aircraft other than that specified in paragraph (a) of this section, under IFR or in extended overwater operations unless it has at least the following radio communication and navigational equipment appropriate to the facilities to be used and which are capable of transmitting to, and receiving from, at any place on the route, at least one ground facility:
(1) A transmitter,
(2) Two microphones,
(3) Two headsets or one headset and one speaker,
(4) A marker beacon receiver,
(5) Two independent receivers for navigation,
(6) Two independent receivers for communications, and
(7) For extended overwater operations only, an additional transmitter.

(c) For the purpose of paragraphs (a)(5), (a)(6), (b)(5), and (b)(6) of this section, a receiver is independent if the function of any part of it does not depend on the functioning of any part of another receiver. However, a receiver that can receive both communications and navigational signals may be used in place of a separate communications receiver and separate navigational signal receiver.

EXPLANATION

Part 298 defines a "Commuter Air Carrier" as "an air taxi operator that carries passengers on at least five round trips per week on at least one route between two or more points according to its published flight schedules that specify the times, days of the week, and places between which those flights are performed."

This regulation addresses Class I navigational requirements (VOR, DME, NDB). Part 135 does not have a section which specifically addresses Class II navigation requirements. Part 135 Class II navigation requirements are specified in Part B of the Operations Specifications (Ops Specs).

CROSS REFERENCES

§1.1, General Definitions, "Extended Over-Water Operation"; 91.183, IFR Radio Communications; 91.185, IFR Operations: Two-Way Radio Communications Failure; 91.215(b), ATC Transponder and Altitude Reporting Equipment and Use; 91.511, Radio Equipment for Overwater Operations; 135.167(c), Emergency Equipment; Extended Overwater Operations; 135.183, Performance Requirements: Land Aircraft Operated Over Water; Part 298, Exemptions for Air Taxi Commuter Air Carrier Operations.

ADVISORY CIRCULARS

AC 90-76B *Flight Operations in Oceanic Airspace* (1990).

AC 90-79 *Recommended Practices and Procedures for the Use of Electronic Long-Range Navigation Equipment* (1980).

AC 90-92 *Guidelines for the Operational Use of Loran-C Navigation Systems Outside the U.S. NAS* (1993).

AIRMAN'S INFORMATION MANUAL

VOR Receiver Check, Para. 1-4;
Marker Beacon, Para. 1-9.

FAA CHIEF COUNSEL OPINIONS

Regarding the language of "appropriate to the facility to be used," the intent of the section is to require Part 135 operators conducting flights under IFR or extended over-water operations to provide a complete secondary (backup) navigation system. If the aircraft can be safely navigated over the same route independently using a VOR and independently using an ADF, the navigation equipment would be considered appropriate to the facilities to be used, but if at any place on the route either navigation receiver is incapable of receiving at least one ground facility, the intent of the section would not be met.

The FAA has determined that the ability to make an approach with the primary or backup navigational system at the airport of intended landing or an alternate airport satisfies the requirements of §135.165(a)(5). Under the hypothetical situation, the airport has "only an NDB approach" and this type of instrument approach (i.e., NDB) requires an ADF receiver. (The two VOR's in the aircraft cannot be used to make this type of approach.) Since under the hypothetical situation the aircraft is equipped with only one independent ADF receiver (which is the only navigation instrument in the airplane capable of navigating to the NDB), that airplane would not comply with the requirements of §135.165(a)(5). However, under the hypothetical situation, if an alternate airport is available (i.e., that alternate airport satisfies all applicable FAR), and if that alternate airport has a VOR approach, then that airplane would comply with the requirements of §135.165(a)(5). (10-31-90).

135.167 EMERGENCY EQUIPMENT: EXTENDED OVERWATER OPERATIONS

(a) No person may operate an aircraft in extended overwater operations unless it carries, installed in conspicuously marked locations easily accessible to the occupants if a ditching occurs, the following equipment:
  (1) An approved life preserver equipped with an approved survivor locator light for each occupant of the aircraft. The life preserver must be easily accessible to each seated occupant.
  (2) Enough approved liferafts of a rated capacity and buoyancy to accommodate the occupants of the aircraft.

(b) Each liferaft required by paragraph (a) of this section must be equipped with or contain at least the following:
  (1) One approved survivor locator light.
  (2) One approved pyrotechnic signaling device.

(3) Either —

(i) One survival kit, appropriately equipped for the route to be flown; or

(ii) One canopy (for sail, sunshade, or rain catcher);

(iii) One radar reflector;

(iv) One liferaft repair kit;

(v) One bailing bucket;

(vi) One signaling mirror;

(vii) One police whistle;

(viii) One raft knife;

(ix) One CO_2 bottle for emergency inflation;

(x) One inflation pump;

(xi) Two oars;

(xii) One 75-foot retaining line;

(xiii) One magnetic compass;

(xiv) One dye marker;

(xv) One flashlight having at least two size "D" cells or equivalent;

(xvi) A 2-day supply of emergency food rations supplying at least 1,000 calories per day for each person;

(xvii) For each two persons the raft is rated to carry, two pints of water or one sea water desalting kit;

(xviii) One fishing kit; and

(xix) One book on survival appropriate for the area in which the aircraft is operated.

(c) No person may operate an aircraft in extended overwater operations unless there is attached to one of the life rafts required by paragraph (a) of this section, a survival type emergency locator transmitter that meets the applicable requirements of TSO-C91. Batteries used in this transmitter must be replaced (or recharged, if the battery is rechargeable) when the transmitter has been in use for more than 1 cumulative hour, and also when 50 percent of their useful life (or for rechargeable batteries, 50 percent of their useful life of charge), as established by the transmitter manufacturer under TSO-C91, paragraph (g)(2) has expired. The new expiration date for the replacement or recharged battery must be legibly marked on the outside of the transmitter. The battery useful life or useful life of charge requirements of this paragraph do not apply to batteries (such as water-activated batteries) that are essentially unaffected during probable storage intervals.

EXPLANATION

The survival kit referred to in §135.167(b)(3)(i) does not have specific standards to which it must conform. The FAA provides guidelines for the contents in AC 120-47.

CROSS REFERENCES

1.1, General Definitions, "Extended Over-Water Operation"; 91.205(b)(ii), Powered Civil Aircraft with Standard Category U.S. Airworthiness Certificates: Instrument and Equipment Requirements; 91.207, Emergency Locator Transmitters; 91.511, Radio Equipment for Overwater Operations; 91.513, Emergency Equipment; 135.19, Emergency Operations; 135.117(a)(5), Briefing of Passengers Before Flight; 135.141, Applicability; 135.165, Radio and Navigational Equipment: Extended Overwater or IFR Operations; 135.177, Emergency Equipment Requirements for Aircraft Having a Passenger Seating Configuration of More Than 19 Passengers.

ADVISORY CIRCULARS

AC 90-76B *Flight Operations in Oceanic Airspace* (1990).

AC 90-79 *Recommended Practices and Procedures for the Use of Electronic Long-Range Navigation Equipment* (1980).

AC 120-47 *Survival Equipment For Use In Overwater Operations* (1987).

AIRMAN'S INFORMATION MANUAL

Emergency Locator Transmitters, Para. 6-14;
Search and Rescue, Para. 6-16.

FAA CHIEF COUNSEL OPINIONS

§135.167 prescribes emergency equipment for **extended** over-water operations. As long as an operator does not engage in extended over-water operations, it need not comply with the provisions of §135.167. However, §135.141 states that the requirements of Subpart C are in addition to the aircraft and equipment requirements of Part 91 of the FAR. Therefore, if an operator operates powered civil aircraft with standard category U.S. airworthiness certificates beyond the power-off gliding distance from shore, approved flotation gear readily available to each occupant and at least one pyrotechnic signaling device are required equipment on those aircraft. [Reference FAR §91.205(b)(11)]. (10-1-85).

135.169 ADDITIONAL AIRWORTHINESS REQUIREMENTS

(a) Except for commuter category airplanes, no person may operate a large airplane unless it meets the additional airworthiness requirements of §§121.213 through 121.283, 121.307, and 121.312 of this chapter.

(b) No person may operate a reciprocating-engine or turbopropeller-powered small airplane that has a passenger seating configuration, excluding pilot seats, of 10 seats or more unless it is type certificated —
- (1) In the transport category;
- (2) Before July 1, 1970, in the normal category and meets special conditions issued by the Administrator for airplanes intended for use in operations under this part;
- (3) Before July 19, 1970, in the normal category and meets the additional airworthiness standards in Special Federal Aviation Regulation No. 23;
- (4) In the normal category and meets the additional airworthiness standards in Appendix A;
- (5) In the normal category and complies with §1.(a) of Special Federal Aviation Regulation No. 41;
- (6) In the normal category and complies with §1.(b) of Special Federal Aviation Regulation No. 41; or
- (7) In the commuter category.

(c) No person may operate a small airplane with a passenger seating configuration, excluding any pilot seat, of 10 seats or more, with a seating configuration greater than the maximum seating configuration used in that type of airplane in operations under this part before August 19, 1977. This paragraph does not apply to —
- (1) An airplane that is type certificated in the transport category; or
- (2) An airplane that complies with —
  - (i) Appendix A of this part provided that its passenger seating configuration, excluding pilot seats, does not exceed 19 seats; or
  - (ii) Special Federal Aviation Regulation No. 41.

(d) Cargo or baggage compartments:
- (1) After March 20, 1991, each Class C or D compartment, as defined in §25.857 of Part 25 of this Chapter, greater than 200 cubic feet in volume in a transport category airplane type certificated after January 1, 1958, must have ceiling and sidewall panels which are constructed of:
  - (i) Glass fiber reinforced resin;
  - (ii) Materials which meet the test requirements of Part 25, Appendix F, Part III of this Chapter; or
  - (iii) In the case of liner installations approved prior to March 20, 1989, aluminum.
- (2) For compliance with this paragraph, the term "liner" includes any design feature, such as a joint or fastener, which would affect the capability of the liner to safely contain a fire.

EXPLANATION

The separate reference to aircraft certificated under SFAR No. 41 is necessary because of the provisions of §135.399.

The commuter category is limited to propeller-driven multi-engine airplanes that have a seating configuration excluding pilot seats, of 19 or less, and a maximum certificated takeoff weight of 19,000 pounds or less, intended for nonacrobatic operation. Nonacrobatic operation includes any maneuver incident to normal flying; stalls (except whip stalls); and lazy eights, chandelles, and steep turns in which the angle of bank is not more than 60 degrees.

CROSS REFERENCES

25.857, Cargo Compartment Classification; 121.213 - 121.283 of Subpart J, Special Airworthiness Requirements; 121.307, Engine Instruments; 121.312, Materials for the Compartment Interiors; SFAR No. 52, Extension of Compliance Date of Seat Cushion Flammability Regulation for Large Airplanes Operated Under Part 135 in Other Than Commuter Air Carrier Operations.

ADVISORY CIRCULARS

AC 120-16C *Continuous Airworthiness Maintenance Programs* (1980).

AC 135.169-1 *Small-Propeller Driven Air Taxi Airplanes That Meet Sections 135.169 (formerly 135.144)* (1979).

135.170 MATERIALS FOR COMPARTMENT INTERIORS

(a) No person may operate an airplane that conforms to an amended or supplemental type certificate issued in accordance with SFAR No. 41 for a maximum certificated takeoff weight in excess of 12,500 pounds, unless within one year after issuance of the initial airworthiness certificate under that SFAR, the airplane meets the compartment interior requirements set forth in §25.853 (a), (b), (b-1), (b-2), and (b-3) of this chapter in effect on September 26, 1978.

CROSS REFERENCES

25.853(a),(b),(b)(1),(b)(2), and (b)(3), Compartment Interiors; SFAR No. 41, Applicability.

135.171 SHOULDER HARNESS INSTALLATION AT FLIGHT CREWMEMBER STATIONS

(a) No person may operate a turbojet aircraft or an aircraft having a passenger seating configuration, excluding any pilot seat, of 10 seats or more unless it is equipped with an approved shoulder harness installed for each flight crewmember station.
(b) Each flight crewmember occupying a station equipped with a shoulder harness must fasten the shoulder harness during takeoff and landing, except that the shoulder harness may be unfastened if the crewmember cannot perform the required duties with the shoulder harness fastened.

EXPLANATION

§91.205(b)(13) requires that each standard category small airplane manufactured after July 18, 1978, have both front seats equipped with shoulder harnesses. If an airplane is equipped with a shoulder harness, a flight crewmember must fasten the shoulder harness for each takeoff and landing unless the crewmember cannot perform necessary duties with the harness fastened. [Reference §91.105(b).] This applies to all Part 135 operations.

CROSS REFERENCES

91.105, Flight Crewmembers at Stations; 91.205, Powered Civil Aircraft with Standard Category U.S. Airworthiness Certificates: Instrument and Equipment Requirements.

ADVISORY CIRCULARS

AC 25.785-1 *Flight Attendant Seat Requirements* (1981).

135.173 AIRBORNE THUNDERSTORM DETECTION EQUIPMENT REQUIREMENTS

(a) No person may operate an aircraft that has a passenger seating configuration, excluding any pilot seat, of 10 seats or more in passenger-carrying operations, except a helicopter operating under day VFR conditions, unless the aircraft is equipped with either approved thunderstorm detection equipment or approved airborne weather radar equipment.
(b) After January 6, 1988, no person may operate a helicopter that has a passenger seating configuration, excluding any pilot seat, of 10 seats or more in passenger-carrying operations, under night VFR when current weather reports indicate that thunderstorms or other potentially hazardous weather conditions that can be detected with airborne thunderstorm detection equipment may reasonably be expected along the route to be flown, unless the helicopter is equipped with either approved thunderstorm detection equipment or approved airborne weather radar equipment.

(c) No person may begin a flight under IFR or night VFR conditions when current weather reports indicate that thunderstorms or other potentially hazardous weather conditions that can be detected with airborne thunderstorm detection equipment, required by paragraph (a) or (b) of this section, may reasonably be expected along the route to be flown, unless the airborne thunderstorm detection equipment is in satisfactory operating condition.

(d) If the airborne thunderstorm detection equipment becomes inoperative en route, the aircraft must be operated under the instructions and procedures specified for that event in the manual required by §135.21.

(e) This section does not apply to aircraft used solely within the State of Hawaii, within the State of Alaska, within that part of Canada west of longitude 130 degrees W, between latitude 70 degrees N, and latitude 53 degrees N, or during any training, test, or ferry flight.

(f) Without regard to any other provision of this part, an alternate electrical power supply is not required for airborne thunderstorm detection equipment.

EXPLANATION

There is no requirement to have this equipment installed on an aircraft during training flights, test flights, or ferry flights.

This section requires that the equipment be approved by the FAA, but does not define or identify acceptable thunderstorm detection equipment. The FAA has approved airborne weather radar and passive detection equipment, such as lightning detection equipment. Technical Standard Order TSO-C110a, "Airborne Passive Thunderstorm Detection Equipment," establishes the minimum operating performance standards and requirements for thunderstorm detection equipment.

CROSS REFERENCES

91.155, Basic VFR Weather Minimums; 91.157, Special VFR Weather Minimums; 135.21, Manual Requirements; 135.175, Airborne Weather Radar Equipment Requirements; 135.205, VFR: Visibility Requirements.

ADVISORY CIRCULARS

AC 00-6A *Aviation Weather* (1975).

AC 00-24B *Thunderstorms* (1983).

AC 20-68B *Recommended Radiation Safety Precautions for Ground Operation of Airborne Weather Radar* (1980).

AIRMAN'S INFORMATION MANUAL

Thunderstorms, Para. 7-25;
Thunderstorm Flying, Para. 7-26.

135.175 AIRBORNE WEATHER RADAR EQUIPMENT REQUIREMENTS

(a) No person may operate a large, transport category aircraft in passenger-carrying operations unless approved airborne weather radar equipment is installed in the aircraft.

(b) No person may begin a flight under IFR or night VFR conditions when current weather reports indicate that thunderstorms, or other potentially hazardous weather conditions that can be detected with airborne weather radar equipment, may reasonably be expected along the route to be flown, unless the airborne weather radar equipment required by paragraph (a) of this section is in satisfactory operating condition.

(c) If the airborne weather radar equipment becomes inoperative enroute, the aircraft must be operated under the instructions and procedures specified for that event in the manual required by §135.21.

(d) This section does not apply to aircraft used solely within the State of Hawaii, within the State of Alaska, within that part of Canada west of longitude 130 degrees W, between latitude 70 degrees, N, and latitude 53 degrees N, or during any training test, or ferry flight.

(e) Without regard to any other provision of this part, an alternate electrical power supply is not required for airborne weather radar equipment.

EXPLANATION

Part B of the Operations Specifications requires weather radar to be installed, operational, and used for ground mapping to assist in navigation when conducting certain operations in the North Pacific near Soviet Airspace.

CROSS REFERENCES

135.173, Airborne Thunderstorm Detection Equipment Requirements; 135.21, Manual Requirements.

ADVISORY CIRCULARS

AC 20-68B *Recommended Radiation Safety Precautions for Ground Operation of Airborne Weather Radar* (1980).

135.177 EMERGENCY EQUIPMENT REQUIREMENTS FOR AIRCRAFT HAVING A PASSENGER SEATING CONFIGURATION OF MORE THAN 19 PASSENGERS

(a) No person may operate an aircraft having a passenger seating configuration, excluding any pilot seat, of more than 19 seats unless it is equipped with the following emergency equipment:

(1) One approved first aid kit for treatment of injuries likely to occur in flight or in a minor accident, which meets the following specifications and requirements:

(i) Each first aid kit must be dust and moisture proof, and contain only materials that either meet Federal Specifications GGK- 319a, as revised, or as approved by the Administrator.

(ii) Required first aid kits must be readily accessible to the cabin flight attendants.

(iii) At time of takeoff, each first aid kit must contain at least the following or other contents approved by the Administrator:

Contents:	Quantity
Adhesive bandage compressors, 1 in	16
Antiseptic swabs	20
Ammonia inhalants	10
Bandage compressors, 4 in	8
Triangular bandage compressors, 40 in	5
Arm splint, noninflatable	1
Leg splint, noninflatable	1
Roller bandage, 4 in	4
Adhesive tape, 1-in standard roll	2
Bandage scissors	1

(2) A crash axe carried so as to be accessible to the crew but inaccessible to passengers during normal operations.

(3) Signs that are visible to all occupants to notify them when smoking is prohibited and when safety belts must be fastened. The signs must be constructed so that they can be turned on during any movement of the aircraft on the surface, for each takeoff or landing, and at other times considered necessary by the pilot in command. "No smoking" signs shall be turned on when required by §135.127.

(b) Each item of equipment must be inspected regularly under inspection periods established in the Operations Specifications to ensure its condition for continued serviceability and immediate readiness to perform its intended emergency purposes.

EXPLANATION

First aid kits are required on aircraft having more than 19 passengers since those are the aircraft that must have flight attendants.

CROSS REFERENCES

135.19(c), Emergency Operations; 135.73, Inspections and Tests; 135.127, Passenger Information; 135.167, Emergency Equipment: Extended Overwater Operations.

ADVISORY CIRCULARS

AC 120-44 *Air Carrier First Aid Programs* (1987).

135.178 ADDITIONAL EMERGENCY EQUIPMENT

No person may operate an airplane having a passenger seating configuration of more than 19 seats, unless it has the additional emergency equipment specified in paragraphs (a) through (l) of this section.

(a) *Means for emergency evacuation.* Each passenger-carrying landplane emergency exit (other than over-the-wing) that is more than 6 feet from the ground, with the airplane on the ground and the landing gear extended, must have an approved means to assist the occupants in descending to the ground. The assisting means for a floor-level emergency exit must meet the requirements of §25.809(f)(1) of this chapter in effect on April 30, 1972, except that, for any airplane for which the application for the type certificate was filed after that date, it must meet the requirements under which the airplane was type certificated. An assisting means that deploys automatically must be armed during taxiing, takeoffs, and landings; however, the Administrator may grant a deviation from the requirement of automatic deployment if he finds that the design of the exit makes compliance impractical, if the assisting means automatically erects upon deployment and, with respect to required emergency exits, if an emergency evacuation demonstration is conducted in accordance with §121.291(a) of this chapter. This paragraph does not apply to the rear window emergency exit of Douglas DC-3 airplanes operated with fewer than 36 occupants, including crewmembers, and fewer than five exits authorized for passenger use.

(b) *Interior emergency exit marking.* The following must be complied with for each passenger-carrying airplane:
   (1) Each passenger emergency exit, its means of access, and its means of opening must be conspicuously marked. The identity and location of each passenger emergency exit must be recognizable from a distance equal to the width of the cabin. The location of each passenger emergency exit must be indicated by a sign visible to occupants approaching along the main passenger aisle. There must be a locating sign —
      (i) Above the aisle near each over-the-wing passenger emergency exit, or at another ceiling location if it is more practical because of low headroom;
      (ii) Next to each floor level passenger emergency exit, except that one sign may serve two such exits if they both can be seen readily from that sign; and
      (iii) On each bulkhead or divider that prevents fore and aft vision along the passenger cabin, to indicate emergency exits beyond and obscured by it, except that if this is not possible, the sign may be placed at another appropriate location.
   (2) Each passenger emergency exit marking and each locating sign must meet the following:
      (i) For an airplane for which the application for the type certificate was filed prior to May 1, 1972, each passenger emergency exit marking and each locating sign must be manufactured to meet the requirement of §25.812(b) of this chapter in effect on April 30, 1972. On these airplanes, no sign may continue to be used if its luminescence (brightness) decreases to below 100 microlamberts. The colors may be reversed if it increases the emergency illumination of the passenger compartment. However, the Administrator may authorize deviation from the 2-inch background requirements if he finds that special circumstances exist that make compliance impractical and that the proposed deviation provides an equivalent level of safety.
      (ii) For an airplane for which the application for the type certificate was filed on or after May 1, 1972, each passenger emergency exit marking and each locating sign must be manufactured to meet the interior emergency exit marking requirements under which the airplane was type certificated. On these airplanes, no sign may continue to be used if its luminescence (brightness) decreases to below 250 microlamberts.

(c) *Lighting for interior emergency exit markings.* Each passenger-carrying airplane must have an emergency lighting system, independent of the main lighting system; however, sources of general cabin illumination may be common to both the emergency and the main lighting systems if the power supply to the emergency lighting system is independent of the power supply to the main lighting system. The emergency lighting system must —
   (1) Illuminate each passenger exit marking and locating sign;

(2) Provide enough general lighting in the passenger cabin so that the average illumination when measured at 40-inch intervals at seat armrest height, on the centerline of the main passenger aisle, is at least 0.05 foot-candles; and
(3) For airplanes type certificated after January 1, 1958, include floor proximity emergency escape path marking which meets the requirements of §25.812(e) of this chapter in effect on November 26, 1984.

(d) *Emergency light operation.* Except for lights forming part of emergency lighting subsystems provided in compliance with §25.812(h) of this chapter (as prescribed in paragraph (h) of this section) that serve no more than one assist means, are independent of the airplane's main emergency lighting systems, and are automatically activated when the assist means is deployed, each light required by paragraphs (c) and (h) of this section must;
(1) Be operable manually both from the flightcrew station and from a point in the passenger compartment that is readily accessible to a normal flight attendant seat;
(2) Have a means to prevent inadvertent operation of the manual controls;
(3) When armed or turned on at either station, remain lighted or become lighted upon interruption of the airplane's normal electric power.
(4) Be armed or turned on during taxiing, takeoff, and landing. In showing compliance with this paragraph a transverse vertical separation of the fuselage need not be considered;
(5) Provide the required level of illumination for at least 10 minutes at the critical ambient conditions after emergency landing; and
(6) Have a cockpit control device that has an "on," "off," and "armed" position.

(e) *Emergency exit operating handles.*
(1) For a passenger-carrying airplane for which the application for the type certificate was filed prior to May 1, 1972, the location of each passenger emergency exit operating handle, and instructions for opening the exit, must be shown by a marking on or near the exit that is readable from a distance of 30 inches. In addition, for each Type I and Type II emergency exit with a locking mechanism released by rotary motion of the handle, the instructions for opening must be shown by —
(i) A red arrow with a shaft at least three-fourths inch wide and a head twice the width of the shaft, extending along at least 70° of arc at a radius approximately equal to three-fourths of the handle length; and
(ii) The word "open" in red letters 1 inch high placed horizontally near the head of the arrow.
(2) For a passenger-carrying airplane for which the application for the type certificate was filed on or after May 1, 1972, the location of each passenger emergency exit operating handle and instructions for opening the exit must be shown in accordance with the requirements under which the airplane was type certificated. On these airplanes, no operating handle or operating handle cover may continue to be used if its luminescence (brightness) decreases to below 100 microlamberts.

(f) *Emergency exit access.* Access to emergency exits must be provided as follows for each passenger-carrying airplane;

(1) Each passageway between individual passenger areas, or leading to a Type I or Type II emergency exit, must be unobstructed and at least 20 inches wide.

(2) There must be enough space next to each Type I or Type II emergency exit to allow a crewmember to assist in the evacuation of passengers without reducing the unobstructed width of the passageway below that required in paragraph (f)(1) of this section; however, the Administrator may authorize deviation from this requirement for an airplane certificated under the provisions of part 4b of the Civil Air Regulations in effect before December 20, 1951, if he finds that special circumstances exist that provide an equivalent level of safety.

(3) There must be access from the main aisle to each Type III and Type IV exit. The access from the aisle to these exits must not be obstructed by seats, berths, or other protrusions in a manner that would reduce the effectiveness of the exit. In addition, for a transport category airplane type certificated after January 1, 1958, there must be placards installed in accordance with §25.813(c)(3) of this chapter for each Type III exit after December 3, 1992.

(4) If it is necessary to pass through a passageway between passenger compartments to reach any required emergency exit from any seat in the passenger cabin, the passageway must not be obstructed. Curtains may, however, be used if they allow free entry through the passageway.

(5) No door may be installed in any partition between passenger compartments.

(6) If it is necessary to pass through a doorway separating the passenger cabin from other areas to reach a required emergency exit from any passenger seat, the door must have a means to latch it in the open position, and the door must be latched open during each takeoff and landing. The latching means must be able to withstand the loads imposed upon it when the door is subjected to the ultimate inertia forces, relative to the surrounding structure, listed in §25.561(b) of this chapter.

(g) *Exterior exit markings.* Each passenger emergency exit and the means of opening that exit from the outside must be marked on the outside of the airplane. There must be a 2-inch colored band outlining each passenger emergency exit on the side of the fuselage. Each outside marking, including the band, must be readily distinguishable from the surrounding fuselage area by contrast in color. The markings must comply with the following:

(1) If the reflectance of the darker color is 15 percent or less, the reflectance of the lighter color must be at least 45 percent.

(2) If the reflectance of the darker color is greater than 15 percent, at least a 30 percent difference between its reflectance and the reflectance of the lighter color must be provided.

(3) Exits that are not in the side of the fuselage must have the external means of opening and applicable instructions marked conspicuously in red or, if red is inconspicuous against the background color, in bright chrome yellow and, when the opening means for such an exit is located on only one side of the fuselage, a conspicuous marking to that effect must be provided on the other side. "Reflectance" is the ratio of the luminous flux reflected by a body to the luminous flux it receives.

(h) *Exterior emergency lighting and escape route.*

(1) Each passenger-carrying airplane must be equipped with exterior lighting that meets the following requirements:

(i) For an airplane for which the application for the type certificate was filed prior to May 1, 1972, the requirements of §24.812(f) and (g) of this chapter in effect on April 30, 1972.

(ii) For an airplane for which the application for the type certificate was filed on or after May 1, 1972, the exterior emergency lighting requirements under which the airplane was type certificated.

(2) Each passenger-carrying airplane must be equipped with a slip-resistant escape route that meets the following requirements:

(i) For an airplane for which the application for the type certificate was filed prior to May 1, 1972, the requirements of §25.803(e) of this chapter in effect on April 30, 1972.

(ii) For an airplane for which the application for the type certificate was filed on or after May 1, 1972, the slip-resistant escape route requirements under which the airplane was type certificated.

(i) *Floor level exits.* Each floor level door or exit in the side of the fuselage (other than those leading into a cargo or baggage compartment that is not accessible from the passenger cabin) that is 44 or more inches high and 20 or more inches wide, but not wider than 48 inches, each passenger ventral exit (except the ventral exits on Martin 404 and Convair 240 airplanes), and each tail cone exit, must meet the requirements of this section for floor level emergency exits. However, the Administrator may grant a deviation from this paragraph if he finds that circumstances make full compliance impractical and that an acceptable level of safety has been achieved.

(j) *Additional emergency exits.* Approved emergency exits in the passenger compartments that are in excess of the minimum number of required emergency exits must meet all of the applicable provisions of this section, except paragraphs (f)(1), (2), and (3) of this section, and must be readily accessible.

(k) On each large passenger-carrying turbojet-powered airplane, each ventral exit and tailcone exit must be —

(1) Designed and constructed so that it cannot be opened during flight; and

(2) Marked with a placard readable from a distance of 30 inches and installed at a conspicuous location near the means of opening the exit, stating that the exit has been designed and constructed so that it cannot be opened during flight.

(l) *Portable lights.* No person may operate a passenger-carrying airplane unless it is equipped with flashlight stowage provisions accessible from each flight attendant seat.

EXPLANATION

Passenger Emergency Exits are defined as follows:

TYPE I —

This type is a floor level exit with a rectangular opening of not less than 24 inches wide by 48 inches high, with corner radii not greater than one-third width of the exit.

TYPE II —

This type is a rectangular opening of not less than 20 inches wide by 44 inches high, with corner radii not greater than one-third the width of the exit. Type II exits must be floor level exits unless located over the wing, in which case they may not have a step-up inside the airplane of more than 10 inches nor a step-down outside the airplane of more than 17 inches.

TYPE III —

This type is a rectangle opening of not less than 20 inches wide by 36 inches high, with corner radii not greater than one-third the width of the exit, and with a step-up inside the airplane of not more than 20 inches. If the exit is located over the wing, the step-down outside the airplane may not exceed 27 inches.

TYPE IV —

This type is a rectangular opening of not less than 19 inches wide by 26 inches high, with corner radii not greater than one-third the width of the exit, located over the wing with a step-up inside the airplane of not more than 29 inches and a step-down outside the airplane of not more than 36 inches.

VENTRAL —

This type is an exit from the passenger compartment through the pressure shell and the bottom fuselage skin. The dimensions and physical configuration of this type of exit must allow at least the same rate of egress as a Type I exit with the airplane in the normal ground attitude, with landing gear extended.

TAIL CONE —

This type is an aft exit from the passenger compartment through the pressure shell and through an openable cone of the fuselage aft of the pressure shell. The means of opening the tailcone must be simple and obvious and must employ a single operation.

TYPE A —

This type is a floor level exit with a rectangle opening of not less than 42 inches wide by 72 inches high with corner radii not greater than one-sixth of the width of the exit.

CROSS REFERENCES

25.561(b), General; 25.803(e), Emergency Evacuation; 25.809, Emergency Exit Arrangement; 25.812(b), (e), (f), (g), and (h), Emergency Lighting; 25.813(c)(3), Emergency Exit Access; 121.291(a), Demonstration of Emergency Evacuation Procedures; 121.310, Additional Emergency Equipment; 135.19(c), Emergency Operations; 135.129, Exit Seating; 135.177, Emergency Equipment Requirements for Aircraft Having a Passenger Seating Configuration of More Than 19 Passengers.

ADVISORY CIRCULARS

AC 20-47 *Exterior Colored Band Around Exits on Transport Airplanes* (1966).

AC 20-118A *Emergency Evacuation Demonstration* (1987).

AC 25.803-1 *Emergency Evacuation Demonstrations* (1989).

AC 25.812-1A *Floor Proximity Emergency Escape Path Marking* (1989).

135.179 INOPERABLE INSTRUMENTS AND EQUIPMENT

(a) No person may take off an aircraft with inoperable instruments or equipment installed unless the following conditions are met:

(1) An approved Minimum Equipment List exists for that aircraft.

(2) The Flight Standards District Office having certification responsibility has issued the certificate holder Operations Specifications authorizing operations in accordance with an approved Minimum Equipment List. The flight crew shall have direct access at all times prior to flight to all of the information contained in the approved Minimum Equipment List through printed or other means approved by the Administrator in the certificate holders Operations Specifications. An approved Minimum Equipment List, as authorized by the Operations Specifications, constitutes an approved change to the type design without requiring recertification.

(3) The approved Minimum Equipment List must:

(i) Be prepared in accordance with the limitations specified in paragraph (b) of this section.

(ii) Provide for the operation of the aircraft with certain instruments and equipment in an inoperable condition.

(4) Records identifying the inoperable instruments and equipment and the information required by paragraph (a)(3)(ii) of this section must be available to the pilot.

(5) The aircraft is operated under all applicable conditions and limitations contained in the Minimum Equipment List and the Operations Specifications authorizing use of the Minimum Equipment List.

(b) The following instruments and equipment may not be included in the Minimum Equipment List:

(1) Instruments and equipment that are either specifically or otherwise required by the airworthiness requirements under which the airplane is type certificated and which are essential for safe operations under all operating conditions.

(2) Instruments and equipment required by an airworthiness directive to be in operable conditions unless the airworthiness directive provides otherwise.

(3) Instruments and equipment required for specific operations by this part.

(c) Notwithstanding paragraphs (b)(1) and (b)(3) of this section, an aircraft with inoperable instruments or equipment may be operated under a special flight permit under §§21.297 and 21.199 of this chapter.

EXPLANATION

The minimum equipment list ("MEL") is intended to permit operation for a minimum period of time until repairs can be accomplished.

The FAA does not consider "direct" access to include information gained from conversations with maintenance personnel by telephone or over the radio prior to dispatch.

Due to the requirements of §39.3, "No person may operate a product to which an airworthiness directive applies except in accordance with the requirements of that airworthiness directive," the airworthiness directive requirements always take precedence over the minimum equipment list (MEL) provisions.

An operator's MEL may be more restrictive than the Master Minimum Equipment List, but under no circumstances may it be less restrictive. An operator's MEL is authorized by Operations Specifications (Ops Specs) paragraph C95.

MELs have certain conditions that must be met prior to deferring items. An operator must ensure that the procedures are accomplished and properly logged. If the procedures include such items as collaring circuit breakers and placarding, the operator should establish a system whereby the required items are checked prior to each flight to ensure that they are not inadvertently removed.

CROSS REFERENCES

21.199, Issue of Special Flight Permits; 91.213, Inoperative Instruments and Equipment; 135.23(e), (f), (g), (h), and (i), Manual Contents; 135.65, Reporting Mechanical Irregularities.

AIRMAN'S INFORMATION MANUAL

Instrument Landing System (ILS), Para. 1-10.

NTSB DECISIONS

Respondent, in his capacity as pilot-in-command, received the aircraft with the left fuel gauge written up as inaccurate. The MEL for the aircraft allowed flight of the airplane with one fuel quantity gauge inoperative, provided that "a reliable, approved means is established to determine fuel quantity on board meets the regulatory requirements for the intended flight." Although the MEL did not have a specific reference to the means to be used, the operator had instructed its pilots on the appropriate use of the dripless stick. On the day in question, the respondent did not use the dripless stick, but only relied on the first officer's observance of fuel being put on board. In finding the respondent in violation of §135.179, the Board held that he "used virtually no means to check the fuel." *Administrator v. Patrizi,* 6 NTSB 861 (1989).

FAA CHIEF COUNSEL OPINIONS

Aircraft with the installed clock inoperative, or one of two installed VHF radio transceivers inoperative, or with its sole transponder inoperative, can not be operated without an approved MEL, the use of which has been authorized by the FAA in the operator's Operations Specifications. (4-23-81).

135.180 TRAFFIC ALERT AND COLLISION AVOIDANCE SYSTEM

(a) After February 9, 1995 no person may operate a turbine powered airplane that has a passenger seating configuration, excluding any pilot seat, of 10 to 30 seats unless it is equipped with an approved traffic alert and collision avoidance system.

(b) The airplane flight manual required by §135.21 of this part shall contain the following information on the TCAS I system required by this section:

- (1) Appropriate procedures for —
  - (i) The use of the equipment; and
  - (ii) Proper flightcrew action with respect to the equipment operation.
- (2) An outline of all input sources that must be operating for the TCAS to function properly.

EXPLANATION

TCAS I provides collision alert warning but no flight guidance.

If an aircraft has an installed operable traffic alert and collision avoidance systems, §91.221(b) requires that system to be on and operating when the aircraft is being operated.

CROSS REFERENCES

1.1, General Definitions, "TCAS I,""TCAS II," "TCAS III," 91.221, Traffic Alert and Collision Avoidance System Equipment and Use; 135.21, Manual Requirements; 135.99, Composition of Flight Crew.

ADVISORY CIRCULARS

AC 20-131A *Airworthiness and Operational Approval of Traffic Alert and Collision Avoidance Systems (TCAS II) and Mode S Transponders* (1993).

AC 120-55A *Air Carrier Operational Approval and Use of TCAS II* (1993).

AIRMAN'S INFORMATION MANUAL

Clearance, Para. 4-80;
Traffic Alert and Collision Avoidance System (TCAS I & II), Para. 4-94.

135.181 PERFORMANCE REQUIREMENTS: AIRCRAFT OPERATED OVER-THE-TOP OR IN IFR CONDITIONS

(a) Except as provided in paragraphs (b) and (c) of this section, no person may —
  (1) Operate a single-engine aircraft carrying passengers over-the-top or in IFR conditions; or
  (2) Operate a multi-engine aircraft carrying passengers over-the-top or in IFR conditions at a weight that will not allow it to climb, with the critical engine inoperative, at least 50 feet a minute when operating at the MEAs of the route to be flown or 5,000 feet MSL, whichever is higher.

(b) Notwithstanding the restrictions in paragraph (a)(2) of this section, multi-engine helicopters carrying passengers offshore may conduct such operations in over-the-top or in IFR conditions at a weight that will allow the helicopter to climb at least 50 feet per minute with the critical engine inoperative when operating at the MEA of the route to be flown or 1,500 feet MSL, whichever is higher.

(c) Without regard to paragraph (a) of this section —
  (1) If the latest weather reports or forecasts, or any combination of them, indicate that the weather along the planned route (including takeoff and landing) allows flight under VFR under the ceiling (if a ceiling exists) and that the weather is forecast to remain so until at least 1 hour after the estimated time of arrival at the destination, a person may operate an aircraft over-the-top; or
  (2) If the latest weather reports or forecasts, or any combination of them, indicate that the weather along the planned route allows flight under VFR under the ceiling (if a ceiling exists) beginning at a point no more than 15 minutes flying time at normal cruise speed from the departure airport, a person may —
    (i) Take off from the departure airport in IFR conditions and fly in IFR conditions to a point no more than 15 minutes flying time at normal cruise speed from that airport;
    (ii) Operate an aircraft in IFR conditions if unforecast weather conditions are encountered while enroute on a flight planned to be conducted under VFR; and
    (iii) Make an IFR approach at the destination airport if unforecast weather conditions are encountered at the airport that do not allow an approach to be completed under VFR.

(d) Without regard to paragraph (a) of this section, a person may operate an aircraft over-the-top under conditions allowing —

   (1) For multi-engine aircraft, descent or continuance of the flight under VFR if its critical engine fails; or

   (2) For single-engine aircraft, descent under VFR if its engine fails.

EXPLANATION

§135.181(d)(1) allows a multi-engine aircraft that can not meet the single-engine enroute climb performance standards to operate over-the-top if adequate weather conditions exist. §135.181(d)(2) allows a single-engine aircraft to operate over-the-top if broken clouds exist that enable the aircraft to make an emergency descent clear of clouds when required due to an inoperative engine.

Weather reports or forecasts used by Part 135 operators to control flight operations must be from National Weather Service or from sources approved by the National Weather Service or the FAA.

While Part 135 has no provisions for the use of fuel dumping or driftdown as an alternate means of compliance with this section, an operator may seek an exemption to allow use of these procedures.

CROSS REFERENCES

1.1, General Definitions, "Critical Engine," and "Over-The-Top"; 11.25, Petitions for Rule Making or Exemptions; 91.155, Basic VFR Weather Minimums; 91.157, Special VFR Weather Minimums; 135.211, VFR: Over-The-Top Carrying Passengers: Operating Limitations; 135.213, Weather Reports and Forecasts; 135.215, IFR: Operating Limitations.

ADVISORY CIRCULARS

AC 90-76B *Flight Operations in Oceanic Airspace* (1990).

AIRMAN'S INFORMATION MANUAL

Abbreviated IFR Departure Clearance (Cleared... As Filed) Procedures, Para. 5-22; VFR-On-Top, Para. 5-82.

FAA CHIEF COUNSEL OPINIONS

The limits of §91.105 [now §91.155] must be used in any descent conducted pursuant to §135.181(c) [now §135.181(d)].

135.183 PERFORMANCE REQUIREMENTS: LAND AIRCRAFT OPERATED OVER WATER

No person may operate a land aircraft carrying passengers over water unless —

(a) It is operated at an altitude that allows it to reach land in the case of engine failure;
(b) It is necessary for takeoff or landing;
(c) It is a multi-engine aircraft operated at a weight that will allow it to climb, with the critical engine inoperative, at least 50 feet a minute, at an altitude of 1,000 feet above the surface; or
(d) It is a helicopter equipped with helicopter flotation devices.

EXPLANATION

While there are no provisions in Part 135 for the use of fuel dumping or driftdown to comply with the provisions of this section, an operator may seek an exemption to allow their use.

CROSS REFERENCES

11.25, Petitions for Rule Making or Exemptions; 91.205, Powered Civil Aircraft with Standard Category U.S. Airworthiness Certificates: Instrument and Equipment Requirements.

ADVISORY CIRCULARS

AC 90-76B *Flight Operations in Oceanic Airspace* (1990).

FAA CHIEF COUNSEL OPINIONS

Aircraft operating under Part 135 may operate over water in accordance with this section. In addition, they must comply with §91.33(b)(11) [now §91.205(b)(11)] relating to flotation equipment, if applicable to the operation. (4-10-75).

135.185 EMPTY WEIGHT AND CENTER OF GRAVITY: CURRENCY REQUIREMENT

(a) No person may operate a multi-engine aircraft unless the current empty weight and center of gravity are calculated from values established by actual weighing of the aircraft within the preceding 36 calendar months.
(b) Paragraph (a) of this section does not apply to —
  (1) Aircraft issued an original airworthiness certificate within the preceding 36 calendar months; and
  (2) Aircraft operated under a weight and balance system approved in the Operations Specifications of the certificate holder.

CROSS REFERENCES

91.605, Transport Category Civil Airplane Weight Limitations; 135.2(e)(2), Air Taxi Operations with Large Aircraft; 135.23(b), Manual Contents; 135.63(c), Recordkeeping Requirements; 135.365, Large Transport Category Airplanes: Reciprocating Engine Powered: Weight Limitations.

ADVISORY CIRCULARS

AC 91-23A *Pilot's Weight and Balance Handbook* (1977).

AC 120-27B *Aircraft Weight and Balance Control* (1990).

SUBPART D — VFR/IFR OPERATING LIMITATIONS AND WEATHER REQUIREMENTS

135.201 APPLICABILITY

This subpart prescribes the operating limitations for VFR/IFR flight operations and associated weather requirements for operations under this part.

135.203 VFR: MINIMUM ALTITUDES

Except when necessary for takeoff and landing, no person may operate under VFR —

(a) An airplane —

 (1) During the day, below 500 feet above the surface or less than 500 feet horizontally from any obstacle; or

 (2) At night, at an altitude less than 1,000 feet above the highest obstacle within a horizontal distance of 5 miles from the course intended to be flown or, in designated mountainous terrain, less than 2,000 feet above the highest obstacle within a horizontal distance of 5 miles from the course intended to be flown; or

(b) A helicopter over a congested area at an altitude less than 300 feet above the surface.

EXPLANATION

The fact that you are making a takeoff or a landing does not, in and of itself, allow operation below the prescribed altitudes. The takeoff or landing site must be an "appropriate site." [Reference §91.119]

CROSS REFERENCES

1.1, General Definitions, "Night"; 91.155, Basic VFR Weather Minimums; 91.157, Special VFR Weather Minimums.

ADVISORY CIRCULARS

AC 91-36C *VFR Flight Near Noise-Sensitive Areas* (1984).

AIRMAN'S INFORMATION MANUAL

Basic VFR Weather Minimums, Para. 3-3;
VFR Cruising Altitudes and Flight Level, Para. 3-4;
Traffic Patterns, Para. 4-53.

135.205 VFR: VISIBILITY REQUIREMENTS

(a) No person may operate an airplane under VFR in uncontrolled airspace when the ceiling is less than 1,000 feet unless flight visibility is at least 2 miles.

(b) No person may operate a helicopter under VFR in Class G airspace at an altitude of 1,200 feet or less above the surface or within the lateral boundaries of the surface areas of Class B, Class C, Class D, or Class E airspace designated for an airport unless the visibility is at least —

(1) During the day — 1/2 mile; or

(2) At night — 1 mile.

CROSS REFERENCES

1.1, General Definitions, "Night"; 91.126, Operating on or in the Vicinity of an Airport in Class G Airspace; 91.127, Operating on or in the Vicinity of an Airport in Class E Airspace; 91.129, Operations in Class D Airspace; 91.130, Operations in Class C Airspace; 91.131, Operations in Class B Airspace; 91.155, Basic VFR Weather Minimums.

AIRMAN'S INFORMATION MANUAL

Basic VFR Weather Minimums, Para. 3-3.

135.207 VFR: HELICOPTER SURFACE REFERENCE REQUIREMENTS

No person may operate a helicopter under VFR unless that person has visual surface reference or, at night, visual surface light reference, sufficient to safely control the helicopter.

CROSS REFERENCES

1.1, General Definitions, "Night"; 91.155, Basic VFR Weather Minimums; 91.157, Special VFR Weather Minimums.

NTSB DECISIONS

The pilot, while admitting a violation of §135.207, argued that a sudden change in the weather caused the situation that made it necessary for him to operate outside the regulations and, that under the provisions of §§91.3 and 135.19, a violation should not be sustained. The Board, in upholding the finding of violations of §§91.105(a) [now 91.155(a)], 135.207 and 91.9 [now 91.13(a)], stated that, because the pilot had not shown he took every step to prevent or avoid an emergency, the emergency was of his own making and therefore, §§91.3 and 135.19 did not excuse the violations. *Administrator v. Rudzek,* EA-3713 (1992).

FAA CHIEF COUNSEL OPINIONS

The FARs permit a properly equipped multiengined helicopter with an appropriately rated crew to fly VFR over-the-top. FARs §§135.211, 135.181, 135.161 and 135.243, allow aircraft to fly VFR over-the-top. The term "aircraft" as used in the FARs includes helicopters. "VFR over-the-top" with respect to the operation of aircraft means the operation of an aircraft over-the-top under VFR when it is not being operated on an IFR flight plan. [14 C.F.R. §1.1] "VFR" means visual flight rules. [14 C.F.R. §1.2].

If the agency's intent was to preclude VFR over-the-top operations in FAR §135.207, it would have stated so. It must be presumed that the drafters of the regulation were aware of the different terms as evidenced by their use in other FARs that pertain to VFR over-the-top operations. §135.207 does not mention VFR over-the-top operations. We therefore conclude that FAR §135.207 does not preclude properly equipped helicopters and instrument rated aircrew from flying VFR over-the-top. (3-3-92).

135.209 VFR: FUEL SUPPLY

(a) No person may begin a flight operation in an airplane under VFR unless, considering wind and forecast weather conditions, it has enough fuel to fly to the first point of intended landing and, assuming normal cruising fuel consumption —
   (1) During the day, to fly after that for at least 30 minutes; or
   (2) At night, to fly after that for at least 45 minutes.

(b) No person may begin a flight operation in a helicopter under VFR unless, considering wind and forecast weather conditions, it has enough fuel to fly to the first point of intended landing and, assuming normal cruising fuel consumption, to fly after that for at least 20 minutes.

EXPLANATION

The fuel-planning requirement of Part 91 and Part 135 are based on IFR and VFR Class I navigation within the contiguous states. Other types of operations or other operations outside the contiguous states may require additional or special training.

CROSS REFERENCES

1.1, General Definitions, "Night"; 91.151, Fuel Requirements for Flight in VFR Conditions; 135.213, Weather Reports and Forecasts.

ADVISORY CIRCULARS

AC 20-24B *Qualification of Fuels, Lubricants, and Additives* (1985).

AC 20-43C *Aircraft Fuel Control* (1976).

AC 20-125 *Water in Aviation Fuels* (1985).

AC 23-10 *Auxiliary Fuel Systems for Reciprocating and Turbine Powered Part 23 Airplanes* (1991).

AC 23.955-1 *Substantiating Flow Rates and Pressures in Fuel Systems of Small Airplanes* (1985).

AC 23.959-1 *Unusable Fuel Test Procedures for Small Airplanes* (1985).

AC 25.8 *Auxiliary Fuel System Installations* (1986).

AC 90-90 *Transcontinental Selected Fuel Conservation Routes* (1990).

AIRMAN'S INFORMATION MANUAL

Minimum Fuel Advisory, Para. 5-84.

NTSB DECISIONS

The pilot, flying on a four-leg Part 135 cargo-carrying operation, was forced to make an emergency landing 36 miles from his intended final destination due to fuel exhaustion. At the stop prior to the final leg, he did not top the tanks, but, after making a visual check of the tanks and gauges and based on his original fuel calculation at the beginning of the trip, he decided to proceed. In upholding the administrative law judge's finding of violations of §§91.5(a) [now 91.103(a)], 135.209(a)(2) and 91.9 [now 91.13(a)], the Board held that reliance on the fuel gauges under the prevailing circumstances was not sufficient. It noted that the elaborate fuel planning for which the airplane's manual provides would not be necessary if fuel gauges could be relied upon. Also, based on the "burn" (consumption) rate, the pilot should have realized the gauges were reading incorrectly prior to the departure on the final leg. *Administrator v. Davis,* 6 NTSB 505 (1988).

135.211 VFR: OVER-THE-TOP CARRYING PASSENGERS: OPERATING LIMITATIONS

Subject to any additional limitations in §135.181, no person may operate an aircraft under VFR over-the-top carrying passengers, unless —

(a) Weather reports or forecasts, or any combination of them, indicate that the weather at the intended point of termination of over-the-top flight —

(1) Allows descent to beneath the ceiling under VFR and is forecast to remain so until at least 1 hour after the estimated time of arrival at that point; or

(2) Allows an IFR approach and landing with flight clear of the clouds until reaching the prescribed initial approach altitude over the final approach facility, unless the approach is made with the use of radar under §91.175(i) of this chapter; or

(b) It is operated under conditions allowing —

(1) For multi-engine aircraft, descent or continuation of the flight under VFR if its critical engine fails; or

(2) For single-engine aircraft, descent under VFR if its engine fails.

EXPLANATION

Since the term "aircraft" is used, helicopters may be operated VFR over-the-top under this section.

The worst weather condition in any of the reports or forecasts used to control a flight movement is the controlling factor. This makes the remarks portion of a forecast (such as "chances of" or "occasionally") as operationally significant as the main body of the forecast.

CROSS REFERENCES

1.1, General Definitions, "Critical Engine," "Over-The-Top"; 91.155, Basic VFR Weather Minimums; 91.157, Special VFR Weather Minimums; 91.175, Takeoff and Landing Under IFR; 135.159, Equipment Requirements: Carrying Passengers Under VFR at Night or Under VFR Over-The-Top Conditions; 135.161, Radio and Navigational Equipment: Carrying Passengers Under VFR at Night or Under VFR Over-The-Top; 135.181, Performance Requirements: Aircraft Operated Over-The-Top or in IFR Conditions; 135.213, Weather Reports and Forecasts; 135.215, IFR: Operating Limitations; 135.225, IFR: Takeoff, Approach, and Landing Minimums.

AIRMAN'S INFORMATION MANUAL

VFR-On-Top, Para. 5-82.

135.213 WEATHER REPORTS AND FORECASTS

(a) Whenever a person operating an aircraft under this part is required to use a weather report or forecast, that person shall use that of the U.S. National Weather Service, a source approved by the U.S. National Weather Service, or a source approved by the Administrator. However, for operations under VFR, the pilot in command may, if such a report is not available, use weather information based on that pilot's own observations or on those of other persons competent to supply appropriate observations.

(b) For the purposes of paragraph (a) of this section, weather observations made and furnished to pilots to conduct IFR operations at an airport must be taken at the airport where those IFR operations are conducted, unless the Administrator issues Operations Specifications allowing the use of weather observations taken at a location not at the airport where the IFR operations are conducted. The Administrator issues such Operations Specifications when, after investigation by the U.S. National Weather Service and the FAA Flight Standards District Office charged with the overall inspection of the certificate holder, it is found that the standards of safety for that operation would allow the deviation from this paragraph for a particular operation for which an ATCO operating certificate has been issued.

EXPLANATION

The purpose of this section is to ensure that IFR operations are not conducted unless reliable weather information for the specific airport is available to the pilot.

"IFR operations" includes operations in VFR weather under an IFR flight plan as well as IFR operations in instrument meteorological conditions.

The authorization for the pilot in command to use his own observations for operations under VFR, where a report is not available, might be exercised in the case of floatplane operations at remote lakes where no weather observer is stationed. However, in such a situation the pilot in command or person exercising operational control still must obtain and use the information that is available, i.e. area forecasts and pilot reports (PIREPs).

The FAA considers certificated commercial pilots, airline transport pilots, dispatchers, air traffic controllers, and trained weather observers competent to provide weather information for Part 135 VFR operations.

Use of U.S. military weather reporting sources is limited to control of those flight operations which use miliary airports as departure, destination, alternate, or diversionary airports.

Automatic reporting systems developed and installed in accordance with Advisory Circular (AC) 91-54, and operated as independent, single-source reporting systems, do not satisfy the requirement of Part 135 for official aviation weather reports. This type of system is approvable only as a source of basic data for a supplementary aviation weather reporting station (SAWRS).

"Weather report" means a report of meteorological conditions observed at a specific time and location.

Automated observing systems installed, operated, and maintained by the National Weather Service (NWS) are approved for use without restriction by Part 135 operators.

CROSS REFERENCES

135.67, Reporting Potentially Hazardous Meteorological Conditions and Irregularities of Communications or Navigational Facilities; 91.155, Basic VFR Weather Minimums; 91.157, Special VFR Weather Minimums.

ADVISORY CIRCULARS

AC 00-6A *Aviation Weather* (1975).

AC 00-24B *Thunderstorms* (1983).

AC 00-45C *Aviation Weather Services* (1985).

AC 121-25 *Additional Weather Information: Domestic and Flag Air Carriers* (1977).

AC 150/5220-16A *Automated Weather Observing Systems (AWOS) for Non-Federal Applications* (1990).

AIRMAN'S INFORMATION MANUAL

National Weather Service Aviation Products, Para. 7-1;
FAA Weather Services, Para. 7-2.

NTSB DECISIONS

Respondent argued that §§135.213(a) and 135.213(b) are solely definitional, and do not prohibit any conduct because they do not contain words such as "no person may." The Board held that the regulations need not, however, be phrased in the negative. These rules are framed in the affirmative, requiring that a person "shall" use particular weather sources (subsection (a)) and that weather observations "must" be taken at a particular airport (subsection (b)). Acting contrary to these requirements is obviously prohibited. *Administrator v. Toups,* EA-3584 (1992).

135.215 IFR: OPERATING LIMITATIONS

(a) Except as provided in paragraphs (b), (c), and (d) of this section, no person may operate an aircraft under IFR outside of controlled airspace or at any airport that does not have an approved standard instrument approach procedure.

(b) The Administrator may issue Operations Specifications to the certificate holder to allow it to operate under IFR over routes outside controlled airspace if —

(1) The certificate holder shows the Administrator that the flight crew is able to navigate, without visual reference to the ground, over an intended track without deviating more than 5 degrees or 5 miles, whichever is less, from that track; and

(2) The Administrator determines that the proposed operations can be conducted safely.

(c) A person may operate an aircraft under IFR outside of controlled airspace if the certificate holder has been approved for the operations and that operation is necessary to —

(1) Conduct an instrument approach to an airport for which there is in use a current approved standard or special instrument approach procedure; or

(2) Climb into controlled airspace during an approved missed approach procedure; or

(3) Make an IFR departure from an airport having an approved instrument approach procedure.

(d) The Administrator may issue Operations Specifications to the certificate holder to allow it to depart at an airport that does not have an approved standard instrument approach procedure when the Administrator determines that it is necessary to make an IFR departure from that airport and that the proposed operations can be conducted safely. The approval to operate at that airport does not include an approval to make an IFR approach to that airport.

EXPLANATION

The term "instrument flight rules" (IFR) is not limited to operations in instrument meteorological conditions.

This regulation specifies the degree of accuracy required when operating IFR outside controlled airspace. It also reflects the concept of "demonstrated ability" to safely conduct operations.

CROSS REFERENCES

1.1, General Definitions, "Controlled Airspace"; 91.175, Takeoff and Landing Under IFR; 91.177, Minimum Altitudes for IFR Operations; 91.179, IFR Cruising Altitude or Flight Level; 135.225, IFR: Takeoff, Approach, and Landing Minimums.

ADVISORY CIRCULARS

AC 61-27C *Instrument Flying Handbook* (1979).

AC 73-2 *IFR Helicopter Operations in the Northeast Corridor* (1979).

AIRMAN'S INFORMATION MANUAL

Instrument Approach Procedures, Para. 5-46;
Instrument Approach, Para. 5-73.

NTSB DECISIONS

A pilot took off on an IFR Part 135 cargo-carrying operation from an airport which was located in uncontrolled airspace and did not have an approved standard instrument approach procedure. The operator's Operations Specifications did not authorize such an operation. The Board held that it was compelled to find a violation of §135.215(a). *Administrator v. Williams,* EA-3588 (1992).

A pilot took off on an IFR Part 135 cargo-carrying operation from an airport which was located in uncontrolled airspace and did not have an approved standard instrument approach procedure. The operator's Operations Specifications did not authorize such an operation. The pilot argued that by giving him the IFR clearance, the FAA condoned the operation. The Board held that even if it were true that the air traffic controller who gave the clearance or the employee who transmitted it to the pilot knew this to be a Part 135 operation, neither individual should be obliged to be aware of all conditions at all airports in his jurisdiction (e.g. whether an airport has an approved weather source and standard instrument approach; whether it is controlled airspace) and act to prevent pilots from FAR violations. In finding §135.215(a) had been violated, the Board concluded that it continues to be the pilot's obligation, as pilot in command, to ensure compliance with all pertinent regulations. *Administrator v. Toups,* EA-3584 (1992).

135.217 IFR: TAKEOFF LIMITATIONS

No person may takeoff an aircraft under IFR from an airport where weather conditions are at or above take off minimums but are below authorized IFR landing minimums unless there is an alternate airport within 1 hour's flying time (at normal cruising speed, in still air) of the airport of departure.

EXPLANATION

Alternate airport must have weather conditions that are at or above IFR landing minimums.

CROSS REFERENCES

91.175, Takeoff and Landing Under IFR; 135.213, Weather Reports and Forecasts; 135.221, IFR: Alternate Airport Weather Minimums; 135.223, IFR: Alternate Airport Requirements; 135.225, IFR: Takeoff, Approach and Landing Minimums.

ADVISORY CIRCULARS

AC 61-27C *Instrument Flying Handbook* (1979).

AIRMAN'S INFORMATION MANUAL

Instrument Departures, Para. 5-25.

135.219 IFR: DESTINATION AIRPORT WEATHER MINIMUMS

No person may take off an aircraft under IFR or begin an IFR or over-the-top operation unless the latest weather reports or forecasts, or any combination of them, indicate that weather conditions at the estimated time of arrival at the next airport of intended landing will be at or above authorized IFR landing minimums.

EXPLANATION

This rule, prior to amendment, required the use of both weather reports and forecasts without regard to any favorable "combination."

CROSS REFERENCES

91.175, Takeoff and Landing Under IFR; 135.213, Weather Reports and Forecasts; 135.225, IFR: Takeoff, Approach and Landing Minimums.

ADVISORY CIRCULARS

AC 61-27C *Instrument Flying Handbook* (1979).

AC 00-6A *Aviation Weather* (1975).

AC 121-26 *Airports — Required Data* (1981).

AIRMAN'S INFORMATION MANUAL

Approach and Landing Minimums, Para. 5-55.

NTSB DECISIONS

A pilot filed two separate IFR flight plans. One was for Martha's Vineyard where, at the time of takeoff from New Bedford, the reported weather was such that a takeoff to that destination was prohibited. The other flight plan had Nantucket as the destination. At Nantucket the weather was sufficient to allow departure for that destination. The pilot said he filed two flight plans because until departure he would not be aware whether he had passengers for both destinations. Once airborne, he changed his destination to Nantucket. The Board nevertheless found a violation of §135.219 on the basis of the flight plan filed with Martha's Vineyard as the destination. *Administrator v. Cunningham*, 5 NTSB 516 (1985).

FAA CHIEF COUNSEL OPINIONS

§§135.219 and 135.221 clearly indicate that the critical time period for purposes of determining whether an aircraft can be dispatched or operated under IFR conditions or whether an airport can be listed as an alternate is the estimated time of arrival. Weather forecasts which indicate that conditions will be at or above minimums at ETA are sufficient for operations under FAR Part 135, even if hourly sequence reports state that weather conditions are currently below minimums. On the other hand, weather forecasts which indicate that conditions at ETA will be below minimums overrule hourly sequence reports that show that the airport is presently above minimums. (7-18-84).

A one-way IFR flight plan from the airport of departure to a DME fix on an approved IFR route would not meet the requirements of §135.219 which clearly contemplates a destination airport and intended landing rather than a DME fix and holding. (12-11-80).

135.221 IFR: ALTERNATE AIRPORT WEATHER MINIMUMS

No person may designate an alternate airport unless the weather reports or forecasts, or any combination of them, indicate that the weather conditions will be at or above authorized alternate airport landing minimums for that airport at the estimated time of arrival.

EXPLANATION

Operations Specifications (Ops Specs) paragraph C55 is issued to all Part 135 operators who conduct IFR operations with airplanes. This paragraph provides a two-part table from which the operator, during the initial dispatch or flight release planning segment of a flight, derives alternate airport IFR weather minimums in those cases where it has been determined that an alternate airport is required. This table frequently produces numbers which are lower than those in §135.221.

CROSS REFERENCES

135.213, Weather Reports and Forecasts; 135.223, IFR: Alternate Airport Requirements; 135.225, IFR: Takeoff, Approach and Landing Minimums.

ADVISORY CIRCULARS

AC 00-6A *Aviation Weather* (1975).

AC 61-27C *Instrument Flying Handbook* (1979).

AC 121-26 *Airports — Required Data* (1981).

FAA CHIEF COUNSEL OPINIONS

[See opinion of 7-18-84, §135.219.]

135.223 IFR: ALTERNATE AIRPORT REQUIREMENTS

(a) Except as provided in paragraph (b) of this section, no person may operate an aircraft in IFR conditions unless it carries enough fuel (considering weather reports or forecasts or any combination of them) to —
   (1) Complete the flight to the first airport of intended landing;
   (2) Fly from that airport to the alternate airport; and
   (3) Fly after that for 45 minutes at normal cruising speed or, for helicopters, fly after that for 30 minutes at normal cruising speed.

(b) Paragraph (a)(2) of this section does not apply if Part 97 of this chapter prescribes a standard instrument approach procedure for the first airport of intended landing and, for at least one hour before and after the estimated time of arrival, the appropriate weather reports or forecasts, or any combination of them, indicate that —
   (1) The ceiling will be at least 1,500 feet above the lowest circling approach MDA; or
   (2) If a circling instrument approach is not authorized for the airport, the ceiling will be at least 1,500 feet above the lowest published minimum or 2,000 feet above the airport elevation, whichever is higher; and
   (3) Visibility for that airport is forecast to be at least three miles, or two miles more than the lower applicable visibility minimums, whichever is the greater, for the instrument approach procedure to be used at the destination airport.

EXPLANATION

While Part 135 does not specifically require a specific increment of contingency fuel, §91.103 does require that such contingencies be considered in preflight planning. Therefore, an increment of fuel to compensate for foreseeable contingencies must be on board. One such contingency would be a delay in receiving takeoff clearance at major terminals.

Part 135 does not specify what action a pilot in command must take if, while enroute, an alternate airport goes below minimums. An operator's general operations manual should contain specific policies and instructions on how the pilot in command is to proceed in foreseeable circumstances that may be encountered in the operator's specific operation.

CROSS REFERENCES

91.103, Preflight Action; 91.167, Fuel Requirements for Flight in IFR Conditions; 91.177, Minimum Altitudes for IFR Operations; 135.69, Restriction or Suspension of Operations: Continuation of Flight in an Emergency; 135.213, Weather Reports and Forecasts; 135.221, IFR: Alternate Airport Requirements; 135.225, IFR: Takeoff, Approach, and Landing Minimums.

ADVISORY CIRCULARS

AC 61-27C *Instrument Flying Handbook* (1979).

AC 121-25 *Additional Weather Information: Domestic and Flag Air Carriers* (1977).

AC 121-26 *Airports — Required Data* (1981).

135.225 IFR: TAKEOFF, APPROACH AND LANDING MINIMUMS

(a) No pilot may begin an instrument approach procedure to an airport unless —
 (1) That airport has a weather reporting facility operated by the U.S. National Weather Service, a source approved by U.S. National Weather Service, or a source approved by the Administrator; and
 (2) The latest weather report issued by that weather reporting facility indicates that weather conditions are at or above the authorized IFR landing minimums for that airport.

(b) No pilot may begin the final approach segment of an instrument approach procedure to an airport unless the latest weather reported by the facility described in paragraph (a)(1) of this section indicates that weather conditions are at or above the authorized IFR landing minimums for that procedure.

(c) If a pilot has begun the final approach segment of an instrument approach to an airport under paragraph (b) of this section and a later weather report indicating below minimum conditions is received after the aircraft is —
 (1) On an ILS final approach and has passed the final approach fix; or
 (2) On an ASR or PAR final approach and has been turned over to the final approach controller; or
 (3) On a final approach using a VOR, NDB, or comparable approach procedure; and the aircraft —
  (i) Has passed the appropriate facility or final approach fix; or
  (ii) Where a final approach fix is not specified, has completed the procedure turn and is established inbound toward the airport on the final approach course within the distance prescribed in the procedure; the approach may be continued and a landing made if the pilot finds, upon reaching the authorized MDA or DH, that actual weather conditions are at least equal to the minimums prescribed for the procedure.

(d) The MDA or DH and visibility landing minimums prescribed in Part 97 of this chapter or in the operator's Operations Specifications are increased by 100 feet and 1/2 mile respectively, but not to exceed the ceiling and visibility minimums for that airport when used as an alternate airport, for each pilot in command of a turbine-powered airplane who has not served at least 100 hours as pilot in command in that type of airplane.

(e) Each pilot making an IFR takeoff or approach and landing at a military or foreign airport shall comply with applicable instrument approach procedures and weather minimums prescribed by the authority having jurisdiction over that airport. In addition, no pilot may, at that airport —
   (1) Take off under IFR when the visibility is less than 1 mile; or
   (2) Make an instrument approach when the visibility is less than 1/2 mile.

(f) If takeoff minimums are specified in Part 97 of this chapter for the takeoff airport, no pilot may take off an aircraft under IFR when the weather conditions reported by the facility described in paragraph (a)(1) of this section are less than the takeoff minimums specified for the takeoff airport in Part 97 or in the certificate holder's Operations Specifications.

(g) Except as provided in paragraph (h) of this section, if takeoff minimums are not prescribed in Part 97 of this chapter for the takeoff airport, no pilot may take off an aircraft under IFR when the weather conditions reported by the facility described in paragraph (a)(1) of this section are less than that prescribed in Part 91 of this chapter or in the certificate holder's Operations Specifications.

(h) At airports where straight-in instrument approach procedures are authorized, a pilot may take off an aircraft under IFR when the weather conditions reported by the facility described in paragraph (a)(1) of this section are equal to or better than the lowest straight-in landing minimums, unless otherwise restricted, if —
   (1) The wind direction and velocity at the time of takeoff are such that a straight-in instrument approach can be made to the runway served by the instrument approach;
   (2) The associated ground facilities upon which the landing minimums are predicated and the related airborne equipment are in normal operation; and
   (3) The certificate holder has been approved for such operations.

EXPLANATION

The object of the flight experience requirement is to ensure that the pilot is fully aware of the aircraft's equipment capabilities and limitations, the available external visual cues, and the aircraft's handling characteristics. It is applicable only in the case of turbojet or turbopropeller aircraft.

Operations Specifications (Ops Specs) paragraph C57 is issued to all Part 135 operators who conduct IFR airplane operations. Only C57a and b will be printed for issuance when an operator is not authorized to use lower-than-standard takeoff minimums. C57a, b, and c will be printed for issuance when the operator is authorized to use takeoff minimums equal to the lowest straight-in landing minimums (§135.225(h)). C57a, b, c, d, and e will be printed for issuance when the operator is restricted to operations only within the United States.

CROSS REFERENCES

91.171, VOR Equipment Check for IFR Operations; 91.175, Takeoff and Landing Minimums Under IFR; 91.177, Minimum Altitudes for IFR Operations; 135.163, Equipment Requirements: Aircraft Carrying Passengers Under IFR; 135.213, Weather Reports and Forecasts; 135.215(c) and (d), IFR: Operating Limitations.

ADVISORY CIRCULARS

AC 25.703-1 *Takeoff Configuration Warning Systems* (1993).

AC 61-27C *Instrument Flying Handbook* (1979).

AC 61-47A *Use of Approach Slope Indicators for Pilot Training* (1979).

AC 90-58C *VOR Course Errors Resulting from 50kHz Channel Mis-Selection* (1975).

AC 120-28C *Criteria for Approval of Category III Landing Weather Minima* (1984).

AC 120-29 *Criteria for Approving Category I and Category II Landing Minima for FAR 121 Operators* (1974).

AIRMAN'S INFORMATION MANUAL

Instrument Departures, Para. 5-25;
Instrument Approach Procedures, Para. 5-46;
Approach and Landing Minimums, Para. 5-55;
Instrument Approach, Para. 5-73;

NTSB DECISIONS

The FAA argued that §135.225(a)(1) prohibits an instrument approach procedure to an airport without an operational weather reporting facility regardless of the weather conditions. The Board did not concur. It stated that, while it is true that the regulation does not expressly except from its coverage instrument approach procedures made in other than instrument weather conditions, it believed that in context that is its proper construction. The regulation is intended to proscribe instrument approaches to airports that do not or may not have weather conditions at or above the authorized IFR landing minimums for ceiling or visibility. Thus, where a pilot cannot determine by visual observation before beginning an instrument approach procedure what actual meteorological conditions exist at the airport, he must obtain such information from the airport's weather reporting facility or, if there is none, proceed to an alternate airport. Where, however, a pilot can see before commencing such an approach that VFR conditions prevail between his aircraft and the airport, there is no need to rely on a weather reporting facility for information the pilot already has observed, and the choice between a landing on the ILS, or by visual reference, or by a combination of elements of both essentially becomes a matter of pilot prerogative. *Administrator v. Beguin,* 5 NTSB 112 (1985).

FAA CHIEF COUNSEL OPINIONS

Question — Are both ceiling and visibility required in order for a FAR Part 135 air carrier pilot to initiate an instrument approach?

Response — FAR 135.225(a) and 135.225(a)(2) forbid a Part 135 pilot from beginning an instrument approach unless reported weather conditions at the destination airport are at or above the authorized IFR landing minimums for the airport. So, even though ceiling is not a criterion on the approach plates, it must be considered by the pilot in his decision to initiate the approach, and in deciding whether the reported ceiling is above or below the decision height or minimum descent altitude for the approach. Similarly, FAR 135.225(b) forbids initiation of a final approach segment unless reported conditions are at or above minimums. Again, the pilot must know the reported ceiling and visibility before deciding whether that approach segment can legally be initiated. (3-21-91).

FAR 135.225(d) raises IFR landing minimums for pilots in command of turbine powered airplanes flown under Part 135 who have not served at least 100 hours as pilot in command in that type of airplane. **Served** and **logged** are not the same in this context, and no matter how the second in command logs his time, he has not served as pilot in command until he has completed the training and check rides necessary for certification as a Part 135 pilot in command. (3-26-92). (12-5-84).

135.227 ICING CONDITIONS: OPERATING LIMITATIONS

(a) No pilot may take off an aircraft that has frost, ice, or snow adhering to any rotor blade, propeller, windshield, wing, stabilizing or control surface, to a powerplant installation, or to an airspeed, altimeter, rate of climb, or flight attitude instrument system, except under the following conditions:
  (1) Takeoffs may be made with frost adhering to the wings, or stabilizing or control surfaces, if the frost has been polished to make it smooth.
  (2) Takeoffs may be made with frost under the wing in the area of the fuel tanks if authorized by the Administrator.

(b) No certificate holder may authorize an airplane to take off and no pilot may take off an airplane any time conditions are such that frost, ice, or snow may reasonably be expected to adhere to the airplane unless the pilot has completed all applicable training as required by §135.341 and unless one of the following requirements is met:
  (1) A pretakeoff contamination check, that has been established by the certificate holder and approved by the Administrator for the specific airplane type, has been completed within 5 minutes prior to beginning takeoff. A pretakeoff contamination check is a check to make sure the wings and control surfaces are free of frost, ice, or snow.
  (2) The certificate holder has an approved alternative procedure and under that procedure the airplane is determined to be free of frost, ice, or snow.
  (3) The certificate holder has an approved deicing/anti-icing program that complies with §121.629(c) of this chapter and the takeoff complies with that program.

(c) Except for an airplane that has ice protection provisions that meet §34 of Appendix A, or those for transport category airplane type certification, no pilot may fly —
  (1) Under IFR into known or forecast light or moderate icing conditions; or
  (2) Under VFR into known light or moderate icing conditions; unless the aircraft has functioning deicing or anti-icing equipment protecting each rotor blade, propeller, windshield, wing, stabilizing or control surface, and each airspeed, altimeter, rate of climb or flight attitude instrument system.

(d) No pilot may fly a helicopter under IFR into known or forecast icing conditions or under VFR into known icing conditions unless it has been type certificated and appropriately equipped for operations in icing conditions.

(e) Except for an airplane that has ice protection provisions that meet §34 of Appendix A, or those for transport category airplane type certification, no pilot may fly an aircraft into known or forecast severe icing conditions.

(f) If current weather reports and briefing information relied upon by the pilot in command indicate that the forecast icing condition that would otherwise prohibit the flight will not be encountered during the flight because of changed weather conditions since the forecast, the restrictions in paragraphs (b), (c) and (d) of this section based on forecast conditions do not apply.

EXPLANATION

This rule does not require Part 135 certificate holders that do not anticipate operating during ground icing conditions to train their pilots or develop pretakeoff contamination check procedures. However, if pilots of a certificate holder that chooses not to train or develop deicing procedures encounter ground icing conditions, they will not be able to takeoff until such conditions no longer exist.

While the requirements of §135.227(b) do not include helicopters, the "clean aircraft" concept of §135.227(a) applies to helicopters.

The "unless" clause in §135.227(c)(2) applies also to §135.227(c)(1).

CROSS REFERENCES

135.213, Weather Reports and Forecasts.

ADVISORY CIRCULARS

AC 20-73 *Aircraft Ice Protection* (1971).

AC 23.1419-2 *Certification of Part 23 Airplanes for Flight in Icing Conditions* (1992).

AC 91-51 *Airplane Deice and Anti-Ice Systems* (1977).

AC 135-XX *Ground Deicing And Anti-Icing Training And Checking (58 Federal Register 6931)* (12-30-93).

AC 135-9 *FAR Part 135 Icing Limitations* (1981).

NTSB DECISIONS

The Board, in a footnote to a case where a violation of §135.227(a)(2) [now 135.227(a)] was upheld, said that, given the weather conditions (high humidity with temperatures hovering around freezing), it was quite possible that ice sufficient to cause a wing stall or buffeting could build up from the time the pilot checked the aircraft in the loading area and the time of actual takeoff roll. It was the pilot's obligation, prior to takeoff, to check the aircraft as often as might be necessary to ensure no ice buildup. That could require a further check of the aircraft **immediately** prior to takeoff. *Administrator v. Connor, III,* EA-3481, Footnote 7 (1-14-92). [This case was prior to Amendment 135-46, 12-30-93, which among other items, required a pretakeoff contamination check within 5 minutes prior to beginning takeoff.]

FAA CHIEF COUNSEL OPINIONS

§135.227(d) [now §135.227(f)] provides that standard aircraft may operate into areas for which icing has been forecast only if (1) "current weather reports" and (2) "briefing information" indicate that weather conditions have changed since the forecast. Pursuant to §135.213(a) "weather reports" must be from the U.S. National Weather Service, a source approved by the U.S. National Weather Service, or a source approved by the Administrator. Pilot reports received from other company pilots would not be sufficient to invoke the provisions of §135.227(d) [now §135.227(f)]. However, such reports would appear to qualify as "briefing information" under §135.227(d) [now §135.227(f)] and could be considered in addition to current official weather reports. (6-1-83).

The deicing and anti-icing equipment requirements in [§135.227(c)(2)] apply to [§135.227(c)(1)] as well. In other words, the deicing and anti-icing equipment requirements in [§135.227(c)(2)] are applicable to aircraft to be operated under VFR or IFR into light or moderate icing conditions. (1-20-75).

135.229 AIRPORT REQUIREMENTS

(a) No certificate holder may use any airport unless it is adequate for the proposed operation, considering such items as size, surface, obstructions, and lighting.

(b) No pilot of an aircraft carrying passengers at night may take off from, or land on, an airport unless —

  (1) That pilot has determined the wind direction from an illuminated wind direction indicator or local ground communications or, in the case of takeoff, that pilot's personal observations; and

  (2) The limits of the area to be used for landing or takeoff are clearly shown —

    (i) For airplanes, by boundary or runway marker lights;

    (ii) For helicopters, by boundary or runway marker lights or reflective material.

(c) For the purpose of paragraph (b) of this section, if the area to be used for takeoff or landing is marked by flare pots or lanterns, their use must be approved by the Administrator.

EXPLANATION

Although the FAA discourages the operation of turbojet aircraft on other than hard-surfaced runways, operation of such equipment from a well compacted non-paved surface is possible. FAA approval is necessary for such operations.

CROSS REFERENCES

1.1, General Definitions, "Night."

ADVISORY CIRCULARS

AC 121-26 Airports — *Required Data* (1981).

AC 139.201-1 *Airport Certification Manual (ACM) and Airport Certification Specification* (1988).

AC 150/5190-1A *Minimum Standards for Commercial Aeronautical Activities on Public Airports* (1985).

AC 150/5300-13 *Airport Design* (1993).

AC 150/5340-1G *Standards for Airport Markings* (1993).

AC 150/5360-12 *Airport Signing and Graphics* (1985).

AIRMAN'S INFORMATION MANUAL

General, Para. 2-30.

SUBPART E — FLIGHT CREWMEMBER REQUIREMENTS

135.241 APPLICABILITY

This subpart prescribes the flight crewmember requirements for operations under this part.

EXPLANATION

"Flight crewmember" means a pilot, flight engineer or flight navigator assigned to duty in an aircraft during flight time. [Reference Part 1, §1.1]

ADVISORY CIRCULARS

AC 25.1523-1 *Minimum Flightcrew* (1993).

135.243 PILOT IN COMMAND QUALIFICATIONS

(a) No certificate holder may use a person, nor may any person serve, as pilot in command in passenger-carrying operations of a turbojet airplane, of an airplane having a passenger seating configuration, excluding any pilot seat, of 10 seats or more, or a multiengine airplane being operated by the "Commuter Air Carrier" (as defined in Part 298 of this title), unless that person holds an airline transport pilot certificate with appropriate category and class ratings and, if required, an appropriate type rating for that airplane.

(b) Except as provided in paragraph (a) of this section, no certificate holder may use a person, nor may any person serve, as pilot in command of an aircraft under VFR unless that person —

(1) Holds at least a commercial pilot certificate with appropriate category and class ratings and, if required, an appropriate type rating for that aircraft; and

(2) Has had at least 500 hours of flight time as a pilot, including at least 100 hours of cross-country flight time, at least 25 hours of which were at night; and

(3) For an airplane, holds an instrument rating or an airline transport pilot certificate with an airplane category rating; or

(4) For helicopter operations conducted VFR over-the-top, holds a helicopter instrument rating, or an airline transport pilot certificate with a category and class rating for that aircraft, not limited to VFR.

(c) Except as provided in paragraph (a) of this section, no certificate holder may use a person, nor may any person serve, as pilot in command of an aircraft under IFR unless that person —
   (1) Holds at least a commercial pilot certificate with appropriate category and class ratings and, if required, an appropriate type rating for that aircraft; and
   (2) Has had at least 1,200 hours of flight time as a pilot, including 500 hours of cross country flight time, 100 hours of night flight time, and 75 hours of actual or simulated instrument time at least 50 hours of which were in actual flight; and
   (3) For an airplane, holds an instrument rating or an airline transport pilot certificate with an airplane category rating; or
   (4) For a helicopter, holds a helicopter instrument rating, or an airline transport pilot certificate with a category and class rating for that aircraft, not limited to VFR.

(d) Paragraph (b)(3) of this section does not apply when —
   (1) The aircraft used is a single reciprocating-engine-powered airplane;
   (2) The certificate holder does not conduct any operation pursuant to a published flight schedule which specifies five or more round trips a week between two or more points and places between which the round trips are performed, and does not transport mail by air under a contract or contracts with the United States Postal Service having total amount estimated at the beginning of any semiannual reporting period (January 1 - June 30: July 1 - December 31) to be in excess of $20,000 over the 12 months commencing with the beginning of the reporting period;
   (3) The area, as specified in the certificate holder's Operations Specifications, is an isolated area, as determined by the Flight Standards district office, if it is shown that —
      (i) The primary means of navigation in the area is by pilotage, since radio navigational aids are largely ineffective; and
      (ii) The primary means of transportation in the area is by air;
   (4) Each flight is conducted under day VFR with a ceiling of not less than 1,000 feet and visibility not less than 3 statute miles;
   (5) Weather reports or forecasts, or any combination of them, indicate that for the period commencing with the planned departure and ending 30 minutes after the planned arrival at the destination the flight may be conducted under VFR with a ceiling of not less than 1,000 feet and visibility of not less than 3 statute miles, except that if weather reports and forecasts are not available, the pilot in command may use that pilot's observations or those of other persons competent to supply weather observations if those observations indicate the flight may be conducted under VFR with the ceiling and visibility required in this paragraph;
   (6) The distance of each flight from the certificate holder's base of operation to destination does not exceed 250 nautical miles for a pilot who holds a commercial pilot certificate with an airplane rating without an instrument rating, provided the pilot's certificate does not contain any limitation to the contrary; and
   (7) The areas to be flown are approved by the certificate-holding FAA Flight Standards district office and are listed in the certificate holder's Operations Specifications.

EXPLANATION

The entire operation, that is, takeoff, enroute travel, and landing must be conducted within the "isolated area" in order for the provisions of §135.243(d) to be applicable.

The FAA considers certificated commercial pilots, airline transport pilots, dispatchers, air traffic controllers, and trained weather observers competent to provide weather information for Part 135 VFR operations.

Pilots in command in intrastate scheduled operations must meet the requirements of §§135.243(a), 135.244, and 135.105(a). This is appropriate since scheduled operation as a "common carrier" would be identical to commuter operation.

"Commuter Air Carrier" means an air taxi operator that carries passengers on at least five round trips per week on at least one route between two or more points according to its published flight schedules that specify the times, days of the week, and places between which those flights are performed. [Reference Part 298, §298.2(f).]

CROSS REFERENCES

135.109, Pilot In Command or Second In Command: Designation Required; 135.113, Passenger Occupancy of Pilot Seat; 135.203, VFR: Minimum Altitudes; 135.205, VFR: Visibility Requirements; 135.211, VFR: Over-The-Top Carrying Passengers: Operating Limitations; 135.213, Weather Reports and Forecasts; 135.297, Pilot In Command: Instrument Proficiency Check Requirements; 135.299, Pilot In Command: Line Checks: Routes and Airports; 298.2(f), Definitions, "Commuter Air Carrier."

ADVISORY CIRCULARS

AC 61-89D *Pilot Certificates: Aircraft Type Ratings* (1991).

AC 121.445-1D *Pilot-In-Command Qualifications For Special Area/Routes and Airports. FAR §121.445* (1990).

AC 120-53 *Crew Qualification and Pilot Type Rating Requirements for Transport Category Aircraft Operated under FAR Part 121* (1991).

NTSB DECISIONS

Where an on-demand operator provided substitute service at the request of and on behalf of a commuter air carrier, the pilot in command was subject to regulations applicable to pilots in command in commuter service. *Administrator v. Miller,* EA-3581 (1992).

FAA CHIEF COUNSEL OPINIONS

"VFR over the top," with respect to the operations of an aircraft, means the operation of an aircraft over-the-top under VFR when it is not being operated on an IFR flight plan. (14 C.F.R. 1.1) "VFR" means visual flight rules. (14.C.F.R. 1.2) (3-3-92).

135.244 OPERATING EXPERIENCE

(a) No certificate holder may use any person, nor may any person serve, as a pilot in command of an aircraft operated by a Commuter Air Carrier (as defined in §298.2 of this title) in passenger-carrying operations, unless that person has completed, prior to designation as pilot in command, on that make and basic model aircraft and in that crewmember position, the following operating experience in each make and basic model of aircraft to be flown:
  (1) Aircraft, single engine — 10 hours.
  (2) Aircraft multi-engine, reciprocating engine-powered — 15 hours.
  (3) Aircraft multi-engine, turbine engine-powered — 20 hours.
  (4) Airplane, turbojet-powered — 25 hours.

(b) In acquiring the operating experience, each person must comply with the following:
  (1) The operating experience must be acquired after satisfactory completion of the appropriate ground and flight training for the aircraft and crewmember position. Approved provisions for the operating experience must be included in the certificate holder's training program.
  (2) The experience must be acquired in flight during commuter passenger- carrying operations under this Part. However, in the case of an aircraft not previously used by the certificate holder in operations under this Part, operating experience acquired in the aircraft during proving flights or ferry flights may be used to meet this requirement.
  (3) Each person must acquire the operating experience while performing the duties of a pilot in command under the supervision of a qualified check pilot.
  (4) The hours of operating experience may be reduced to not less than 50 percent of the hours required by this section by the substitution of one additional takeoff and landing for each hour of flight.

EXPLANATION

The basis for requiring operating experience as set forth in this regulation is the fact that accidents and general operating experience have shown that extensive total time or multi-engine time does not establish that a pilot in command can safely operate a particular make or model of aircraft.

Because of the differences between charter or on-demand operations and commuter operations, experience obtained on charter or on-demand operations cannot be used to satisfy the requirements of this section.

Operating experience can be transferred by the pilot to another certificate holder provided satisfactory documentation is provided to the new certificate holder and the experience is obtained in the same make and basic model of aircraft.

The intent of make and model aircraft in this section is to permit the pilot to acquire the necessary experience in any make and "**basic**" model of the aircraft involved. For instance, all series models of Piper PA-31, Cessna 310, Beech 99 or DeHavilland DHC-6 aircraft can be flown to meet the operating experience in that particular make and model aircraft.

Second in commands who serve in commuter operations are not required to acquire operating experience.

CROSS REFERENCES

135.243, Pilot In Command Qualifications; 135.327, Training Program: Curriculum; 135.337, Training Program: Check Airmen and Instructor Qualifications; 135.341, Pilot and Flight Attendant Crewmember Training Programs; 298.2, Definitions.

ADVISORY CIRCULARS

AC 61-66 *Annual Pilot in Command Proficiency Checks* (1973).

AC 61-89D *Pilot Certificates: Aircraft Type Ratings* (1991).

AC 61-98A *Currency and Additional Qualification Requirements for Certificated Pilots* (1991).

AC 120-53 *Crew Qualification and Pilot Type Rating Requirements for Transport Category Aircraft Operated Under FAR Part 121* (1991).

NTSB DECISIONS

Pilots of an on-demand charter operation providing substitute service for a commuter operator are subject to the regulations applicable to pilots in command in commuter service. *Administrator v. Miller,* EA-3581 (1992).

FAA CHIEF COUNSEL OPINIONS

Question — Does a new Captain [in a multi-engine turbine engine-powered aircraft] only require 10 hours and 10 landings [using the 50% reduction] to satisfy the operating experience [requirements] of §135.244?

> Response — The number of required hours is 20 per §135.244(a)(3). However, §135.244(b)(4) provides for the reduction of the required number of operating hours by the substitution of one additional takeoff and landing for each hour of flight. This means that for each takeoff and landing completed, one hour of the required operating experience can be substituted. However, the hours of operating experience may not be reduced to less than 50 per cent of the required 20 hours. It is important to note that 10 landings are not enough to reduce the required number of hours for multi-engine turbine engine-powered aircraft to 10; 10 takeoffs must be completed as well. The regulation reads "takeoff **and** landing," not takeoff **or** landing." (5-21-90).

135.245 SECOND IN COMMAND QUALIFICATIONS

(a) Except as provided in paragraph (b), no certificate holder may use any person, nor may any person serve, as second in command of an aircraft unless that person holds at least a commercial pilot certificate with appropriate category and class ratings and an instrument rating. For flight under IFR, that person must meet the recent instrument experience requirements of Part 61 of this chapter.

(b) A second in command of a helicopter operated under VFR, other than over- the-top, must have at least a commercial pilot certificate with an appropriate aircraft category and class rating.

EXPLANATION

If for any reason a pilot is designated a second in command on an aircraft in a Part 135 operation, he or she must meet all the regulatory requirements for a second in command.

If the person chartering an aircraft requests or contracts for a copilot, the regulatory requirements for second in command must be met, even if a second in command is neither required by the type certificate of the aircraft nor by the regulations for the type of operation being conducted.

"Recent instrument experience requirements of Part 61" refers to §61.57(e), even though that regulation sets recent flight experience requirements for pilots in command.

CROSS REFERENCES

61.55, Second-In-Command Qualifications; 61.65, Instrument Rating Requirements; 61.57, Recent Flight Experience: Pilot In Command; 135.101, Second In Command Required in IFR Conditions; 135.103, Exception to Second In Command Requirement: IFR Operations; 135.105, Exception to Second In Command Requirement: Approval for Use of Autopilot System; 135.109, Pilot In Command or Second In Command: Designation Required; 135.293, Initial and Recurrent Pilot Testing Requirements.

ADVISORY CIRCULARS

AC 61-89D *Pilot Certificates: Aircraft Type Ratings* (1991).

AC 61-65C *Certification: Pilot and Flight Instructors* (1991).

AC 120-53 *Crew Qualification and Pilot Type Rating Requirements for Transport Category Aircraft Operated Under Part §121* (1991).

FAA CHIEF COUNSEL OPINIONS

It is important not to confuse a "current instrument rating" with "recent instrument experience." A current instrument rating merely means that a person holds an instrument rating, and that it has not been revoked, suspended, or surrendered. The term carries no implication of recent experience required in §61.57(e). §135.245 clearly requires recent instrument experience, not merely an instrument rating. It is also important to note that the 6 month instrument currency requirement of Part 61 is in addition to the second in command annual competency check required in §135.293(b). (6-18-91).

135.247 PILOT QUALIFICATIONS: RECENT EXPERIENCE

(a) No certificate holder may use any person, nor may any person serve, as pilot in command of an aircraft carrying passengers unless, within the preceding 90 days, that person has —

(1) Made three takeoffs and three landings as the sole manipulator of the flight controls in an aircraft of the same category and class and, if a type rating is required, of the same type in which that person is to serve; or

(2) For operation during the period beginning 1 hour after sunset and ending 1 hour before sunrise (as published in the Air Almanac), made three takeoffs and three landings during that period as the sole manipulator of the flight controls in an aircraft of the same category and class and, if a type rating is required, of the same type in which that person is to serve.

A person who complies with paragraph (a)(2) of this paragraph need not comply with paragraph (a)(1) of this paragraph.

(b) For the purpose of paragraph (a) of this section, if the aircraft is a tailwheel airplane, each takeoff must be made in a tailwheel airplane and each landing must be made to a full stop in a tailwheel airplane.

EXPLANATION

The requirements of this section do not apply to Part 135 cargo carrying operations.

The requirements of this section do not apply to second in commands.

CROSS REFERENCES

135.63(a)(4), Record-keeping Requirements; 135.243, Pilot In Command Qualifications.

ADVISORY CIRCULARS

AC 61-89D *Pilot Certificates: Aircraft Type Ratings* (1991).

AC 61-98A *Currency and Additional Qualification Requirements for Certificated Pilots* (1991).

AC 120-53 *Crew Qualification and Pilot Type Rating Requirements for Transport Category Aircraft Operated Under FAR Part 121* (1991).

135.249 USE OF PROHIBITED DRUGS

(a) This section applies to persons who perform a function listed in Appendix I to Part 121 of this chapter for a certificate holder or an operator. For the purpose of this section, a person who performs such a function pursuant to a contract with the certificate holder or the operator is considered to be performing that function for the certificate holder or the operator.

(b) No certificate holder or operator may knowingly use any person to perform, nor may any person perform for a certificate holder or an operator, either directly or by contract, any function listed in Appendix I to Part 121 of this chapter while that person has a prohibited drug, as defined in that appendix in his or her system.

(c) Except as provided in paragraph (d) of this section, no certificate holder or operator may knowingly use any person to perform, nor may any person perform for a certificate holder or an operator, either directly or by contract, any function listed in Appendix I to Part 121 of this chapter if that person has failed a test or refused to submit to a test required by that appendix given by any certificate holder or any operator.

(d) Paragraph (c) of this section does not apply to a person who has received a recommendation to be hired or to return to duty from a medical review officer in accordance with Appendix I to Part 121 of this chapter or who has received a special issuance medical certificate after evaluation by the Federal Air Surgeon for drug dependency in accordance with Part 67 of this chapter.

EXPLANATION

This section applies to persons conducting non-stop sightseeing flights for compensation or hire in an airplane or rotorcraft that begin and end at the same airport and are conducted within a 25-statute mile radius of that airport, even though a Part 135 certificate is not required to conduct such operations.

CROSS REFERENCES

61.14, Refusal to Submit to a Drug Test; 61.15, Offenses Involving Alcohol or Drugs; 61.16, Refusal to Submit to an Alcohol Test or to Furnish Test Results; 63.12b, Refusal to Submit to a Drug or Alcohol Test; 65.23, Refusal to Submit to Drug or Alcohol Test; 65.46a, Misuse of Alcohol; 65.46b, Testing for Alcohol; 91.17, Alcohol or Drugs; Part 121, Appendix I; Part 121, Appendix J; 135.251, Testing for Prohibited Drugs; 135.253, Misuse of Alcohol; 135.255, Testing for Alcohol; §614 of the Federal Aviation Act of 1958, as amended (14 U.S.C. App. §1434), Alcohol and Controlled Substances Testing; 49 C.F.R. Part 40 (DOT), Procedures For Transportation Workplace Drug Testing Programs.

ADVISORY CIRCULARS

AC 91.11-1 *Guide to Drug Hazards in Aviation Medicine* (1963).

AC 121-30 *Guidelines for Developing an Anti-Drug Plan for Aviation Personnel* (1989).

135.251 TESTING FOR PROHIBITED DRUGS

(a) Each certificate holder or operator shall test each of its employees who performs a function listed in Appendix I to Part 121 of this chapter in accordance with that appendix.
(b) No certificate holder or operator may use any contractor to perform a function listed in Appendix I to Part 121 of this chapter unless that contractor tests each employee performing such a function for the certificate holder or operator in accordance with that appendix.

EXPLANATION

This regulation requires the testing of all employees, including temporary employees, no matter how brief their length of employment.

Flight crewmembers of aviation entities holding Part 121 or 135 certificates are not required to be drug tested if the flight operations they conduct are not subject to Parts 121 or 135, e.g. corporate flights conducted under Part 91.

Employees of Part 121 and 135 certificate holders performing security functions unrelated to aviation operations under Parts 121 and 135 are not covered by this regulation, e.g. security guards at corporate headquarters.

A contractor employee covered by one aviation entity's anti-drug program can provide services for any entity subject to this regulation.

Part 121 and 135 certificate holder's employees located outside the United States are not subject to the testing requirements of this regulation.

An individual does not "fail" a drug test until the test results have been verified by a medical review officer.

For small operators, participation in an FAA approved consortium may be advisable from a practical standpoint.

CROSS REFERENCES

61.14, Refusal to Submit to a Drug Test; 61.15, Offenses Involving Alcohol or Drugs; 61.16, Refusal to Submit to an Alcohol Test or to Furnish Test Results; 63.12b, Refusal to Submit to a Drug or Alcohol Test; 65.23, Refusal to Submit to Drug or Alcohol Test; 65.46a, Misuse of Alcohol; 65.46b, Testing for Alcohol; 91.17, Alcohol or Drugs; Part 121, Appendix I; Part 121, Appendix J; 135.249, Use of Prohibited Drugs; 135.253, Misuse of Alcohol; 135.255, Testing for Alcohol; §614 of the Federal Aviation Act of 1958, as amended (14 U.S.C. App. §1434), Alcohol and Controlled Substances Testing; 49 C.F.R. Part 40 (DOT), Procedures For Transportation Workplace Drug Testing Programs.

ADVISORY CIRCULARS

AC 91.11-1 *Guide to Drug Hazards in Aviation Medicine* (1963).

AC 121-30 *Guidelines for Developing an Anti-Drug Plan for Aviation Personnel* (1989).

135.253 MISUSE OF ALCOHOL

(a) This section applies to employees who perform a function listed in Appendix J to Part 121 of this chapter for a certificate holder or operator (*covered employees*). For the purpose of this section, a person who meets the definition of covered employee in Appendix J is considered to be performing the function for the certificate holder or operator.

(b) *Alcohol concentration.* No covered employee shall report for duty or remain on duty requiring the performance of safety-sensitive functions while having an alcohol concentration of 0.04 or greater. No certificate holder or operator having actual knowledge that an employee has an alcohol concentration of 0.04 or greater shall permit the employee to perform or continue to perform safety-sensitive functions.

(c) *On-duty use.* No covered employee shall use alcohol while performing safety-sensitive functions. No certificate holder or operator having actual knowledge that a covered employee is using alcohol while performing safety-sensitive functions shall permit the employee to perform or continue to perform safety-sensitive functions.

(d) *Pre-duty use.*

(1) No covered employee shall perform flight crewmember or flight attendant duties within 8 hours after using alcohol. No certificate holder or operator having actual knowledge that such an employee has used alcohol within 8 hours shall permit the employee to perform or continue to perform the specified duties.

(2) No covered employee shall perform safety-sensitive duties other than those specified in paragraph (d)(1) of this section within 4 hours after using alcohol. No certificate holder or operator having actual knowledge that such an employee has used alcohol within 4 hours shall permit the employee to perform or continue to perform safety-sensitive functions.

(e) *Use following an accident.* No covered employee who has actual knowledge of an accident involving an aircraft for which he or she performed a safety-sensitive function at or near the time of the accident shall use alcohol for 8 hours following the accident, unless he or she has been given a post-accident test under Appendix J of Part 121 of this chapter, or the employer has determined that the employee's performance could not have contributed to the accident.

(f) *Refusal to submit to a required alcohol test.* No covered employee shall refuse to submit to a post-accident, random, reasonable suspicion, or follow-up alcohol test required under Appendix J to Part 121 of this chapter. No operator or certificate holder shall permit a covered employee who refuses to submit to such a test to perform or continue to perform safety-sensitive functions.

EXPLANATION

The identification of the activities that will subject employees to this regulation shall be determined by the employer based on the requirements of the FAA's regulations and the employer's experience and knowledge of the employees' duties. The identification of the activities shall be included in the company policy required by Appendix J, Part 121 and is subject to FAA approval.

This regulation does not limit the employer's authority to remove the employee from the performance of safety-sensitive duties if the employer believes, notwithstanding an alcohol test result of less than 0.04 or no test at all, that the employee is impaired.

The restrictions regarding on-duty use do not apply to on-call or reserve employees who are not at work; however, these employees, if called in, are subject to the prohibitions on pre-duty use of alcohol.

Use of medication containing alcohol while on duty will violate this regulation. Steps should be taken to ensure employees are aware of this fact.

The "use following an accident" provision applies only where the employee has actual notice of the accident and that their performance of duties may be implicated. The performance of duties must have occurred at or near the time of the accident. The regulation does not affect individuals who performed maintenance on the aircraft days or weeks prior to the accident.

Refusal to submit to a preemployment or return to duty testing is the basis for precluding an employee from performing a safety-sensitive function, but is not the basis for action by the FAA against any airman certificate held by the employee.

CROSS REFERENCES

61.14, Refusal to Submit to a Drug Test; 61.15, Offenses Involving Alcohol or Drugs; 61.16, Refusal to Submit to an Alcohol Test or to Furnish Test Results; 63.12b, Refusal to Submit to a Drug or Alcohol Test; 65.23, Refusal to Submit to Drug or Alcohol Test; 65.46a, Misuse of Alcohol; 65.46b, Testing for Alcohol; 91.17, Alcohol or Drugs; Part 121, Appendix J; 135.249, Use of Prohibited Drugs; 135.251, Testing for Prohibited Drugs; 135.255, Testing for Alcohol; §614 of the Federal Aviation Act of 1958, as amended (14 U.S.C. App. §1434), Alcohol and Controlled Substances Testing; 49 C.F.R. Part 40 (DOT), Procedures For Transportation Workplace Drug Testing Programs.

135.255 TESTING FOR ALCOHOL

(a) Each certificate holder and operator must establish an alcohol misuse prevention program in accordance with the provisions of Appendix J to Part 121 of this chapter.

(b) No certificate holder or operator shall use any person who meets the definition of "covered employee" in Appendix J to Part 121 to perform a safety-sensitive function listed in that appendix unless such person is subject to testing for alcohol misuse in accordance with the provisions of Appendix J.

EXPLANATION

No mixing of employer-directed and FAA-mandated programs is permitted.

This regulation is applicable to sightseeing operators who meet the criteria of §135.1(c).

"Pre-employment testing" does not have to occur prior to hiring an individual, but must occur before that individual is used to perform a safety-sensitive function.

In the case of random testing, the employees selected for testing must proceed immediately to the testing site. If the employee is performing a safety-sensitive function at the time of the notification, the employee should arrange for a replacement or otherwise cease performing the function as soon as it can be safely terminated.

Testing is not required of employees located outside the territory of the United States. At such time as employees begins to perform functions wholly or partially within the territory of the United States, they must be returned to the random testing pool.

Employees must be provided with educational materials that explain the alcohol misuse requirements and the employer's policies and procedures with respect to meeting those requirements. An employer must also establish an alcohol misuse prevention program.

If a covered employee, who holds a medical certificate under Part 67, is determined by an employer to have violated the provisions of §§65.46a, 121.458 or 135.253, the employer is required to notify the FAA Federal Air Surgeon of the fact within 2 working days.

CROSS REFERENCES

61.14, Refusal to Submit to a Drug Test; 61.15, Offenses Involving Alcohol or Drugs; 61.16, Refusal to Submit to an Alcohol Test or to Furnish Test Results; 63.12b, Refusal to Submit to a Drug or Alcohol Test; 65.23, Refusal to Submit to Drug or Alcohol Test; 65.46a, Misuse of Alcohol; 65.46b, Testing for Alcohol; 91.17, Alcohol or Drugs; Part 121, Appendix I; Part 121, Appendix J; 135.253, Misuse of Alcohol; §614 of the Federal Aviation Act of 1958, as amended (14 U.S.C. App. §1434), Alcohol and Controlled Substances Testing; 49 C.F.R. Part 40 (DOT), Procedures For Transportation Workplace Drug Testing Programs.

SUBPART F — FLIGHT CREWMEMBER FLIGHT TIME LIMITATIONS AND REST REQUIREMENTS

135.261 APPLICABILITY

§§135.263 through 135.271 prescribe flight time limitations and rest requirements for operations conducted under this part as follows:

(a) §135.263 applies to all operations under this subpart.

(b) §135.265 applies to:

(1) Scheduled passenger-carrying operations except those conducted solely within the state of Alaska. "Scheduled passenger-carrying operations" means passenger-carrying operations that are conducted in accordance with a published schedule which covers at least five round trips per week on at least one route between two or more points, includes dates or times (or both), and is openly advertised or otherwise made readily available to the general public, and

(2) Any other operation under this part, if the operator elects to comply with §135.265 and obtains an appropriate operations specification amendment.

(c) §§135.267 and 135.269 apply to any operation that is not a scheduled passenger-carrying operation and to any operation conducted solely within the State of Alaska, unless the operator elects to comply with §135.265 as authorized under paragraph (b)(2) of this section.

(d) §135.271 contains special daily flight time limits for operations conducted under the helicopter emergency medical evacuation service (HEMES).

EXPLANATION

A pilot flying Part 121 domestic flights and Part 135 scheduled flights could legally fly both types of flights interchangeably up to 1000 hours in a calendar year. The pilot could then continue to fly Part 135 scheduled flights for an additional 200 hours, but could no longer fly Part 121 domestic flights. The same principle would apply for the monthly and weekly limits.

Dual operators, Part 135 scheduled and Part 135 non-scheduled, on a daily basis, where requirements are not parallel, must comply with the most restrictive limits. To avoid scheduling complications for dual operations, §135.261(c) allows, through an appropriate Operations Specifications amendment, a dual operator to conduct all operations in accordance with §135.265.

CROSS REFERENCES

135.263, Flight Time Limitations and Rest Requirements: All Certificate Holders; 135.265, Flight Time Limitations and Rest Requirements: Scheduled Operations; 135.267, Flight Time Limitations and Rest Requirements: Unscheduled One- and Two-Pilot Crews; 135.269, Flight Time Limitations and Rest Requirements: Three- and Four-Pilot Crews; 135.271, Helicopter Hospital Emergency Medical Evacuation Service (HEMES).

135.263 FLIGHT TIME LIMITATIONS AND REST REQUIREMENTS: ALL CERTIFICATE HOLDERS

(a) A certificate holder may assign a flight crewmember and a flight crewmember may accept an assignment for flight time only when the applicable requirements of §§135.263 through 135.271 are met.
(b) No certificate holder may assign any flight crewmember to any duty with the certificate holder during any required rest period.
(c) Time spent in transportation, not local in character, that a certificate holder requires of a flight crewmember and provides to transport the crewmember to an airport at which he is to serve on a flight as a crewmember, or from an airport at which he was relieved from duty to return to his home station, is not considered part of a rest period.
(d) A flight crewmember is not considered to be assigned flight time in excess of flight time limitations if the flights to which he is assigned normally terminate within the limitations, but due to circumstances beyond the control of the certificate holder or flight crewmember (such as adverse weather conditions), are not at the time of departure expected to reach their destination within the planned flight time.

EXPLANATION

These regulations are intended to protect against acute (short-term) fatigue by requiring specific rest periods in the 24 hours preceding the completion of scheduled flight time and to protect against chronic or long term fatigue by setting cumulative flight time limits.

"Rest" has been defined by the FAA as "an absence of any work-related duties for the air carrier." Time spent answering the phone or performing other administrative duties for the certificate holder cannot be considered rest time.

In a nutshell, the FAA's position on rest time is this:

- Rest time must be determined prospectively;
- Rest time must be free from all duty;
- Rest time must be free from all responsibility for work or duty.

The FAA takes the position that if a crewmember carries a pager or cell phone because he is "on call," then he is not on rest time.

Merely possessing a cell phone or pager during a predesignated rest period does not invalidate that rest period.

A "calendar quarter" refers to the four periods of 3 months each, beginning in January, April, July, and October.

The rest requirement is based on the number of flight hours looking back 24 hours from the completion of each flight segment. If a pilot is scheduled for 4 hours of flight time late on the first day and receives a reduced rest of 8 hours, he or she can only be scheduled for up to 5 hours of flight time the following morning, since the flight crewmember cannot be scheduled for 9 or more flight hours in 24 consecutive hours, based on an 8-hour reduced rest period.

Both the certificate holder and the flight crewmember are responsible for complying with the flight time limitations and rest requirements. The flight crewmember may have logged commercial flying other than the flight time logged for the operator of which the operator is not aware. Therefore, the flight crewmember must also be responsible for compliance.

§135.263(d) applies to unscheduled as well as scheduled operations.

Part 135 operators must, in scheduling flights, provide adequate time for flight crewmembers to perform pre- and post-flight duties, and at least the minimum rest periods required by the rules.

CROSS REFERENCES

135.261, Applicability; 135.265, Flight Time Limitations and Rest Requirements: Scheduled Operations; 135.267, Flight Time Limitations and Rest Requirements: Unscheduled One- and Two-Pilot Crews; 135.269, Flight Time Limitations and Rest Requirements: Unscheduled Three-and Four-Pilot Crews; 135.271, Helicopter Hospital Emergency Medical Evacuation Service (HEMES).

ADVISORY CIRCULARS

AC 120-51A *Crew Resource Management Training* (1993).

AC 120-59 *Air Carrier Internal Evaluation Programs* (1992).

FAA CHIEF COUNSEL OPINIONS

A flight conducted for the purpose of re-positioning an aircraft under Part 91, AFTER the completion of an assigned flight conducted under Part 135, cannot be considered a new assignment under Part 135 and, therefore, is not subject to the flight time limitations and rest requirements of Part 135. "Other commercial flying" under Part 91 must be counted against the daily flight time limitations of Part 135 if it PRECEDES the flight conducted under Part 135. All Part 91 commercial flight time is counted against the pilot's quarterly and yearly flight time limitations. If a pilot reached the yearly Part 135 flight limit, the pilot could still fly under Part 91 in that calendar year. (4-9-93).

Delay caused by late passenger arrivals is a circumstance beyond the control of the certificate holder and the flightcrew. The flightcrew may therefore complete their assigned schedule. (8-30-93).

The FAA has consistently interpreted delays due to weather, ATC, and mechanical delays as examples of circumstances beyond the control of the certificate holder under §135.263(d). This flexibility results in a requirement to add a flight crewmember's actual flight time accumulated in the previous days to the flight time scheduled to be flown for the particular day that is under review. If the total flight time, actual plus scheduled, is not in excess of the limitations under §135.265, then the flight crewmember may complete all flight segments for that day. (7-15-92).

Travel between a crewmember's residence and the airport is "local" and therefore may be considered as part of a rest period. (7-14-92).

A ferry flight does not fall under the "transportation" described in §135.263(c), UNLESS it is at the direction of the certificate holder, in which case it is a duty assignment and considered "other commercial flying" under §135.267(b). Ferry flight time reduces the hours a crewmember has available to fly in a 24 consecutive hour period under Part 135 if the ferry flight is conducted before the Part 135 flight. (3-27-92).

The Agency has interpreted "duty" as including actual work for a certificate holder or present responsibility for work if the occasion should arise.

The Agency has interpreted provisions substantively identical to §135.263(b) to the effect that a flight crewmember's receipt of one telephone call from his air carrier employer during a required rest period does not violate a regulation such as §135.263(b). (10-5-87).

The words "local in character" are intended to encompass transportation **normally** used from one's residence to one's **place of business** or from a hotel to an airport. Performing duties as flight crewmembers does not fall within the "local in character" exception. Therefore, piloting an airplane on a Part 91 positioning or repositioning flight may not be performed during a required rest period. (4-4-91).

135.265 FLIGHT TIME LIMITATIONS AND REST REQUIREMENTS: SCHEDULED OPERATIONS

(a) No certificate holder may schedule any flight crewmember, and no flight crewmember may accept an assignment, for flight time in scheduled operations or in other commercial flying if that crewmember's total flight time in all commercial flying will exceed —
  (1) 1,200 hours in any calendar year.
  (2) 120 hours in any calendar month.
  (3) 34 hours in any 7 consecutive days.
  (4) 8 hours during any 24 consecutive hours for a flight crew consisting of one pilot.
  (5) 8 hours between required rest periods for a flight crew consisting of two pilots qualified under this part for the operation being conducted.

(b) Except as provided in paragraph (c) of this section, no certificate holder may schedule a flight crewmember, and no flight crewmember may accept an assignment, for flight time during the 24 consecutive hours preceding the scheduled completion of any flight segment without a scheduled rest period during that 24 hours of at least the following:
  (1) 9 consecutive hours of rest for less than 8 hours of scheduled flight time.
  (2) 10 consecutive hours of rest for 8 or more but less than 9 hours of scheduled flight time.
  (3) 11 consecutive hours of rest for 9 or more hours of scheduled flight time.

(c) A certificate holder may schedule a flight crewmember for less than the rest required in paragraph (b) of this section or may reduce a scheduled rest under the following conditions:
  (1) A rest required under paragraph (b)(1) of this section may be scheduled for or reduced to a minimum of 8 hours if the flight crewmember is given a rest period of at least 10 hours that must begin no later than 24 hours after the commencement of the reduced rest period.
  (2) A rest required under paragraph (b)(2) of this section may be scheduled for or reduced to a minimum of 8 hours if the flight crewmember is given a rest period of at least 11 hours that must begin no later than 24 hours after the commencement of the reduced rest period.
  (3) A rest required under paragraph (b)(3) of this section may be scheduled for or reduced to a minimum of 9 hours if the flight crewmember is given a rest period of at least 12 hours that must begin no later than 24 hours after the commencement of the reduced rest period.

(d) Each certificate holder shall relieve each flight crewmember engaged in scheduled air transportation from all further duty for at least 24 consecutive hours during any 7 consecutive days.

EXPLANATION

While §135.265 deals primarily with daily scheduled flight hours, actual flight hours determine compliance with weekly monthly, and annual limits.

[For the FAA's position on rest time see the explanation under §135.263.]

If a flight crewmember is scheduled for 7:45 hours of flight and 9 hours of rest in the 24 hours preceding the scheduled completion of the flight, and because of enroute delays, the crewmember actually flies 8:05 hours, the subsequent rest does not have to be 10 hours. No penalty exists under §135.265 for circumstances under which actual flight time exceeds scheduled flight time. However, if actual flight hours infringe on a required minimum reduced rest or makeup rest, the full required minimum rest must be given at the completion of the late flight. For example, if a flight crewmember is scheduled for 5 hours of flight followed immediately by 9 hours of rest and because of reasons beyond the control of the operator or flight crewmember the flight infringes on the scheduled rest, one of two events could occur: (1) If the total scheduled time in the 24 consecutive hours is less than 8, the required rest could be reduced to 8 hours with a compensatory rest of 10 hours given at the next scheduled rest; (2) If the rest is already a minimum rest, the flight crewmember must be given that rest, which means that subsequent scheduled flights will have to be delayed.

In scheduled operations, while there is a limit to the number of scheduled flight time hours (8 hours) between required rest periods, except for one-pilot crews, there is no specific limit to actual daily flight time.

CROSS REFERENCES

135.261, Applicability; 135.263, Flight Time Limitations and Rest Requirements: All Certificate Holders; 135.267, Flight Time Limitations and Rest Requirements: Unscheduled One- and Two-Pilot Crews; 135.269, Flight Time Limitations and Rest Requirements: Unscheduled Three-and Four-Pilot Crews; 135.271, Helicopter Hospital Emergency Medical Evacuation Service (HEMES).

ADVISORY CIRCULARS

AC 120-51A *Crew Resource Management Training* (1993).

AC 120-59 *Air Carrier Internal Evaluation Programs* (1992).

FAA CHIEF COUNSEL OPINIONS

The FAA has consistently interpreted the word "duty" to mean either actual work for the air carrier or present responsibility should the occasion arise. (4-14-90). "24 consecutive hours" is not synonymous with a calendar day. Thus, if a period of 24 consecutive hours of relief from all duty is given (for example, from 3:00 p.m. of one day to 3:00 p.m. of the next day) during the 7 consecutive days, then the certificate holder has complied with the regulation. (4-14-90).

135.267 FLIGHT TIME LIMITATIONS AND REST REQUIREMENTS: UNSCHEDULED ONE- AND TWO-PILOT CREWS

(a) No certificate holder may assign any flight crewmember, and no flight crewmember may accept an assignment, for flight time as a member of a one- or two-pilot crew if that crewmember's total flight time in all commercial flying will exceed —
  (1) 500 hours in any calendar quarter.
  (2) 800 hours in any two consecutive calendar quarters.
  (3) 1,400 hours in any calendar year.

(b) Except as provided in paragraph (c) of this section, during any 24 consecutive hours the total flight time of the assigned flight when added to any other commercial flying by that flight crewmember may not exceed —
  (1) 8 hours for a flight crew consisting of one pilot; or
  (2) 10 hours for a flight crew consisting of two pilots qualified under this Part for the operation being conducted.

(c) A flight crewmember's flight time may exceed the flight time limits of paragraph (b) of this section if the assigned flight time occurs during a regularly assigned duty period of no more than 14 hours and —
  (1) If this duty period is immediately preceded by and followed by a required rest period of at least 10 consecutive hours of rest;
  (2) If flight time is assigned during this period, that total flight time when added to any other commercial flying by the flight crewmember may not exceed —
    (i) 8 hours for a flight crew consisting of one pilot; or
    (ii) 10 hours for a flight crew consisting of two pilots; and
  (3) If the combined duty and rest periods equal 24 hours.

(d) Each assignment under paragraph (b) of this section must provide for at least 10 consecutive hours of rest during the 24-hour period that precedes the planned completion time of the assignment.

(e) When a flight crewmember has exceeded the daily flight time limitations in this section, because of circumstances beyond the control of the certificate holder or flight crewmember (such as adverse weather conditions), that flight crewmember must have a rest period before being assigned or accepting an assignment for flight time of at least —
  (1) 11 consecutive hours of rest if the flight time limitation is exceeded by not more than 30 minutes;
  (2) 12 consecutive hours of rest if the flight time limitation is exceeded by more than 30 minutes, but not more than 60 minutes; and
  (3) 16 consecutive hours of rest if the flight time limitation is exceeded by more than 60 minutes.

(f) The certificate holder must provide each flight crewmember at least 13 rest periods of at least 24 consecutive hours each in each calendar quarter.

(g) The Director, Flight Standards Service may issue Operations Specifications authorizing a deviation from any specific requirement of this section if he finds that the deviation is justified to allow a certificate holder additional time, but in no case beyond October 1, 1987, to bring its operations into full compliance with the requirements of this section. Each application for a deviation must be submitted to the Director, Flight Standards Service before October 1, 1986. Each applicant for a deviation may continue to operate under the requirements of Subpart F of this part as in effect on September 30, 1985, until the Director, Flight Standards Service has responded to the deviation request.

EXPLANATION

[For the FAA's position on rest time see the explanation under §135.263.]

Quarterly limits, as opposed to monthly limits, allow flexible scheduling for seasonable and on-demand operations.

Instead of 24 hours off in 7 days, this regulation requires 13 rest periods of at least 24 hours in each calendar quarter.

§135.267(c) allows an operator and flight crewmember to use a schedule of regular daily duty hours rather than a rolling 24-hour clock. If the flight crewmember's duty time fluctuates from day to day or week to week, then the rolling 24-hour clock must be used.

CROSS REFERENCES

135.261, Applicability; 135.263, Flight Time Limitations and Rest Requirements: All Certificate Holders; 135.265, Flight Time Limitations and Rest Requirements: Scheduled Operations; 135.269, Flight Time Limitations and Rest Requirements: Unscheduled Three- and Four-Pilot Crews; 135.271, Helicopter Hospital Emergency Medical Evacuation Service (HEMES).

ADVISORY CIRCULARS

AC 120-51A *Crew Resource Management Training* (1993).

AC 120-59 *Air Carrier Internal Evaluation Programs* (1992).

FAA CHIEF COUNSEL OPINIONS

§135.267(d) does not contain an explicit limitation on duty time. This regulation provides limits on flight time rather than duty time. Thus, §135.267(d) cannot be construed as a hard and fast rule that 14 hours of duty time must never, under any circumstances, be exceeded. The key to the applicability of §135.267(d) is in the final phrase "planned completion time of the assignment." If the original planning is upset for reasons beyond the control of the crew and operator, the flight may nevertheless be conducted, though crew duty time may extend beyond the planned completion. This assumes that the original planning was realistic. (1-16-92).

Both the crew and the certificate holder would be in violation of §91.13(a) if crewmembers fly when their state of fatigue would potentially endanger others. (3-30-92).

There are no precise standards to determine if a schedule is "realistic." The original scheduling must represent a normal occurrence in the flight operations conducted by the carrier. A schedule designed to circumvent the overall intent of a regulation will not be considered "realistic." (3-30-92).

An infrequent deviation from an otherwise regularly assigned work schedule does NOT require abandonment of the flexibility afforded by §135.267(c) and compliance instead with §135.267(b). (7-22-89).

Technically, it is not a violation of §135.267(b) for a pilot to fly during the required rest period if the flying is not assigned by the certificate holder. However, it is a violation of [§91.13] if the certificate holder allows or the crewmember performs any flying when the pilot's lack of rest may endanger others. (8-9-89).

Central to the rationale of §135.267(c) is the idea that a certificate holder may not move from section (b) to (c) and back because section (c) contemplates that the certificate holder's pilots will be on a regularly scheduled day to day work pattern. If the certificate holder constantly moves the pilot from the coverage of section (b) to (c), he is clearly not maintaining a regularly scheduled work pattern and, therefore, cannot fall within the scope of section (c). (1-21-91).

If the same company or organization which is the Part 135 certificate holder is also assigning the "other commercial flying" under Parts 61, 91, or 141, it is still the pilot's employer in Part 135 operations, and the pilot may not consider that flight time as rest time. (10-31-90).

135.269 FLIGHT TIME LIMITATIONS AND REST REQUIREMENTS: UNSCHEDULED THREE- AND FOUR-PILOT CREWS

(a) No certificate holder may assign any flight crewmember, and no flight crewmember may accept an assignment for flight time as a member of a three- or four-pilot crew if that crewmember's total flight time in all commercial flying will exceed —
   (1) 500 hours in any calendar quarter.
   (2) 800 hours in any two consecutive calendar quarters.
   (3) 1,400 hours in any calendar year.

(b) No certificate holder may assign any pilot to a crew of three or four pilots, unless that assignment provides —
   (1) At least 10 consecutive hours of rest immediately preceding the assignment;
   (2) No more than 8 hours of flight deck duty in any 24 consecutive hours;
   (3) No more than 18 duty hours for a three-pilot crew or 20 duty hours for a four-pilot crew in any 24 consecutive hours;
   (4) No more than 12 hours aloft for a three-pilot crew or 16 hours aloft for a four-pilot crew during the maximum duty hours specified in paragraph (b)(3) of this section;
   (5) Adequate sleeping facilities on the aircraft for the relief pilot;
   (6) Upon completion of the assignment, a rest period of at least 12 hours;
   (7) For a three-pilot crew, a crew which consists of at least the following:
      (i) A pilot in command (PIC) who meets the applicable flight crewmember requirements of Subpart E of Part 135;
      (ii) A PIC who meets the applicable flight crewmember requirements of Subpart E of Part 135, except those prescribed in §§135.244 and 135.247; and
      (iii) A second in command (SIC) who meets the SIC qualifications of §135.245.
   (8) For a four-pilot crew, at least three pilots who meet the conditions of paragraph (b)(7) of this section; plus a fourth pilot who meets the SIC qualifications of §135.245.

(c) When a flight crewmember has exceeded the daily flight deck duty limitation in this section by more than 60 minutes; because of circumstances beyond the control of the certificate holder or flight crewmember, that flight crewmember must have a rest period before the next duty period of at least 16 consecutive hours.

(d) A certificate holder must provide each flight crewmember at least 13 rest periods of at least 24 consecutive hours each in each calendar quarter.

EXPLANATION

[For the FAA's position on rest time see the explanation under §135.263.]

This regulation limits not only hours of flight deck duty, but also hours of duty and hours aloft.

CROSS REFERENCES

135.243, Pilot In Command Qualifications; 135.244, Operating Experience; 135.245, Second In Command Qualifications; 135.247, Pilot Qualifications: Recent Experience; 135.261, Applicability; 135.263, Flight Time Limitations and Rest Requirements: All Certificate Holders; 135.265, Flight Time Limitations and Rest Requirements: Scheduled Operations; 135.267, Flight Time Limitations and Rest Requirements: Unscheduled One- and Two-Pilot Crews; 135.269, Flight Time Limitations and Rest Requirements: Unscheduled Three- and Four-Pilot Crews; 135.271, Helicopter Hospital Emergency Medical Evacuation Service (HEMES).

ADVISORY CIRCULARS

AC 120-51A *Crew Resource Management Training* (1993).

AC 120-59 *Air Carrier Internal Evaluation Programs* (1992).

135.271 HELICOPTER HOSPITAL EMERGENCY MEDICAL EVACUATION SERVICE (HEMES)

(a) No certificate holder may assign any flight crewmember, and no flight crewmember may accept an assignment for flight time if that crewmember's total flight time in all commercial flight will exceed —
  (1) 500 hours in any calendar quarter.
  (2) 800 hours in any two consecutive calendar quarters.
  (3) 1,400 hours in any calendar year.

(b) No certificate holder may assign a helicopter flight crewmember, and no flight crewmember may accept an assignment, for hospital emergency medical evacuation service helicopter operations unless that assignment provides for at least 10 consecutive hours of rest immediately preceding reporting to the hospital for availability for flight time.

(c) No flight crewmember may accrue more than 8 hours of flight time during any 24-consecutive hour period of a HEMES assignment, unless an emergency medical evacuation operation is prolonged. Each flight crewmember who exceeds the daily 8 hour flight time limitation in this paragraph must be relieved of the HEMES assignment immediately upon the completion of that emergency medical evacuation operation and must be given a rest period in compliance with paragraph (h) of this section.

(d) Each flight crewmember must receive at least 8 consecutive hours of rest during any 24 consecutive hour period of a HEMES assignment. A flight crewmember must be relieved of the HEMES assignment if he or she has not or cannot receive at least 8 consecutive hours of rest during any 24 consecutive hour period of a HEMES assignment.

(e) A HEMES assignment may not exceed 72 consecutive hours at the hospital.

(f) An adequate place of rest must be provided at, or in close proximity to, the hospital at which the HEMES assignment is being performed.

(g) No certificate holder may assign any other duties to a flight crewmember during a HEMES assignment.

(h) Each pilot must be given a rest period upon completion of the HEMES assignment and prior to being assigned any further duty with the certificate holder of —
   (1) At least 12 consecutive hours for an assignment of less than 48 hours.
   (2) At least 16 consecutive hours for an assignment of more than 48 hours.

(i) The certificate holder must provide each flight crewmember at least 13 rest periods of at least 24 consecutive hours each in each calendar quarter.

EXPLANATION

[For the FAA's position on rest time see the explanation under §135.263.]

The HEMES assignment is not to be used for the routine transport of patients to, from, or between hospitals. It is intended to be used in bona fide emergency situations.

Fixed-wing aircraft are excluded because they are not truly hospital based and the flight crewmember of an airplane does not work in the same closely controlled environment experienced by a helicopter flight crewmember based at a hospital heliport.

The required place of rest should be in an area away from the general flow of vehicle and pedestrian traffic. It should provide adequate facilities including but not limited to a shower, a closet, a bed with sheets, and the space environmentally controlled for comfort. The space should be available on a continuous basis.

Operator should maintain a record that distinctly distinguishes flight time, rest time, and off-duty or unassigned time.

When a flight crewmember is assigned to HEMES under §135.271, the flight crewmember may not be assigned to any other duties.

§§135.267 or 135.271 should be identified in the company training program and Operations Specifications and specify which regulation the operator has chosen to comply with in its particular operation.

CROSS REFERENCES

135.261, Applicability; 135.263, Flight Time Limitations and Rest Requirements: All Certificate Holders; 135.265, Flight Time Limitations and Rest Requirements: Scheduled Operations; 135.267, Flight Time Limitations and Rest Requirements: Unscheduled One- and Two-Pilot Crews; 135.269, Flight Time Limitations and Rest Requirements: Unscheduled Three-and Four-Pilot Crews.

ADVISORY CIRCULARS

AC 135-14A *Emergency Medical Services/-Helicopter (EMS/H)* (1991).

FAA CHIEF COUNSEL OPINIONS

A pilot on 24-hour standby duty must be available for duty anytime during the 24-hour period. Even if the standby pilot is not called to duty during the 24-hour standby period, that 24-hour standby period cannot be considered rest. The rest period cannot be determined retrospectively. For example, if a pilot was not called while on standby, the standby period cannot be redefined as a rest period. The rest period must be determined in advance. (11-9-90).

When an aircraft is owned by a hospital with a Part 135 certificate and all the people carried aboard the aircraft during a particular flight are employees of that hospital (no patient aboard), a flight could be conducted under Part 91. This flight would, however, be considered "other commercial flying" and must be counted against the daily flight time limitations under Part 135. (6-7-90).

SUBPART G — CREWMEMBER TESTING REQUIREMENTS

135.291 APPLICABILITY

This subpart prescribes the tests and checks required for pilot and flight attendant crewmembers and for the approval of check pilots in operations under this part.

EXPLANATION

Although this section indicates that this subpart speaks to Part 135 check pilots, §135.303 was deleted and the check airman training and checking are now contained in Subpart H, §§135.337 and 135.339.

CROSS REFERENCES

135.337, Training Program: Check Airmen and Instructor Qualifications; 135.339, Check Airmen and Flight Instructors: Initial and Transition Training.

135.293 INITIAL AND RECURRENT PILOT TESTING REQUIREMENTS

(a) No certificate holder may use a pilot, nor may any person serve as a pilot, unless, since the beginning of the 12th calendar month before that service, that pilot has passed a written or oral test, given by the Administrator or an authorized check pilot, on that pilot's knowledge in the following areas —

(1) The appropriate provisions of Parts 61, 91, and 135 of this chapter and the Operations Specifications and the manual of the certificate holder;

(2) For each type of aircraft to be flown by the pilot, the aircraft powerplant, major components and systems, major appliances, performance and operating limitations, standard and emergency operating procedures, and the contents of the approved Aircraft Flight Manual or equivalent, as applicable;

(3) For each type of aircraft to be flown by the pilot, the method of determining compliance with weight and balance limitations for takeoff, landing and enroute operations;

(4) Navigation and use of air navigation aids appropriate to the operation or pilot authorization, including, when applicable, instrument approach facilities and procedures;

(5) Air traffic control procedures, including IFR procedures when applicable;

(6) Meteorology in general, including the principles of frontal systems, icing, fog , thunderstorms, and windshear, and if appropriate for the operation of the certificate holder, high altitude weather;

(7) Procedures for —
(i) Recognizing and avoiding severe weather situations;
(ii) Escaping from severe weather situations, in case of inadvertent encounters, including low-altitude windshear (except that rotorcraft pilots are not required to be tested on escaping from low-altitude windshear); and
(iii) Operating in or near thunderstorms (including best penetrating altitudes), turbulent air (including clear air turbulence), icing, hail, and other potentially hazardous meteorological conditions; and
(8) New equipment, procedures, or techniques, as appropriate.

(b) No certificate holder may use a pilot, nor may any person serve as a pilot, in any aircraft unless, since the beginning of the 12th calendar month before that service, that pilot has passed a competency check given by the Administrator or an authorized check pilot in that class of aircraft, if single- engine airplane other than turbojet, or that type of aircraft, if helicopter, multi-engine airplane, or turbojet airplane, to determine the pilot's competence in practical skills and techniques in that aircraft or class of aircraft. The extent of the competency check shall be determined by the Administrator or authorized check pilot conducting the competency check. The competency check may include any of the maneuvers and procedures currently required for the original issuance of the particular pilot certificate required for the operations authorized and appropriate to the category, class and type of aircraft involved. For the purposes of this paragraph, type, as to an airplane, means any one of a group of airplanes determined by the Administrator to have a similar means of propulsion, the same manufacturer, and no significantly different handling or flight characteristics. For the purposes of this paragraph, type, as to a helicopter, means a basic make and model.

(c) The instrument proficiency check required by §135.297 may be substituted for the competency check required by this section for the type of aircraft used in the check.

(d) For the purposes of this part, competent performance of a procedure or maneuver by a person to be used as a pilot requires that the pilot be the obvious master of the aircraft, with the successful outcome of the maneuver never in doubt.

(e) The Administrator or authorized check pilot certifies the competency of each pilot who passes the knowledge or flight check in the certificate holder's pilot records.

(f) Portions of a required competency check may be given in an aircraft simulator or other appropriate training device, if approved by the Administrator.

EXPLANATION

When a flight check is conducted for an airline transport pilot certificate or for an additional type rating to an airline transport pilot certificate, if successfully accomplished, it may be simultaneously credited for a Part 135 competency check (§135.293(b)) or a Part 135 instrument-proficiency check (§135.297(a)), as applicable.

Rotorcraft pilots' exclusion from being tested on escaping from low-altitude windshear was based on the fact that there was insufficient data on helicopter response to windshear encounters.

The definition of "type" as it pertains to airplanes in §135.293(b) relaxes the definition of "type" as set forth in Part 1. However, for §§135.293(a)(2) and (a)(3) and 135.293(b), the Part 1 definition of "type" still applies to helicopters.

There are no provisions in Part 135 which allow recurrent training under §135.351 to be substituted for the competency check required by §135.293(b).

While the regulation states that the extent of the check is determined by the Administration or check airman, FAA Order 8400.10 contains specific guidance in Volume III, Chapter 2 regarding the content of the check (now called a checking module under new training programs). The same standards, guidance and direction are applicable to both FAA inspectors and check airmen.

The maneuvers and procedures (sometimes referred to as events) contained in an operator's checking module are drawn from the practiced test standards (PTS) for the particular pilot certificate required to be held.

In accordance with Volume III, Chapter 2 of FAA Order 8400.10, FAA inspectors and check airmen may waive certain events ordinarily required. This provision does **not** extend to checks involving pilot certification. Waiver authority is not automatic and only applies when a pilot demonstrates a high level of performance.

When a check airman determines an event is unsatisfactory, the check airman may conduct training and repeat the testing of that event. Training may not be conducted, however, without recording the failure of these events. Training and checking cannot be conducted simulateously.

When training is required, the §135.293(b) check must be temporarily suspended, training conducted, and then the check resumed. This training to proficiency is not an option when testing is administered by an FAA inspector.

"Type," as used for airplanes in §135.293(b) refers to make and model of airplane equivalent to other models in a series. FAA Order 8400.10 lists the following as equivalent:

Multi-engine, General-Purpose

Beechcraft reciprocating: B-50, 55, 56, 57, 58, 60, 70 and 95. Cessna reciprocating: C-310, 320, 340 and 400 series.
Cessna: 336, 337.
Piper reciprocating: PA 23, 30, 31, 34 and 39.
Rockwell Commander reciprocating: 500, 560, 680, 685, and 720.

Multi-engine, Turbopropeller

Beechcraft Turbopropeller: B65-A90, 90, 99, 100 and 220
Cessna Turbopropeller: 400 series.
Piper Turbopropeller: Cheyenne series.
Rockwell Commander Turbopropeller: 680T, 690V, 680W and 69L
Fairchild SA 226-227 series.

A pilot with a current §135.293(a) and (b) competency check in one make and model in a series may be qualified in another airplane in that series simply by passing a written or oral test prescribed by §135.293(a).

A pilot with a current §135.293(a) and (b) competency check in any single engine airplane of a given class (ASEL or ASES), may be qualified in another airplane of that class simply by passing a written or oral test prescribed by §135.293(a). This does not apply if the airplane is turbojet powered.

There are no provisions in Part 135 which allow recurrent flight and recurrent ground training under §135.351 to be substituted for the competency check required by §135.293(b). However, satisfactory completion of the competency check may be substituted for recurrent flight training (only).

A §135.293(b) competency check may not be performed during passenger-carrying operations conducted under Part 135.

A higher standard of pilot proficiency is required under Part 135 compared to Part 61 requirements for the original issuance of the certificate or rating. Contrast with §61.43(a)(6), where the successful outcome of a maneuver may never be seriously in doubt.

Recording of proficiency/competency checks may be accomplished on FAA Form 8410-3 or any other form developed by the operator. While pilots are advised to keep a copy for their own personal records, it is not a requirement under the FARs for a pilot to possess a copy of the proficiency/competency check form while conducting operations under Part 135.

As a matter of policy the FAA requires that there be some demonstration of competency on the part of the pilot to maneuver the aircraft solely by reference to instruments on a VFR competency check. The demonstration will be appropriate to the aircraft's installed equipment and the operating environment.

While an instrument proficiency check under §135.297 may be substituted for the competency check required by §135.293(b), the oral or written test requirements of §135.293(a) still must be accomplished.

CROSS REFERENCES

61.121, Applicability (Subpart — E Commercial Pilots); 61.151, Eligibility Requirements: General (Subpart F — Airline Transport Pilots); 135.19, Emergency Operations; 135.21(d)(1)(e), Manual Requirements; 135.63(a)(4)(vi), Record-keeping Requirements; 135.123, Emergency and Emergency Evacuation Duties; 135.297, Pilot In Command: Instrument Proficiency Check Requirements; 135.327, Training Program: Curriculum; 135.335, Approval of Aircraft Simulators and Other Training Devices; 135.337, Training Program: Check Airmen and Instructor Qualifications; 135.341, Pilot and Flight Attendant Crewmember Training Programs.

ADVISORY CIRCULARS

AC 61-65C *Certification: Pilot and Flight Instructors* (1991).

AC 61-89D *Pilot Certificates: Aircraft Type Ratings* (1991).

AC 61-98A *Currency and Additional Qualification Requirements for Certificated Pilots* (1991).

AC 120-53 *Crew Qualification and Pilot Type Rating Requirements for Transport Category Aircraft Operated Under FAR Part 121* (1991).

AIRMAN'S INFORMATION MANUAL

Low Level Wind Shear Alert System (LLWAS), Para. 4-56;
Clearance, Para. 4-80;
Instrument Approach Procedures, Para. 5-46;
Wind Shear PIREPs, Para. 7-22.

FAA CHIEF COUNSEL OPINIONS

FAR 135.293 sets out criteria for the annual written or oral test and competency flight check which must be given to all pilots, regardless of position. The regulation applies to all pilots and is not restricted to PIC's only. (6-4-92).

Even if it is assumed that a second in command is not required on the flights, if the employee were used as a second in command, it would be necessary that you comply with the various requirements, including §§135.95, 135.245 and 135.293. In this respect, the word "pilot" in §135.293 includes pilot in command and second in command. (4-10-79).

135.295 INITIAL AND RECURRENT FLIGHT ATTENDANT CREWMEMBER TESTING REQUIREMENTS

No certificate holder may use a flight attendant crewmember, nor may any person serve as a flight attendant crewmember unless, since the beginning of the 12th calendar month before that service, the certificate holder has determined by appropriate initial and recurrent testing that the person is knowledgeable and competent in the following areas as appropriate to assigned duties and responsibilities —

(a) Authority of the pilot in command;

(b) Passenger handling, including procedures to be followed in handling deranged persons or other persons whose conduct might jeopardize safety;

(c) Crewmember assignments, functions, and responsibilities during ditching and evacuation of persons who may need the assistance of another person to move expeditiously to an exit in an emergency;

(d) Briefing of passengers;

(e) Location and operation of portable fire extinguishers and other items of emergency equipment;

(f) Proper use of cabin equipment and controls;

(g) Location and operation of passenger oxygen equipment;

(h) Location and operation of all normal and emergency exits, including evacuation chutes and escape ropes; and

(i) Seating of persons who may need assistance of another person to move rapidly to an exit in an emergency as prescribed by the certificate holder's operations manual.

EXPLANATION

The "other items of emergency equipment" include such items as the megaphones, crash ax, oxygen devices, and first aid kits.

CROSS REFERENCES

135.21(d)(1) and (e), Manual Requirements; 135.117, Briefing of Passengers Before Flight; 135.129, Exit Seating; 135.155, Fire Extinguishers: Passenger- Carrying Aircraft; 135.167, Emergency Equipment: Extended Overwater Operations; 135.177, Emergency Equipment Requirements for Aircraft Having a Passenger Seating Configuration of More Than 19 Passengers; 135.178, Additional Emergency Equipment; 135.341, Pilot and Flight Attendant Crewmember Training Programs.

ADVISORY CIRCULARS

AC 120-51A *Crew Resource Management Training* (1993).

AC 120-53 *Crew Qualification and Pilot Type Rating Requirements for Transport Category Aircraft Operated Under FAR Part 121* (1991).

135.297 PILOT IN COMMAND: INSTRUMENT PROFICIENCY CHECK REQUIREMENTS

(a) No certificate holder may use a pilot, nor may any person serve, as a pilot in command of an aircraft under IFR unless, since the beginning of the sixth calendar month before that service, that pilot has passed an instrument proficiency check under this section administered by the Administrator or an authorized check pilot.

(b) No pilot may use any type of precision instrument approach procedure under IFR unless, since the beginning of the sixth calendar month before that use, the pilot has satisfactorily demonstrated that type of approach procedure. No pilot may use any type of nonprecision approach procedure under IFR unless, since the beginning of the sixth calendar month before that use, the pilot has satisfactorily demonstrated either that type approach procedure or any other two different types of nonprecision approach procedures. The instrument approach procedure or procedures must include at least one straight-in approach, one circling approach, and one missed approach. Each type of approach procedure demonstrated must be conducted to published minimums for that procedure.

(c) The instrument proficiency check required by paragraph (a) of this section consists of an oral or written equipment test and a flight check under simulated or actual IFR conditions. The equipment test includes questions on emergency procedures, engine operation, fuel and lubrication systems, power settings, stall speeds, best engine-out speed, propeller and supercharger operations, and hydraulic, mechanical, and electrical systems, as appropriate. The flight check includes navigation by instruments, recovery from simulated emergencies, and standard instrument approaches involving navigational facilities which that pilot is to be authorized to use. Each pilot taking the instrument proficiency check must show that standard of competence required by §135.293(d).

(1) The instrument proficiency check must —
   (i) For a pilot in command of an airplane under §135.243(a), include the procedures and maneuvers for an airline transport pilot certificate in the particular type of airplane, if appropriate; and
   (ii) For a pilot in command of an airplane or helicopter under §135.243(c), include the procedures and maneuvers for a commercial pilot certificate with an instrument rating and, if required, for the appropriate type rating.

(2) The instrument proficiency check must be given by an authorized check airman or by the Administrator.

(d) If the pilot in command is assigned to pilot only one type of aircraft, that pilot must take the instrument proficiency check required by paragraph (a) of this section in that type of aircraft.

(e) If the pilot in command is assigned to pilot more than one type of aircraft, that pilot must take the instrument proficiency check required by paragraph (a) of this section in each type of aircraft to which that pilot is assigned, in rotation, but not more than one flight check during each period described in paragraph (a) of this section.

(f) If the pilot in command is assigned to pilot both single-engine and multi-engine aircraft, that pilot must initially take the instrument proficiency check required by paragraph (a) of this section in a multi-engine aircraft, and each succeeding check alternately in single-engine and multi-engine aircraft, but not more than one flight check during each period described in paragraph (a) of this section. Portions of a required flight check may be given in an aircraft simulator or other appropriate training device, if approved by the Administrator.

(g) If the pilot in command is authorized to use an autopilot system in place of a second in command, that pilot must show, during the required instrument proficiency check, that the pilot is able (without a second in command) both with and without using the autopilot to —
   (1) Conduct instrument operations competently; and
   (2) Properly conduct air-ground communications and comply with complex air traffic control instructions.
   (3) Each pilot taking the autopilot check must show that, while using the autopilot, the airplane can be operated as proficiently as it would be if a second in command were present to handle air-ground communications and air traffic control instructions. The autopilot check need only be demonstrated once every 12 calendar months during the instrument proficiency check required under paragraph (a) of this section.

EXPLANATION

When a flight check is conducted for an airline transport pilot certificate or for an additional type rating to an airline transport pilot certificate, if successfully accomplished, it may be simultaneously credited for a Part 135 competency check (§135.293(b)) or a Part 135 instrument-proficiency check (§135.297(a)), as applicable.

Examples of nonprecision approaches are localizer, localizer (back course), VOR, VOR-DME, NDB, and ASR.

The keeping of accurate records is imperative especially in those cases where, by reason of the nature of the operations, pilots are required to take checks in rotation in the case of different types of aircraft and alternately in the case of single- and multi-engine aircraft.

The requirements of this section are not aircraft specific; that is, a single check fulfilling the requirements of §135.297 is sufficient to qualify a pilot in command to conduct IFR operations in all types of aircraft in which the pilot in command is qualified according to §135.293.

A proficiency check conducted to satisfy §135.297 simultaneously satisfies the requirements of §135.293 for the type of aircraft in which the check is accomplished. However, the oral or written test requirement of §135.293 must be completed.

There are very limited circumstances under which a pilot may carry passengers in instrument meteorological conditions in single engine aircraft without an SIC or autopilot (see §135.103 and §135.181). However, the pilot under those circumstances must still have the instrument proficiency check required under §135.297 and meet the pilot in command requirements of §135.243(c).

Approvals for lower-than-standard takeoff minimums authorized under §135.225(h) and Operations Specifications paragraph C57 may be granted based upon testing conducted during the §135.297 proficiency check.

Circling approaches will not be tested if the operator prohibits circling approaches in revenue service.

Precision approaches shall be conducted to DH. Nonprecision approaches shall be conducted to MDA, with the view limiting device removed at the minimum published viability appropriate for the approach category (A, B, C or D) of aircraft used, if a landing is to be performed.

Instrument approaches tested will consist of any standard instrument approach authorized in the operator's Operations Specifications, paragraph C52.

The pilot must demonstrate the ability to use all installed equipment, including autopilots and flight directors.

A higher standard of pilot proficiency is required under Part 135 compared to Part 61 requirements for the original issuance of an instrument rating. Contrast with 61.43(a)(6), where the successful outcome of a maneuver may never be seriously in doubt.

CROSS REFERENCES

61.65, Instrument Rating Requirements; 135.105, Exception to Second In Command Requirement: Approval for Use of Autopilot System; 135.225, IFR: Takeoff, Approach and Landing Minimums; 135.243(a),(c), and (d), Pilot In Command Qualifications; 135.335, Approval of Aircraft Simulators and Other Training Devices.

ADVISORY CIRCULARS

AC 61-66 *Annual Pilot in Command Proficiency Checks* (1973).

AC 61-98A *Currency and Additional Qualification Requirements for Certificated Pilots* (1991).

AIRMAN'S INFORMATION MANUAL

Practice Instrument Approaches, Para. 4-70;
Instrument Approach Procedures, Para. 5-46.

135.299 PILOT IN COMMAND: LINE CHECKS: ROUTES AND AIRPORTS

(a) No certificate holder may use a pilot, nor may any person serve, as a pilot in command of a flight unless, since the beginning of the 12th calendar month before that service, that pilot has passed a flight check in one of the types of aircraft which that pilot is to fly. The flight check shall —
   (1) Be given by an approved check pilot or by the Administrator;
   (2) Consist of at least one flight over one route segment; and
   (3) Include takeoffs and landings at one or more representative airports. In addition to the requirements of this paragraph, for a pilot authorized to conduct IFR operations, at least one flight shall be flown over a civil airway, an approved off-airway route, or a portion of either of them.

(b) The pilot who conducts the check shall determine whether the pilot being checked satisfactorily performs the duties and responsibilities of a pilot in command in operations under this part, and shall so certify in the pilot training record.

(c) Each certificate holder shall establish in the manual required by §135.21 a procedure which will ensure that each pilot who has not flown over a route and into an airport within the preceding 90 days will, before beginning the flight become familiar with all available information required for the safe operation of that flight.

EXPLANATION

The requirements of this section apply to all Part 135 operators i.e. single pilot owner-operator, helicopter operator, on-demand air taxi operator, or commuter air carrier.

A line check may be as brief or as extensive as the person giving the check deems necessary to determine the pilot's competence.

When a pilot in command serves in both Part 121 and Part 135 operations, a line check conducted in a Part 121 aircraft satisfies the Part 135 line check requirement.

For scheduled operators, the route segment will be typically flown in revenue service, and may or may not be conducted during the same flight as the §135.293(b) check. In other words, a line check could be administered during a passenger-carrying flight in revenue service, while a competency check under §135.293(b) never could.

While there are provisions that permit certain operators to conduct the §135.293(b) competency check and the §135.297 proficiency check in an approved simulator, the §135.299 line check must be performed in an aircraft in flight.

Recording of the line check may be accomplished on FAA Form 8410-3 or any other form developed by the operator.

The manual is not a requirement for single pilot and single pilot-in-command operators.

CROSS REFERENCES

135.21, Manual Requirements; 135.243, Pilot In Command Qualifications; 135.337, Training Program: Check Airmen and Instructor Qualifications.

ADVISORY CIRCULARS

AC 61-98A *Currency and Additional Qualification Requirements for Certificated Pilots* (1991).

AC 121.445-1D *Pilot-In-Command Qualifications For Special Areas/Routes and Airports. FAR §121.445* (1990).

135.301 CREWMEMBER: TESTS AND CHECKS, GRACE PROVISIONS, TRAINING TO ACCEPTED STANDARDS

(a) If a crewmember who is required to take a test or a flight check under this part, completes the test or flight check in the calendar month before or after the calendar month in which it is required, that crewmember is considered to have completed the test or check in the calendar month in which it is required.

(b) If a pilot being checked under this subpart fails any of the required maneuvers, the person giving the check may give additional training to the pilot during the course of the check. In addition to repeating the maneuvers failed, the person giving the check may require the pilot being checked to repeat any other maneuvers that are necessary to determine the pilot's proficiency. If the pilot being checked is unable to demonstrate satisfactory performance to the person conducting the check, the certificate holder may not use the pilot, nor may the pilot serve, as a flight crewmember in operations under this part until the pilot has satisfactorily completed the check.

EXPLANATION

If a test or check is required to be taken in January 1995 and it is satisfactorily completed in December 1994 or February 1995, then the test or check would be considered to have been completed in the month, January 1995, in which it was required. The date of the next required test or check would be based on the January 1995 date, not on the December 1994 or February 1995 date.

The prohibition against the use of a pilot in §135.301(b) relates to all Part 135 operations, not just the one for which the check was a requirement.

When a check is interrupted to conduct training, that check must still be completed within the time frame the operator originally scheduled for the check. If the training is so extensive that the check cannot be completed in the allotted time frame, the check airman must consider the check to be unsatisfactory and place the airman in requalification training.

ADVISORY CIRCULARS

AC 61-66 *Annual Pilot in Command Proficiency Checks* (1973).

AC 61-89D *Pilot Certificates: Aircraft Type Ratings* (1991).

AC 61-98A *Currency and Additional Qualification Requirements for Certificated Pilots* (1991).

AIRMAN'S INFORMATION MANUAL

Flight Inspection/Flight Check Aircraft in Terminal Areas, Para. 4-73.

FAA CHIEF COUNSEL OPINIONS

If the certificate holder's Operations Specifications authorize single- and multi-engine operations and the pilot fails his multi-engine checkride, §135.301(b) appears to prohibit the operator from using that pilot in any Part 135 operation until the pilot passes the multi-engine checkride. The result would appear to be the same if that pilot failed an instrument check ride where the Operations Specifications authorized instrument operations. (5-21-90).

Question — Do the words "under this part" in §135.301(a) allow an instrument competency check required by §61.57(e)(2) to be completed in the calendar month before or after the calendar month in which the instrument competency check is required.

> Response — Negative. When §135.301(a) uses the words "under this part", the reference is to Part 135 only. Therefore, the "grace month" provision of §135.301(a) does not apply to an instrument competency check required by §61.57(e)(2). (5-10-89).
>
> If a pilot conducted several flights in the grace month after the required flight check was due and then terminated his employment with the certificate holder without first completing the flight check, that subsequent failure to complete the flight check would NOT operate after the fact to make operations during the grace month illegal. (10-30-79).

SUBPART H — TRAINING

135.321 APPLICABILITY AND TERMS USED

(a) This subpart prescribes requirements for establishing and maintaining an approved training program for crewmembers, check airmen and instructors, and other operations personnel, and for the approval and use of aircraft simulators and other training devices in the conduct of that program.

(b) For the purposes of this subpart, the following terms and definitions apply:

(1) Initial training. The training required for crewmembers who have not qualified and served in the same capacity on an aircraft.

(2) Transition training. The training required for crewmembers who have qualified and served in the same capacity on another aircraft.

(3) Upgrade training. The training required for crewmembers who have qualified and served as second in command on a particular aircraft type, before they serve as pilot in command on that aircraft.

(4) Differences training. The training required for crewmembers who have qualified and served on a particular type aircraft, when the Administrator finds differences training is necessary before a crewmember serves in the same capacity on a particular variation of that aircraft.

(5) Recurrent training. The training required for crewmembers to remain adequately trained and currently proficient for each aircraft crewmember position, and type of operation in which the crewmember serves.

(6) In flight. The maneuvers, procedures, or functions that must be conducted in the aircraft.

EXPLANATION

For a program to be "approved" it must be evaluated and specifically approved by the FAA.

Certain training centers and manufacturers have FAA approval to train flight crews in certain aircraft types used in Part 135 operations.

Difference training may be required where the concerned aircraft has differences relating to configuration, handling qualities, performance, procedures, limitations, controls, instruments, indicators, systems, equipment, options, or modifications.

Single pilot and single pilot-in-command operators are not required to have pilot training programs.

Certain training centers and manufacturers can be included in an operator's pilot training program for the purpose of providing ground training, flight training, and simulator training. These sources can also provide check airman services to the operator on the basis of exemption.

[Editor's Note: The FAA is developing two new ACs which will provide examples of training programs for Part 121 and Part 135 operators. Publication and distribution of these new ACs was expected during 1993. As of this book's publication, the FAA may accept and grant approval for new training programs that are not in the modular format specified in FAA Order 8400.10 Volume III, Chapter 2. Operators are encouraged, nonetheless, to use the new modular format. After publication of the ACs, new training programs and revisions to existing training programs will only be accepted and approved in the modular format. Existing training programs with final approval need not be converted to the modular format if the FAA finds them to be effective and safe. Training programs currently being prepared using other than the modular format may be accepted for approval consideration for up to one year after the effective date of the new ACs.]

CROSS REFERENCES

135.63(a)(4), Recordkeeping Requirements; 135.333, Training Requirements: Handling and Carriage of Hazardous Materials; 135.335, Approval of Aircraft Simulators and Other Training Devices; 135.341, Pilot and Flight Attendant Crewmember Training Programs.

135.323 TRAINING PROGRAM: GENERAL

(a) Each certificate holder required to have a training program under §135.341 shall:
  (1) Establish, obtain the appropriate initial and final approval of, and provide a training program that meets this subpart and that ensures that each crewmember, flight instructor, check airman, and each person assigned duties for the carriage and handling of hazardous materials (as defined in 49 CFR 171.8) is adequately trained to perform their assigned duties.
  (2) Provide adequate ground and flight training facilities and properly qualified ground instructors for the training required by this subpart.
  (3) Provide and keep current for each aircraft type used and, if applicable, the particular variations within the aircraft type, appropriate training material, examinations, forms, instructions, and procedures for use in conducting the training and checks required by this subpart.
  (4) Provide enough flight instructors, check airmen, and simulator instructors to conduct required flight training and flight checks, and simulator training courses allowed under this subpart.

(b) Whenever a crewmember who is required to take recurrent training under this subpart completes the training in the calendar month before, or the calendar month after, the month in which that training is required, the crewmember is considered to have completed it in the calendar month in which it was required.

(c) Each instructor, supervisor, or check airman who is responsible for a particular ground training subject, segment of flight training, course of training, flight check, or competence check under this part shall certify as to the proficiency and knowledge of the crewmember, flight instructor, or check airman concerned upon completion of that training or check. The certification shall be made a part of the crewmember's record. When the certification required by this paragraph is made by an entry in a computerized recordkeeping system, the certifying instructor, supervisor, or check airman, must be identified with that entry. However, the signature of the certifying instructor, supervisor, or check airman, is not required for computerized entries.

(d) Training subjects that apply to more than one aircraft or crewmember position and that have been satisfactorily completed during previous training while employed by the certificate holder for another aircraft or another crewmember position, need not be repeated during subsequent training other than recurrent training.

(e) Aircraft simulators and other training devices may be used in the certificate holder's training program if approved by the Administrator.

EXPLANATION

A certificate holder may include in the training program submitted to the FAA for approval training provided by factory-approved ground schools or their equivalent. If determined satisfactory by the FAA, it will be approved.

§135.323(a)(2) does not limit instructor personnel to certificated ground instructors. Other properly qualified persons identified by the certificate holder and approved by the FAA may be used in the approved training program.

The expiration date assigned to an initially approved program cannot exceed 24 months from the date of initial approval. Initial approval is granted by letter.

A check airman is an airman designated by the FAA who has the appropriate training, experience, and demonstrated ability to evaluate and certify to the knowledge and skills of other airmen.

If the training program calls for the use of an aircraft simulator, it should specifically provide for the use of an aircraft when the simulator is out of service.

Single pilot and single pilot in command operators are not required to have a training program under §135.341.

The FAA can grant initial approval of up to two years to a training program to evaluate its effectiveness. If found to be effective, parts or all of the training program can be granted final approval any time during the initial approval period. Final approval must be obtained prior to expiration of initial approval. Initial and final approval are both granted by letter. FAA surveillance of facilities, courseware, instructors, and records will be conducted to monitor training program effectiveness.

The grace month concept applies to recurrent training. There is a three-month eligibility period during which recurrent training may be completed.

Accurate and detailed records are essential for determination of FAR compliance. Smaller operators often combine training records with the pilot record required by §135.63(a)4.

CROSS REFERENCES

135.63, Recordkeeping Requirements; 135.293, Initial and Recurrent Pilot Testing Requirements; 135.301, Crewmember: Tests and Checks, Grace Provisions, Training to Accepted Standards; 135.333, Training Requirements: Handling and Carriage of Hazardous Materials; 135.335, Approval of Aircraft Simulators and Other Training Devices; 135.337, Training Program: Check Airmen and Instructor Qualifications; 135.339, Check Airmen and Flight Instructors: Initial and Transition Training; 135.341, Pilot and Flight Attendant Crewmember Training Programs.

ADVISORY CIRCULARS

AC 141-1A *Pilot School Certification* (1993).

FAA CHIEF COUNSEL OPINIONS

There is no specific method of compliance with §135.323(c). The rule requires that the person responsible for each subject of the course of training given a crewmember certify for that part of the training program. However, if one instructor conducts all training given, that person could certify the training records in a manner acceptable to the principal operations inspector. (7-17-81).

135.325 TRAINING PROGRAM AND REVISION: INITIAL AND FINAL APPROVAL

(a) To obtain initial and final approval of a training program, or a revision to an approved training program, each certificate holder must submit to the Administrator —
   (1) An outline of the proposed or revised curriculum, that provides enough information for a preliminary evaluation of the proposed training program or revision; and
   (2) Additional relevant information that may be requested by the Administrator.

(b) If the proposed training program or revision complies with this subpart, the Administrator grants initial approval in writing after which the certificate holder may conduct the training under that program. The Administrator then evaluates the effectiveness of the training program and advises the certificate holder of deficiencies, if any, that must be corrected.

(c) The Administrator grants final approval of the proposed training program or revision if the certificate holder shows that the training conducted under the initial approval in paragraph (b) of this section ensures that each person who successfully completes the training is adequately trained to perform that person's assigned duties.

(d) Whenever the Administrator finds that revisions are necessary for the continued adequacy of a training program that has been granted final approval, the certificate holder shall, after notification by the Administrator, make any changes in the program that are found necessary by the Administrator. Within 30 days after the certificate holder receives the notice, it may file a petition to reconsider the notice with the Administrator. The filing of a petition to reconsider stays the notice pending a decision by the Administrator. However, if the Administrator finds that there is an emergency that requires immediate action in the interest of safety, the Administrator may, upon a statement of the reasons, require a change effective without stay.

EXPLANATION

A petition for reconsideration of changes to the training program directed by the FAA is available only where the program has been finally approved. Changes directed by the FAA prior to final approval of the program are not covered by this section.

The additional information that may be requested will consist of that necessary for the FAA to determine that the training program is feasible and adequately supported. Notification by the FAA of the necessity of changes to a training program effectively withdraws the final approval. The FAA maintains close control over the content of air carrier training programs. No training may be conducted from a training program that has not been at least initially approved. The FAA can grant initial approval of up to two years to a training program to evaluate its effectiveness. If the FAA requests a change to an initially approved program, it must be made. Once final approval is granted, an operator may petition the FAA for reconsideration if it does not agree with a requested change. If the requested change originated from an emergency requiring immediate action in the interest of safety, the foregoing petition will not prevent the FAA from requiring the change. FAA surveillance of facilities, courseware, instructors, and records will be conducted to monitor training program effectiveness.

135.327 TRAINING PROGRAM: CURRICULUM

(a) Each certificate holder must prepare and keep current a written training program curriculum for each type of aircraft for each crewmember required for that type aircraft. The curriculum must include ground and flight training required by this subpart.

(b) Each training program curriculum must include the following:

(1) A list of principal ground training subjects, including emergency training subjects, that are provided.

(2) A list of all the training devices, mockups, systems trainers, procedures trainers, or other training aids that the certificate holder will use.

(3) Detailed descriptions or pictorial displays of the approved normal, abnormal, and emergency maneuvers, procedures and functions that will be performed during each flight training phase or flight check, indicating those maneuvers, procedures and functions that are to be performed during the inflight portions of flight training and flight checks.

EXPLANATION

In meeting the requirements of §135.327(b)(3), operators should use the Airline Transport Pilot and Type Rating Practical Test Standard (FAA-S-8081-5), any applicable Flight Standardization Boards (FSB) reports, the manufacturer's recommendations, and Volume 5 of FAA Order 8400.10, Air Transportation Operations Inspector's Handbook.

AIRMAN'S INFORMATION MANUAL.

Flight Inspection/Flight Check Aircraft in Terminal Areas, Para. 4-73.

135.329 CREWMEMBER TRAINING REQUIREMENTS

(a) Each certificate holder must include in its training program the following initial and transition ground training as appropriate to the particular assignment of the crewmember:
  (1) Basic indoctrination ground training for newly hired crewmembers including instruction in at least the —
    (i) Duties and responsibilities of crewmembers as applicable;
    (ii) Appropriate provisions of this chapter;
    (iii) Contents of the certificate holder's operating certificate and Operations specifications (not required for flight attendants); and
    (iv) Appropriate portions of the certificate holder's operating manual.
  (2) The initial and transition ground training in §§135.345 and 135.349, as applicable.
  (3) Emergency training in §135.331
(b) Each training program must provide the initial and transition flight training in §135.347, as applicable.
(c) Each training program must provide recurrent ground and flight training in §135.351.
(d) Upgrade training in §§135.345 and 135.347 for a particular type aircraft may be included in the training program for crewmembers who have qualified and served as second in command on that aircraft.
(e) In addition to initial, transition, upgrade and recurrent training, each training program must provide ground and flight training, instruction, and practice necessary to ensure that each crewmember —
  (1) Remains adequately trained and currently proficient for each aircraft, crewmember position, and type of operation in which the crewmember serves; and
  (2) Qualifies in new equipment, facilities, procedures, and techniques, including modifications to aircraft.

EXPLANATION

The basic indoctrination ground training has as its objective the introduction of the new hire crewmember to the operator and its manner of conducting operations in air transportation. Part 135 does not specify the number of hours that must be programmed for this training. The national norms range from 16 to 32 hours depending on the complexity of the operation and aircraft.

CROSS REFERENCES

135.5, Certificate and Operations Specifications Required; 135.21(d) and (e), Manual Requirements; 135.293, Initial and Recurrent Pilot Testing Requirements; 135.295, Initial and Recurrent Flight Attendant Crewmember Testing Requirements; 135.331, Crewmember Emergency Training; 135.341, Pilot and Flight Attendant Crewmember Training Programs; 135.351, Recurrent Training.

ADVISORY CIRCULARS

AC 120-51A *Crew Resource Management Training* (1993).

AC 120-53 *Crew Qualification and Pilot Type Rating Requirements for Transport Category Aircraft Operated Under FAR Part 121* (1991).

135.331 CREWMEMBER EMERGENCY TRAINING

(a) Each training program must provide emergency training under this section for each aircraft type, model, and configuration, each crewmember, and each kind of operation conducted, as appropriate for each crewmember and the certificate holder.

(b) Emergency training must provide the following:

(1) Instruction in emergency assignments and procedures, including coordination among crewmembers.

(2) Individual instruction in the location, function, and operation of emergency equipment including —

(i) Equipment used in ditching and evacuation;

(ii) First aid equipment and its proper use; and

(iii) Portable fire extinguishers, with emphasis on the type of extinguisher to be used on different classes of fires.

(3) Instruction in the handling of emergency situations including —

(i) Rapid decompression;

(ii) Fire in flight or on the surface and smoke control procedures with emphasis on electrical equipment and related circuit breakers found in cabin areas;

(iii) Ditching and evacuation;

(iv) Illness, injury, or other abnormal situations involving passengers or crewmembers; and

(v) Hijacking and other unusual situations.

(4) Review of the certificate holder's previous aircraft accidents and incidents involving actual emergency situations.

(c) Each crewmember must perform at least the following emergency drills, using the proper emergency equipment and procedures, unless the Administrator finds that, for a particular drill, the crewmember can be adequately trained by demonstration:

(1) Ditching, if applicable.

(2) Emergency evacuation.

(3) Fire extinguishing and smoke control.

(4) Operation and use of emergency exits, including deployment and use of evacuation chutes, if applicable.

(5) Use of crew and passenger oxygen.

(6) Removal of life rafts from the aircraft, inflation of the life rafts, use of life lines, and boarding of passengers and crew, if applicable.
(7) Donning and inflation of life vests and the use of other individual flotation devices, if applicable.

(d) Crewmembers who serve in operations above 25,000 feet must receive instruction in the following:
(1) Respiration.
(2) Hypoxia.
(3) Duration of consciousness without supplemental oxygen at altitude.
(4) Gas expansion.
(5) Gas bubble formation.
(6) Physical phenomena and incidents of decompression.

EXPLANATION

"Emergency drill" training provides instruction and practice in the actual use of certain items of emergency equipment, such as fire extinguishers, life vests, oxygen bottles, and first aid equipment.

"Emergency situation" training consists of instruction on the factors involved, as well as the procedures to be followed, when emergency situations occur.

When an operator uses a number of different aircraft, it should consider dividing the training into two types of training. "General" emergency training would be on emergency items common to all aircraft. "Aircraft specific" emergency training would cover those items which are specific to each aircraft.

HALON fire extinguishers should not be discharged during the required drills unless procedures for protecting the environment from the HALON are in effect.

CROSS REFERENCES

135.19, Emergency Operations; 135.123, Emergency and Emergency Evacuation Duties; 135.155, Fire Extinguishers: Passenger-Carrying Aircraft; 135.157, Oxygen Equipment Requirements; 135.167, Emergency Equipment: Extended Overwater Operations; 135.177, Emergency Equipment Requirements for Aircraft Having a Passenger Seating Configuration of More Than 19 Passengers; 135.178, Additional Emergency Equipment.

ADVISORY CIRCULARS

AC 25.803-1 *Emergency Evacuation Demonstrations* (1989).

AC 120-44 *Air Carrier First Aid Programs* (1987).

AC 120-51A *Crew Resource Management Training* (1993).

AIRMAN'S INFORMATION MANUAL

Emergency Condition — Request Assistance Immediately, Para. 6-2;
Ditching Procedures, Para. 6-22;
Special Emergency (Air Piracy), Para. 6-23;
Effects of Altitude, Para. 8-2;
Hyperventilation in Flight, Para. 8-3;
Carbon Monoxide Poisoning in Flight, Para. 8-4.

135.333 TRAINING REQUIREMENTS: HANDLING AND CARRIAGE OF HAZARDOUS MATERIALS

(a) Except as provided in paragraph (d) of this section, no certificate holder may use any person to perform, and no person may perform, any assigned duties and responsibilities for the handling or carriage of hazardous materials (as defined in 49 CFR 171.8), unless within the preceding 12 calendar months that person has satisfactorily completed initial or recurrent training in an appropriate training program established by the certificate holder, which includes instruction regarding —
   (1) The proper shipper certification, packaging, marking, labeling, and documentation for hazardous materials; and
   (2) The compatibility, loading, storage, and handling characteristics of hazardous materials.

(b) Each certificate holder shall maintain a record of the satisfactory completion of the initial and recurrent training given to crewmembers and ground personnel who perform assigned duties and responsibilities for the handling and carriage of hazardous materials.

(c) Each certificate holder that elects not to accept hazardous materials shall ensure that each crewmember is adequately trained to recognize those items classified as hazardous materials.

(d) If a certificate holder operates into or out of airports at which trained employees or contract personnel are not available, it may use persons not meeting the requirements of paragraphs (a) and (b) of this section to load, offload, or otherwise handle hazardous materials if these persons are supervised by a crewmember who is qualified under paragraphs (a) and (b) of this section.

EXPLANATION

Operators that choose not to carry hazardous materials must have a hazardous materials recognition program. The program should include identification of hazardous materials, ensuring that no packages containing hazardous material are accepted, and procedures for reporting damaged packages that are found to contain, or that are suspected of containing, hazardous materials. (49 CFR §175.45, Reporting Hazardous Materials Incidents)

The requirement for training regarding hazardous materials extends not only to crewmembers, but also to ground personnel whose duties include handling such materials.

CROSS REFERENCES

135.85(c), Carriage of Persons Without Compliance With the Passenger-Carrying Provisions of This Part; 135.323(a)(1), Training Program: General.

ADVISORY CIRCULARS

AC 121-21B *Information Guide for Training Programs and Manual Requirements in the Air Transportation of Hazardous Materials* (1983).

AC 121-27 *Guide for Air Carriers, Freight Forwarders, and Shippers in Obtaining Information Dealing with the Transportation of Hazardous Materials by Air* (1984).

135.335 APPROVAL OF AIRCRAFT SIMULATORS AND OTHER TRAINING DEVICES

(a) Training courses using aircraft simulators and other training devices may be included in the certificate holder's training program if approved by the Administrator.

(b) Each aircraft simulator and other training device that is used in a training course or in checks required under this subpart must meet the following requirements:

   (1) It must be specifically approved for —

      (i) The certificate holder; and

      (ii) The particular maneuver, procedure, or crewmember function involved.

   (2) It must maintain the performance, functional and other characteristics that are required for approval.

   (3) Additionally, for aircraft simulators, it must be —

      (i) Approved for the type aircraft and, if applicable, the particular variation within type for which the training or check is being conducted; and

      (ii) Modified to conform with any modification to the aircraft being simulated that changes the performance, functional, or other characteristics required for approval.

(c) A particular aircraft simulator or other training device may be used by more than one certificate holder.

(d) In granting initial and final approval of training programs or revisions to them, the Administrator considers the training devices, methods, and procedures listed in the certificate holder's curriculum under §135.327.

EXPLANATION

While the requirements of 135.335(b)(1) and (2) are applicable to aircraft simulators and other training devices, 135.335(b)(3) applies only to aircraft simulators.

CROSS REFERENCES

135.293(f), Initial and Recurrent Pilot Testing Requirements; 135.297(f), Pilot In Command: Instrument Proficiency Check Requirements; 135.321(e), Applicability and Terms Used; 135.327, Training Program: Curriculum; 135.347(c), Pilots: Initial, Transition, Upgrade, and Differences Flight Training.

ADVISORY CIRCULARS

AC 120-40B *Airplane Simulator Qualification* (1993).

AC 120-45A *Airplane Flight Training Device Qualification* (1992).

AC 120-46 *Use of Advanced Training Devices* (Airplane Only) (1987).

135.337 TRAINING PROGRAM: CHECK AIRMEN AND INSTRUCTOR QUALIFICATIONS

(a) No certificate holder may use a person, nor may any person serve, as a flight instructor or check airman in a training program established under this subpart unless, for the particular aircraft type involved, that person —
  (1) Holds the airman certificate and ratings that must be held to serve as a pilot in command in operations under this part;
  (2) Has satisfactorily completed the appropriate training phases for the aircraft, including recurrent training, required to serve as a pilot in command in operations under this part;
  (3) Has satisfactorily completed the appropriate proficiency or competency checks required to serve as a pilot in command in operations under this part;
  (4) Has satisfactorily completed the applicable training requirements of §135.339;
  (5) Holds a Class I or Class II medical certificate required to serve as a pilot in command in operations under this part;
  (6) In the case of a check airman, has been approved by the Administrator for the airman duties involved; and
  (7) In the case of a check airman used in an aircraft simulator only, holds a Class III medical certificate.

(b) No certificate holder may use a person, nor may any person serve, as a simulator instructor for a course of training given in an aircraft simulator under this subpart unless that person —
  (1) Holds at least a commercial pilot certificate; and
  (2) Has satisfactorily completed the following as evidenced by the approval of a check airman —
    (i) Appropriate initial pilot and flight instructor ground training under this subpart; and
    (ii) A simulator flight training course in the type simulator in which that person instructs under this subpart.

EXPLANATION

The check airman used in an aircraft simulator requires only a Class III medical certificate, but still must meet all the other requirements of the FAR for being a check airman.

For operators that do not have a training program or only use a single pilot in command, a check airman, who performs competency and line checks, may qualify and maintain currency by receiving the necessary checks from a check airman from another operator or training center approved by the operator's principal operations inspector or by receiving the checks from an FAA inspector.

CROSS REFERENCES

61.123, Eligibility Requirements: General (Commercial Pilots); 61.129, Airplane Rating: Aeronautical Experience; 61.181, Applicability (Flight Instructors); 67.13, First-Class Medical Certificate; 67.15, Second-Class Medical Certificate; 67.17, Third-Class Medical Certificate; 135.63(a)(4)(viii), Recordkeeping Requirements; 135.243, Pilot In Command Qualifications; 135.293, Initial and Recurrent Pilot Testing Requirements; 135.297, Pilot In Command: Instrument Proficiency Check Requirements; 135.299, Pilot In Command: Line Checks: Routes and Airports; 135.335, Approval of Aircraft Simulators and Other Training Devices; 135.339, Check Airmen and Flight Instructors: Initial and Transition Training; 135.351, Recurrent Training.

ADVISORY CIRCULARS

AC 61-89D *Pilot Certificates: Aircraft Type Ratings* (1991).

AC 61-98A *Currency and Additional Qualification Requirements for Certificated Pilots* (1991).

NTSB DECISIONS

Respondent, who signed off a checkride, claimed that the FAA inspector had given him oral authorization to conduct the check. The inspector denied doing so and the administrative law judge believed him. The Board went on to say that an informal authorization to act as check airman is not contemplated by the regulations and policies of the FAA. *Administrator v. Newman* 6 NTSB 413 (1988).

[Editor's Note: This case cited, in support of its position, §§135.303 and 135.337. In 1992, §135.303 was deleted because it was obsolete. However, the FAA policy regarding approval of check airman has not changed. Approval must be in writing.]

135.339 CHECK AIRMEN AND FLIGHT INSTRUCTORS: INITIAL AND TRANSITION TRAINING

(a) The initial and transition ground training for pilot check airmen must include the following:
   (1) Pilot check airman duties, functions, and responsibilities.
   (2) The applicable provisions of this chapter and certificate holder's policies and procedures.
   (3) The appropriate methods, procedures, and techniques for conducting the required checks.
   (4) Proper evaluation of pilot performance including the detection of —
      (i) Improper and insufficient training; and
      (ii) Personal characteristics that could adversely affect safety.
   (5) The appropriate corrective action for unsatisfactory checks.
   (6) The approved methods, procedures, and limitations for performing the required normal, abnormal, and emergency procedures in the aircraft.

(b) The initial and transition ground training for pilot flight instructors, except for the holder of a valid flight instructor certificate, must include the following:
   (1) The fundamental principles of the teaching-learning process.
   (2) Teaching methods and procedures.
   (3) The instructor-student relationship.

(c) The initial and transition flight training for pilot check airmen and pilot flight instructors must include the following:
   (1) Enough inflight training and practice in conducting flight checks from the left and right pilot seats in the required normal, abnormal, and emergency maneuvers to ensure that person's competence to conduct the pilot flight checks and flight training under this subpart.
   (2) The appropriate safety measures to be taken from either pilot seat for emergency situations that are likely to develop in training.
   (3) The potential results of improper or untimely safety measures during training.

   The requirements of paragraphs (2) and (3) of this paragraph may be accomplished in flight or in an approved simulator.

EXPLANATION

§135.339(c)(3) does not require the demonstration of unsafe practices in flight. It is intended to ensure that the training program includes a discussion or an appropriate demonstration of the need for timely action in response to a dangerous in-flight situation. The training regarding appropriate safety measures may be and should be accomplished in a simulator when one is available.

CROSS REFERENCES

61.181, Applicability (Flight Instructors); 135.337, Training Program: Check Airmen and Instructor Qualifications.

ADVISORY CIRCULARS

AC 61-89D *Pilot Certificates: Aircraft Type Ratings* (1991).

AC 61-98A *Currency and Additional Qualification Requirements for Certificated Pilots* (1991).

AC 61-103 *Announcement of Availability: Industry-Developed Transition Training Guidelines for High Performance Aircraft* (1989).

AC 120-51A *Crew Resource Management Training* (1993).

135.341 PILOT AND FLIGHT ATTENDANT CREWMEMBER TRAINING PROGRAMS

(a) Each certificate holder, other than one who uses only one pilot in the certificate holder's operation, shall establish and maintain an approved pilot training program, and each certificate holder who uses a flight attendant crewmember shall establish and maintain an approved flight attendant training program, that is appropriate to the operations to which each pilot and flight attendant is to be assigned, and will ensure that they are adequately trained to meet the applicable knowledge and practical testing requirements of §§135.293 through 135.301. However, the Administrator may authorize a deviation from this section if the Administrator finds that, because of the limited size and scope of the operation, safety will allow a deviation from these requirements.

(b) Each certificate holder required to have a training program by paragraph (a) of this section shall include in that program ground and flight training curriculums for —
- (1) Initial training;
- (2) Transition training;
- (3) Upgrade training;
- (4) Differences training; and
- (5) Recurrent training.

(c) Each certificate holder required to have a training program by paragraph (a) of this section shall provide current and appropriate study materials for use by each required pilot and flight attendant.

(d) The certificate holder shall furnish copies of the pilot and flight attendant crewmember training program, and all changes and additions, to the assigned representative of the Administrator. If the certificate holder uses training facilities of other persons, a copy of those training programs or appropriate portions used for those facilities shall also be furnished. Curricula that follow FAA published curricula may be cited by reference in the copy of the training program furnished to the representative of the Administrator and need not be furnished with the program.

EXPLANATION

The FAA may allow deviation from the requirements of this section when the operator shows that literal compliance with the rule is not necessary in the interest of safety.

This section does not apply to individual certificate holders serving as the only pilot in their operations or to a corporation or other legal entity that uses only one pilot.

A Basic Part 135 Operator may obtain deviations from the requirements of this section. [See explanation under §135.21 for the definition of Basic Part 135 Operator.] For those operators conducting on-demand passenger or cargo carrying operations or only scheduled cargo carrying operations, the deviations may be approved by the Flight Standards District Office which has been assigned certification responsibilities. For those proposing to conduct scheduled passenger (commuter) operations the deviations must be approved by the appropriate Regional Flight Standards District Office.

CROSS REFERENCES

135.21, Manual Requirements; 135.293, Initial and Recurrent Pilot Testing Requirements; 135.295, Initial and Recurrent Flight Attendant Crewmember Testing Requirements; 135.297, Pilot In Command: Instrument Proficiency Check Requirements; 135.299, Pilot In Command: Line Checks: Routes and Airports; 135.301, Crewmember: Tests and Checks, Grace Provisions, Training to Accepted Standards; 135.343, Crewmember Initial and Recurrent Training Requirements; 135.345, Pilots: Initial, Transition, and Upgrade Ground Training; 135.347, Pilots: Initial, Transition, Upgrade, and Differences Flight Training; 135.349, Flight Attendants: Initial and Transition Ground Training; 135.351, Recurrent Training; SFAR No. 58, Advanced Qualification Program.

ADVISORY CIRCULARS

AC 120-51A *Crew Resource Management Training* (1993).

AC 120-53 *Crew Qualification and Pilot Type Rating Requirements for Transport Category Aircraft Operated Under FAR Part 121* (1991).

135.343 CREWMEMBER INITIAL AND RECURRENT TRAINING REQUIREMENTS

No certificate holder may use a person, nor may any person serve, as a crewmember in operations under this part unless that crewmember has completed the appropriate initial or recurrent training phase of the training program appropriate to the type of operation in which the crewmember is to serve since the beginning of the 12th calendar month before that service. This section does not apply to a certificate holder who uses only one pilot in the certificate holder's operation.

EXPLANATION

This section does not apply to individual certificate holders serving as the only pilot in their operations or to a corporation or other legal entity that uses only one pilot.

CROSS REFERENCES

135.293, Initial and Recurrent Pilot Testing Requirements; 135.295, Initial and Recurrent Flight Attendant Crewmember Testing Requirements.

ADVISORY CIRCULARS

AC 120-51A *Crew Resource Management Training* (1993).

135.345 PILOTS: INITIAL, TRANSITIONS, AND UPGRADE GROUND TRAINING

Initial, transition, and upgrade ground training for pilots must include instruction in at least the following, as applicable to their duties:

(a) General subjects —
- (1) The certificate holder's flight locating procedures;
- (2) Principles and methods for determining weight and balance, and runway limitations for takeoff and landing;
- (3) Enough meteorology to ensure a practical knowledge of weather phenomena, including the principles of frontal systems, icing, fog, thunderstorms, windshear and, if appropriate, high altitude weather situations;
- (4) Air traffic control systems, procedures, and phraseology;
- (5) Navigation and the use of navigational aids, including instrument approach procedures;
- (6) Normal and emergency communication procedures;
- (7) Visual cues before and during descent below DH or MDA; and
- (8) Other instructions necessary to ensure the pilot's competence.

(b) For each aircraft type —
- (1) A general description;
- (2) Performance characteristics;

(3) Engines and propellers;
(4) Major components;
(5) Major aircraft systems (i.e., flight controls, electrical, and hydraulic,) other systems, as appropriate, principles of normal, abnormal, and emergency operations, appropriate procedures and limitations;
(6) Knowledge and procedures for —
  (i) Recognizing and avoiding severe weather situations;
  (ii) Escaping from severe weather situations, in case of inadvertent encounters, including low-altitude windshear (except that rotorcraft pilots are not required to be trained in escaping from low-altitude windshear);
  (iii) Operating in or near thunderstorms (including best penetrating altitudes), turbulent air (including clear air turbulence), icing, hail, and other potentially hazardous meteorological conditions; and
  (iv) Operating airplanes during ground icing conditions, (i.e., any time conditions are such that frost, ice, or snow may reasonably be expected to adhere to the airplane), if the certificate holder expects to authorize takeoffs in ground icing conditions, including:
    (A) The use of holdover times when using deicing/anti-icing fluids;
    (B) Airplane deicing/anti-icing procedures, including inspection and check procedures and responsibilities;
    (C) Communications;
    (D) Airplane surface contamination (i.e., adherence of frost, ice, or snow) and critical area identification, and knowledge of how contamination adversely affects airplane performance and flight characteristics;
    (E) Types and characteristics of deicing/anti-icing fluids, if used by the certificate holder;
    (F) Cold weather preflight inspection procedures;
    (G) Techniques for recognizing contamination on the airplane;
(7) Operating limitations;
(8) Fuel consumption and cruise control;
(9) Flight planning;
(10) Each normal and emergency procedure; and
(11) The approved Aircraft Flight Manual, or equivalent.

EXPLANATION

If an operator does not anticipate operating during ground icing conditions, the rule does not require that the training set forth in §135.345(b)(6)(iv) be given to its pilots. However, if operator elects not to give training and encounters such conditions, it can not takeoff until the icing conditions no longer exist.

§135.345(b)(6)(ii), insofar as low altitude windshear, and (b)(6)(iv) do not apply to helicopters.

CROSS REFERENCES

135.79, Flight Locating Requirements; 135.213, Weather Reports and Forecasts; 135.227, Icing Conditions: Operating Limitations; 135.293, Initial and Recurrent Pilot Testing Requirements; 135.295, Initial and Recurrent Flight Attendant Crewmember Testing Requirements; 135.341(d), Pilot and Flight Attendant Crewmember Training Programs.

ADVISORY CIRCULARS

AC 61-9B *Pilot Transition Courses for Complex Single Engine and Light, Twin-Engine Airplanes* (1974).

AC 61-65C *Certification: Pilot and Flight Instructors* (1991).

AC 61-66 *Annual Pilot in Command Proficiency Checks* (1973).

AC 61-89D *Pilot Certificates: Aircraft Type Ratings* (1991).

AC 61-98A *Currency and Additional Qualification Requirements for Certificated Pilots* (1991).

AC 91-13C *Cold Weather Operation of Aircraft* (1979).

135.347 PILOTS: INITIAL, TRANSITION, UPGRADE, AND DIFFERENCES FLIGHT TRAINING

(a) Initial, transition, upgrade, and differences training for pilots must include flight and practice in each of the maneuvers and procedures in the approved training program curriculum.

(b) The maneuvers and procedures required by paragraph (a) of this section must be performed in flight, except to the extent that certain maneuvers and procedures may be performed in an aircraft simulator, or an appropriate training device, as allowed by this subpart.

(c) If the certificate holder's approved training program includes a course of training using an aircraft simulator or other training device, each pilot must successfully complete —

- (1) Training and practice in the simulator or training device in at least the maneuvers and procedures in this subpart that are capable of being performed in the aircraft simulator or training device; and
- (2) A flight check in the aircraft or a check in the simulator or training device to the level of proficiency of a pilot in command or second in command, as applicable, in at least the maneuvers and procedures that are capable of being performed in an aircraft simulator or training device.

CROSS REFERENCES

135.293, Initial and Recurrent Pilot Testing Requirements; 135.295, Initial and Recurrent Flight Attendant Crewmember Testing Requirements; 135.327, Training Program: Curriculum; 135.335, Approval of Aircraft Simulators and Other Training Devices; 135.341(d), Pilot and Flight Attendant Crewmember Training Programs.

ADVISORY CIRCULARS

AC 61-66 *Annual Pilot in Command Proficiency Checks* (1973).

AC 61-89D *Pilot Certificates: Aircraft Type Ratings* (1991).

AC 61-98A *Currency and Additional Qualification Requirements for Certificated Pilots* (1991).

135.349 FLIGHT ATTENDANTS: INITIAL AND TRANSITION GROUND TRAINING

Initial and transition ground training for flight attendants must include instruction in at least the following —

(a) General subjects —
  (1) The authority of the pilot in command; and
  (2) Passenger handling, including procedures to be followed in handling deranged persons or other persons whose conduct might jeopardize safety.

(b) For each aircraft type —
  (1) A general description of the aircraft emphasizing physical characteristics that may have a bearing on ditching, evacuation, and inflight emergency procedures and on other related duties;
  (2) The use of both the public address system and the means of communicating with other flight crewmembers, including emergency means in the case of attempted hijacking or other unusual situations; and
  (3) Proper use of electrical galley equipment and the controls for cabin heat and ventilation.

EXPLANATION

The subject matters referred to in §135.349 should be included in the flight attendant manual and the flight attendants trained on the content of the manual.

CROSS REFERENCES

135.123, Emergency and Emergency Evacuation Duties; 135.150, Public Address and Crewmember Interphone Systems; 135.341(d), Pilot and Flight Attendant Crewmember Training Programs.

ADVISORY CIRCULARS

AC 120-48 *Communication and Coordination Between Flight Crewmembers and Flight Attendants* (1988).

AC 120-51A *Crew Resource Management Training* (1993).

135.351 RECURRENT TRAINING

(a) Each certificate holder must ensure that each crewmember receives recurrent training and is adequately trained and currently proficient for the type aircraft and crewmember position involved.

(b) Recurrent ground training for crewmembers must include at least the following:

  (1) A quiz or other review to determine the crewmember's knowledge of the aircraft and crewmember position involved.

  (2) Instruction as necessary in the subjects required for initial ground training by this subpart, as appropriate, including low-altitude windshear training and training on operating during ground icing conditions, as prescribed in §135.341 and described in §135.345, and emergency training.

(c) Recurrent flight training for pilots must include, at least, flight training in the maneuvers or procedures in this subpart, except that satisfactory completion of the check required by §135.293 within the preceding 12 calendar months may be substituted for recurrent flight training.

EXPLANATION

While the satisfactory completion of the check required by §135.293 within the preceding 12 calendar months may be substituted for recurrent flight training, there is no provision in Part 135 which allows recurrent training to substitute for required checks or tests.

Recurrent general emergency training consists of all the items required by §135.331.

CROSS REFERENCES

135.293, Initial and Recurrent Pilot Testing Requirements; 135.331, Crewmember Emergency Training; 135.345, Pilots: Initial, Transition, and Upgrade Ground Training.

ADVISORY CIRCULARS

AC 61-98A *Currency and Additional Qualification Requirements for Certificated Pilots* (1991).

135.353 PROHIBITED DRUGS

(a) Each certificate holder or operator shall provide each employee performing a function listed in Appendix I to Part 121 of this chapter and his or her supervisor with the training specified in that appendix.
(b) No certificate holder or operator may use any contractor to perform a function specified in Appendix I to Part 121 of this chapter unless that contractor provides each of its employees performing that function for the certificate holder or the operator and his or her supervisor with the training specified in that appendix.

EXPLANATION

The regulations relating to the misuse of alcohol and the testing for alcohol do not include any requirements for formal training of employees as is required in the case of prohibited drugs. The determination of the best means of educating employees beyond the minimum requirement to distribute informational material is left to the discretion of the operators.

ADVISORY CIRCULARS

AC 121-30 *Guidelines for Developing an Anti-Drug Plan for Aviation Personnel* (1989).

SUBPART I — AIRPLANE PERFORMANCE OPERATING LIMITATIONS

135.361 APPLICABILITY

(a) This subpart prescribes airplane performance operating limitations applicable to the operation of the categories of airplanes listed in §135.363 when operated under this part.
(b) For the purpose of this subpart, "effective length of the runway," for landing means the distance from the point at which the obstruction clearance plane associated with the approach end of the runway intersects the centerline of the runway to the far end of the runway.
(c) For the purpose of this subpart, "obstruction clearance plane" means a plane sloping upward from the runway at a slope of 1:20 to the horizontal, and tangent to or clearing all obstructions within a specified area surrounding the runway as shown in a profile view of that area. In the plan view, the centerline of the specified area coincides with the centerline of the runway, beginning at the point where the obstruction clearance plane intersects the centerline of the runway and proceeding to a point at least 1,500 feet from the beginning point. After that the centerline coincides with the takeoff path over the ground for the runway (in the case of takeoffs) or with the instrument approach counterpart (for landings), or, where the applicable one of these paths has not been established, it proceeds consistent with turns of at least 4,000-foot radius until a point is reached beyond which the obstruction clearance plane clears all obstructions. This area extends laterally 200 feet on each side of the centerline at the point where the obstruction clearance plane intersects the runway and continues at this width to the end of the runway; then it increases uniformly to 500 feet on each side of the centerline at a point 1,500 feet from the intersection of the obstruction clearance plane with the runway; after that it extends laterally 500 feet on each side of the centerline.

EXPLANATION

This subpart applies to the type of aircraft being operated rather than the type of operation. All aircraft operating under Part 135 must comply.

The certificate holder is responsible for obtaining the required data for each airport into which its operations are conducted. Sources of the necessary information are: Airport Obstruction Charts (OC) produced by National Ocean Service; Obstruction Data Sheets (ODS), digital derivatives of the OC; Terrain Charts produced by National Geographic Survey; FAA Form 5010-1, Airport Master Records, available in the Airports Division of the appropriate FAA regional office; Notice To Airmen contain temporary and immediate changes; Airport owners/operators have basic data available; and there are commercial services providing the necessary information, such as Jeppesen's Ops Data Service. For more information, contact Jeppesen at (303) 799-9090.

135.363 GENERAL

(a) Each certificate holder operating a reciprocating engine powered large transport category airplane shall comply with §§135.365 through 135.377.
(b) Each certificate holder operating a turbine engine powered large transport category airplane shall comply with §§135.379 through 135.387, except that when it operates a turbo-propeller-powered large transport category airplane certificated after August 29, 1959, but previously type certificated with the same number of reciprocating engines, it may comply with §§135.365 through 135.377.
(c) Each certificate holder operating a large nontransport category airplane shall comply with §§135.389 through 135.395 and any determination of compliance must be based only on approved performance data. For the purpose of this subpart, a large nontransport category airplane is an airplane that was type certificated before July 1, 1942.
(d) Each certificate holder operating a small transport category airplane shall comply with §135.397.
(e) Each certificate holder operating a small nontransport category airplane shall comply with §135.399.
(f) The performance data in the Airplane Flight Manual applies in determining compliance with §§135.365 through 135.387. Where conditions are different from those on which the performance data is based, compliance is determined by interpolation or by computing the effects of change in the specific variables, if the results of the interpolation or computations are substantially as accurate as the results of direct tests.
(g) No person may take off a reciprocating engine powered large transport category airplane at a weight that is more than the allowable weight for the runway being used (determined under the runway takeoff limitations of the transport category operating rules of this subpart) after taking into account the temperature operating correction factors in §4a.749a-T or §4b.117 of the Civil Air Regulations in effect on January 31, 1965, and in the applicable Airplane Flight Manual.
(h) The Administrator may authorize in the Operations Specifications deviations from this subpart if special circumstances make a literal observance of a requirement unnecessary for safety.
(i) The 10-mile width specified in §§135.369 through 135.373 may be reduced to 5 miles, for not more than 20 miles, when operating under VFR or where navigation facilities furnish reliable and accurate identification of high ground and obstructions located outside of 5 miles, but within 10 miles, on each side of the intended track.
(j) Each certificate holder operating a commuter category airplane shall comply with §135.398.

EXPLANATION

A large airplane type certificated after July 1, 1942, must meet performance operating limitations for a transport category airplane to operate under Part 135. §§91.9 and 91.13(a) are the regulations that make the Airplane Flight Manual limitations applicable to Part 135 operations.

In the case of reciprocating engine powered large transport category airplanes, takeoff performance must be corrected for ambient temperatures.

Once an airplane is certified, it normally remains in production and in service under the original rules even though those rules have been superseded. Subpart I of Part 121 and of Part 135 containing a number of sets of rules to account for the progressive enhancement of safety standards. These rules frequently refer to superseded airplane certification rules and effective certification dates. When determining which performance rules apply to a specific airplane, you must determine the airplane certification category, the aircraft size, and whether the aircraft has been modified by STCs. This information can be found on the type certification data sheet. The table below contains a summary of the categories into which airplanes have been divided for purposes of performance computations under Part 121 and Part 135.

LARGE NONTRANSPORT CATEGORY (More than 12,500 lbs. MTOW)

- Certified prior to July 1, 1942 under Aero Bulletin 7A.

LARGE TRANSPORT CATEGORY (More than 12,500 lbs. MTOW)

- Certified under CAR 4, 4A, 4B, SR,422, SR 422A, SR 422B, or FAR 25.

SMALL TRANSPORT CATEGORY (Not more than 12,500 lbs. MTOW)

- Certified under CAR 4, 4A, 4B, SR 422, SR 422A, SR 422B, or FAR 25

COMMUTER CATEGORY (Up to 19,000 lbs. MTOW)

- 19 passenger seats
- Reciprocating or Turbopropeller
- Certified under Part 23
- Redefined as small for performance computation purposes and large for purposes of pilot certification.

NORMAL CATEGORY (Over 12,500 lbs. up to 19,000 lbs. MTOW)

- Certified under FAR 23 and SFAR 41.1(b)
- 10 to 19 Passengers
- Defined as a small airplanes for performance computation purposes and large airplanes for pilot certification by SFAR 41

NORMAL CATEGORY (12,500 lbs. or less MTOW)

- 10 to 19 Passengers
- Certified under CAR 3 or FAR 23 and one of the following (including STCs):
  — Special conditions of the Administrator, SFAR 23, & SFAR 41, Paragraph 1(a)

NORMAL CATEGORY (12,500 lbs. or less MTOW)

- 9 or less Passenger Seats
- Certified under CAR 3 or FAR 23

CROSS REFERENCES

135.365, Large Transport Category Airplanes: Reciprocating Engine Powered: Weight Limitations; 135.367, Large Transport Category Airplanes: Reciprocating Engine Powered: Takeoff Limitations; 135.369, Large Transport Category Airplanes: Reciprocating Engine Powered: En Route Limitations: All Engines Operating; 135.371, Large Transport Category Airplanes: Reciprocating Engine Powered: En Route Limitations: One Engine Inoperative; 135.373, Part 25 Transport Category Airplanes with Four or More Engines: Reciprocating Engine Powered: En Route Limitations: Two Engines Inoperative; 135.375, Large Transport Category Airplanes: Reciprocating Engine Powered: Landing Limitations: Destination Airports; 135.377, Large Transport Category Airplanes: Reciprocating Engine Powered: Landing Limitations: Alternate Airports; 135.379, Large Transport Category Airplanes: Turbine Engine Powered: Takeoff Limitations; 135.381, Large Transport Category Airplanes: Turbine Engine Powered: En Route Limitations: One Engine Inoperative; 135.383, Large Transport Category Airplanes: Turbine Engine Powered: En Route Limitations: Two Engines Inoperative; 135.385, Large Transport Category Airplanes: Turbine Engine Powered: Landing Limitations: Destination Airports; 135.387, Large Transport Category Airplanes: Turbine Engine Powered: Landing Limitations: Alternate Airports; 135.389, Large Nontransport Category Airplanes: Takeoff Limitations; 135.391, Large Nontransport Category Airplanes: En Route Limitations: One Engine Inoperative; 135.393, Large Nontransport Category Airplanes: Landing Limitations: Destination Airports; 135.395, Large Nontransport Category Airplanes: Landing Limitations: Alternate Airports; 135.397, Small Transport Category Airplane Performance Operating Limitations; 135.398, Commuter Category Airplanes Performance Operating Limitations; 135.399, Small Nontransport Category Airplane Performance Operating Limitations.

ADVISORY CIRCULARS

AC 125-1 *Operations of Large Airplanes Subject to Federal Aviation Regulations Part 125* (1981).

135.365 LARGE TRANSPORT CATEGORY AIRPLANES: RECIPROCATING ENGINE POWERED: WEIGHT LIMITATIONS

(a) No person may take off a reciprocating engine powered large transport category airplane from an airport located at an elevation outside of the range for which maximum takeoff weights have been determined for that airplane.
(b) No person may take off a reciprocating engine powered large transport category airplane for an airport of intended destination that is located at an elevation outside of the range for which maximum landing weights have been determined for that airplane.
(c) No person may specify, or have specified, an alternate airport that is located at an elevation outside of the range for which maximum landing weights have been determined for the reciprocating engine powered large transport category airplane concerned.
(d) No person may take off a reciprocating engine powered large transport category airplane at a weight more than the maximum authorized takeoff weight for the elevation of the airport.
(e) No person may take off a reciprocating engine powered large transport category airplane if its weight on arrival at the airport of destination will be more than maximum authorized landing weight for the elevation of that airport, allowing for normal consumption of fuel and oil enroute.

EXPLANATION

With a constant weight as airport elevation increases, the takeoff run required before the airplane reaches V1, VR, and V2 speeds increase. Also, the stopping distance from V1 increases. A greater air distance is traversed from the lift-off to the specified runway crossing height because of the increased true airspeed at the indicated V2 speed. Therefore, to achieve similar V1, VR, and V2 speeds, weight must be reduced.

ADVISORY CIRCULARS

AC 23-7 *Substantiation for an Increase in Maximum Weight, Maximum Landing Weight, or Maximum Zero Fuel Weight* (1987).

AC 125-1 *Operations of Large Airplanes Subject to Federal Aviation Regulations Part 125* (1981).

135.367 LARGE TRANSPORT CATEGORY AIRPLANES: RECIPROCATING ENGINE POWERED: TAKEOFF LIMITATIONS

(a) No person operating a reciprocating engine powered large transport category airplane may take off that airplane unless it is possible —
  (1) To stop the airplane safely on the runway, as shown by the accelerate-stop distance data, at any time during takeoff until reaching critical engine failure speed;
  (2) If the critical engine fails at any time after the airplane reaches critical-engine failure speed V1, to continue the takeoff and reach a height of 50 feet, as indicated by the takeoff path data, before passing over the end of the runway; and
  (3) To clear all obstacles either by at least 50 feet vertically (as shown by the takeoff path data) or 200 feet horizontally within the airport boundaries and 300 feet horizontally beyond the boundaries, without banking before reaching a height of 50 feet (as shown by the takeoff path data) and after that without banking more than 15 degrees.

(b) In applying this section, corrections must be made for any runway gradient. To allow for wind effect, takeoff data based on still air may be corrected by taking into account not more than 50 percent of any reported headwind component and not less than 150 percent of any reported tailwind component.

EXPLANATION

The aircraft must be able to stop on the runway. Clearways and stopways cannot be considered in making the determination.

Any object inside the airport boundary which is within a horizontal distance of 200 feet of the flightpath or outside the airport boundary within 300 feet of the flightpath, must be considered an obstacle for takeoff computations.

Runway gradient corrections are usually made using the average runway gradient. This is determined by dividing the difference in the elevation of the two ends of the runway by the runway length.

ADVISORY CIRCULARS

AC 25-13 *Reduced and Derated Takeoff Thrust (Power) Procedures* (1988).

AC 125-1 *Operations of Large Airplanes Subject to Federal Aviation Regulations Part 125* (1981).

135.369 LARGE TRANSPORT CATEGORY AIRPLANES: RECIPROCATING ENGINE POWERED: ENROUTE LIMITATIONS: ALL ENGINES OPERATING

(a) No person operating a reciprocating engine powered large transport category airplane may take off that airplane at a weight, allowing for normal consumption of fuel and oil, that does not allow a rate of climb (in feet per minute), with all engines operating, of at least 6.90 V_{SO} (that is, the number of feet per minute obtained by multiplying the number of knots by 6.90) at an altitude of at least 1,000 feet above the highest ground or obstruction within ten miles of each side of the intended track.

(b) This section does not apply to large transport category airplanes certificated under Part 4a of the Civil Air Regulations.

EXPLANATION

Compliance with this section does not relieve the operator from complying with the provisions of §135.181, which can be more restrictive.

ADVISORY CIRCULARS

AC 125-1 *Operations of Large Airplanes Subject to Federal Aviation Regulations Part 125* (1981).

135.371 LARGE TRANSPORT CATEGORY AIRPLANES: RECIPROCATING ENGINE POWERED: ENROUTE LIMITATIONS: ONE ENGINE INOPERATIVE

(a) Except as provided in paragraph (b) of this section, no person operating a reciprocating engine powered large transport category airplane may take off that airplane at a weight, allowing for normal consumption of fuel and oil, that does not allow a rate of climb (in feet per minute), with one engine inoperative, of at least (0.079-0.106/N) V_{SO}^2 (where N is the number of engines installed and V_{SO} is expressed in knots) at an altitude of at least 1,000 feet above the highest ground or obstruction within 10 miles of each side of the intended track. However, for the purposes of this paragraph the rate of climb for transport category airplanes certificated under Part 4a of the Civil Air Regulations is 0.026 V_{SO}^2.

(b) In place of the requirements of paragraph (a) of this section, a person, may, under an approved procedure, operate a reciprocating engine powered large transport category airplane at an all-engines-operating altitude that allows the airplane to continue, after an engine failure, to an alternate airport where a landing can be made under §135.377, allowing for normal consumption of fuel and oil. After the assumed failure, the flight path must clear the ground and any obstruction within five miles on each side of the intended track by at least 2,000 feet.

(c) If an approved procedure under paragraph (b) of this section is used, the certificate holder shall comply with the following:

(1) The rate of climb (as prescribed in the Airplane Flight Manual for the appropriate weight and altitude) used in calculating the airplane's flight path shall be diminished by an amount in feet per minute, equal to (0.079-0.106/N) VSO^2 (where N is the number of engines installed and VSO is expressed in knots) for airplanes certificated under Part 25 of this chapter and by 0.026 VSO^2 for airplanes certificated under Part 4a for the Civil Air Regulations.

(2) The all-engines-operating altitude shall be sufficient so that in the event the critical engine becomes inoperative at any point along the route, the flight will be able to proceed to a predetermined alternate airport by use of this procedure. In determining the takeoff weight, the airplane is assumed to pass over the critical obstruction following engine failure at a point no closer to the critical obstruction than the nearest approved radio navigational fix, unless the Administrator approves a procedure established on a different basis upon finding that adequate operational safeguards exist.

(3) The airplane must meet the provisions of paragraph (a) of this section at 1,000 feet above the airport used as an alternate in this procedure.

(4) The procedure must include an approved method of accounting for winds and temperatures that would otherwise adversely affect the flight path.

(5) In complying with this procedure, fuel jettisoning is allowed if the certificate holder shows that it has an adequate training program, that proper instructions are given to the flight crew, and all other precautions are taken to ensure a safe procedure.

(6) The certificate holder and the pilot in command shall jointly elect an alternate airport for which the appropriate weather reports or forecasts, or any combination of them, indicate that weather conditions will be at or above the alternate weather minimum specified in the certificate holder's Operations Specifications for that airport when the flight arrives.

EXPLANATION

If an operator elects, under §135.371(b), to utilize an approved procedure instead of complying with §135.371(a), the procedure must be approved by the FAA principal operations inspector and set forth in a company flight manual or a portion of the general operating manual.

The provisions of §135.181 must be complied with fully.

Any procedure approved under §135.371 must be set forth in the operator's manual and training program.

CROSS REFERENCES

135.213, Weather Reports and Forecasts; 135.377, Large Transport Category Airplanes: Reciprocating Engine Powered: Landing Limitations: Alternate Airports.

ADVISORY CIRCULARS

AC 20-105A *Engine Power-Loss Accident Prevention* (1980).

AC 125-1 *Operations of Large Airplanes Subject to Federal Aviation Regulations Part 125* (1981).

135.373 PART 25 TRANSPORT CATEGORY AIRPLANES WITH FOUR OR MORE ENGINES: RECIPROCATING ENGINE POWERED: ENROUTE LIMITATIONS: TWO ENGINES INOPERATIVE

(a) No person may operate an airplane certificated under Part 25 and having four or more engines unless —
- (1) There is no place along the intended track that is more than 90 minutes (with all engines operating at cruising power) from an airport that meets §135.377; or
- (2) It is operated at a weight allowing the airplane, with the two critical engines inoperative, to climb at 0.013 V_{SO}^2 feet per minute (that is, the number of feet per minute obtained by multiplying the number of knots squared by 0.013) at an altitude of 1,000 feet above the highest ground or obstruction within 10 miles on each side of the intended track, or at an altitude of 5,000 feet, whichever is higher.

(b) For the purposes of paragraph (a)(2) of this section, it is assumed that —
- (1) The two engines fail at the point that is most critical with respect to the takeoff weight;
- (2) Consumption of fuel and oil is normal with all engines operating up to the point where the two engines fail with two engines operating beyond that point;
- (3) Where the engines are assumed to fail at an altitude above the prescribed minimum altitude, compliance with the prescribed rate of climb at the prescribed minimum altitude need not be shown during the descent from the cruising altitude to the prescribed minimum altitude, if those requirements can be met once the prescribed minimum altitude is reached, and assuming descent to be along a net flight path and the rate of descent to be 0.013 V_{SO}^2 greater than the rate in the approved performance data; and
- (4) If fuel jettisoning is provided, the airplane's weight at the point where the two engines fail is considered to be not less than that which would include enough fuel to proceed to an airport meeting §135.377 and to arrive at an altitude of at least 1,000 feet directly over that airport.

EXPLANATION

If an operator elects to jettison fuel to comply with this section, enough fuel must remain after jettison to allow the airplane to proceed to a suitable alternate airport and to arrive at an altitude of at least 1000 feet directly over that airport.

The provisions of §135.181 can be more restrictive and must be complied with fully.

CROSS REFERENCES

135.377, Large Transport Category Airplanes: Reciprocating Engine Powered: Landing Limitations: Alternate Airports.

ADVISORY CIRCULARS

AC 125-1 *Operations of Large Airplanes Subject to Federal Aviation Regulations Part 125* (1981).

135.375 LARGE TRANSPORT CATEGORY AIRPLANES: RECIPROCATING ENGINE POWERED: LANDING LIMITATIONS: DESTINATION AIRPORTS

(a) Except as provided in paragraph (b) of this section, no person operating a reciprocating engine powered large transport category airplane may take off that airplane, unless its weight on arrival, allowing for normal consumption of fuel and oil in flight, would allow a full stop landing at the intended destination within 60 percent of the effective length of each runway described below from a point 50 feet directly above the intersection of the obstruction clearance plane and the runway. For the purposes of determining the allowable landing weight at the destination airport the following is assumed:
  (1) The airplane is landed on the most favorable runway and in the most favorable direction in still air.
  (2) The airplane is landed on the most suitable runway considering the probable wind velocity and direction (forecast for the expected time of arrival), the ground handling characteristics of the type of airplane, and other conditions such as landing aids and terrain, and allowing for the effect of the landing path and roll of not more than 50 percent of the headwind component or not less than 150 percent of the tailwind component.

(b) An airplane that would be prohibited from being taken off because it could not meet paragraph (a)(2) of this section may be taken off if an alternate airport is selected that meets all of this section except that the airplane can accomplish a full stop landing within 70 percent of the effective length of the runway.

EXPLANATION

For dispatch planning, reciprocating-powered airplanes must be able to land within 60% of the effective runway at the destination. A flight may also be dispatched to a destination at which the airplane can land within 70% of the effective runway, if the designated alternate airport is one at which the airplane can land within 70% of the effective runway distance.

ADVISORY CIRCULARS

AC 125-1 *Operations of Large Airplanes Subject to Federal Aviation Regulations Part 125* (1981).

135.377 LARGE TRANSPORT CATEGORY AIRPLANES: RECIPROCATING ENGINE POWERED: LANDING LIMITATIONS: ALTERNATE AIRPORTS

No person may list an airport as an alternate airport in a flight plan unless the airplane (at the weight anticipated at the time of arrival at the airport), based on the assumptions in §135.375(a)(1) and (2), can be brought to a full stop landing within 70 percent of the effective length of the runway.

CROSS REFERENCES

135.375, Large Transport Category Airplanes: Reciprocating Engine Powered: Landing Limitations: Destination Airports.

ADVISORY CIRCULARS

AC 125-1 *Operations of Large Airplanes Subject to Federal Aviation Regulations Part 125* (1981).

135.379 LARGE TRANSPORT CATEGORY AIRPLANES: TURBINE ENGINE POWERED: TAKEOFF LIMITATIONS

(a) No person operating a turbine engine powered large transport category airplane may take off that airplane at a weight greater than that listed in the Airplane Flight Manual for the elevation of the airport and for the ambient temperature existing at takeoff.

(b) No person operating a turbine engine powered large transport category airplane certificated after August 26, 1957, but before August 30, 1959 (SR422, 422A), may take off that airplane at a weight greater than that listed in the Airplane Flight Manual for the minimum distance required for takeoff. In the case of an airplane certificated after September 30, 1958 (SR422A, 422B), the takeoff distance may include a clearway distance but the clearway distance included may not be greater than one-half of the takeoff run.

(c) No person operating a turbine engine powered large transport category airplane certificated after August 29, 1959 (SR422B), may take off that airplane at a weight greater than that listed in the Airplane Flight Manual at which compliance with the following may be shown:

(1) The accelerate-stop distance, as defined in §25.109 of this chapter, must not exceed the length of the runway plus the length of any stopway.

(2) The takeoff distance must not exceed the length of the runway plus the length of any clearway except that the length of any clearway included must not be greater than one-half the length of the runway.

(3) The takeoff run must not be greater than the length of the runway.

(d) No person operating a turbine engine powered large transport category airplane may takeoff that airplane at a weight greater than that listed in the Airplane Flight Manual —

(1) For an airplane certificated after August 26, 1957, but before October 1, 1958 (SR422), that allows a takeoff path that clears all obstacles either by at least (35 + 0.01 D) feet vertically (D is the distance along the intended flight path from the end of the runway in feet), or by at least 200 feet horizontally within the airport boundaries and by at least 300 feet horizontally after passing the boundaries; or

(2) For an airplane certificated after September 30, 1958 (SR422A, 422B), that allows a net takeoff flight path that clears all obstacles either by a height of at least 35 feet vertically, or by at least 200 feet horizontally within the airport boundaries and by at least 300 feet horizontally after passing the boundaries.

(e) In determining maximum weights, minimum distances and flight paths under paragraphs (a) through (d) of this section, correction must be made for the runway to be used, the elevation of the airport, the effective runway gradient, and the ambient temperature and wind component at the time of takeoff.

(f) For the purposes of this section, it is assumed that the airplane is not banked before reaching a height of 50 feet, as shown by the takeoff path or net takeoff flight path data (as appropriate) in the Airplane Flight Manual, and after that the maximum bank is not more than 15 degrees.

(g) For the purposes of this section, the terms, "takeoff distance," "takeoff run," "net takeoff flight path," have the same meanings as set forth in the rules under which the airplane was certificated.

EXPLANATION

Effective August 27, 1957, Special Regulation (SR) 422 was the basis for certification of the first turbine-powered transport airplanes, such as the Boeing 707, the Lockheed Electra, and the Fairchild 27. SR422A became effective July 2, 1958, and was superseded by SR422B effective August 29, 1959. Only a few airplanes were certified under SR422A, such as the Gulfstream I and the CL44. The majority of the turbine-powered transport category airplanes now in service, such as DC-8, DC-9, and B-727, were originally certified under SR422B. SR422B was recodified with minor changes to Part 25, which became effective in February 1965.

"Clearway" and "stopway" are defined in Part 1.

CROSS REFERENCES

25.109, Accelerate-Stop Distance.

ADVISORY CIRCULARS

AC 25.939-1 *Evaluating Turbine Engine Operating Characteristics* (1986).

AC 125-1 *Operations of Large Airplanes Subject to Federal Aviation Regulations Part 125* (1981).

135.381 LARGE TRANSPORT CATEGORY AIRPLANES: TURBINE ENGINE POWERED: ENROUTE LIMITATIONS: ONE ENGINE INOPERATIVE

(a) No person operating a turbine engine powered large transport category airplane may take off that airplane at a weight, allowing for normal consumption of fuel and oil, that is greater than that which (under the approved, one engine inoperative, enroute net flight path data in the Airplane Flight Manual for that airplane) will allow compliance with subparagraph (1) or (2) of this paragraph, based on the ambient temperatures expected en route.

(1) There is a positive slope at an altitude of at least 1,000 feet above all terrain and obstructions within five statute miles on each side of the intended track, and, in addition, if that airplane was certificated after August 29, 1958 (SR422B), there is a positive slope at 1,500 feet above the airport where the airplane is assumed to land after an engine fails.

(2) The net flight path allows the airplane to continue flight from the cruising altitude to an airport where a landing can be made under §135.387 clearing all terrain and obstructions within five statute miles of the intended track by at least 2,000 feet vertically and with a positive slope at 1,000 feet above the airport where the airplane lands after an engine fails, or, if that airplane was certificated after September 30, 1958 (SR422A, 422B), with a positive slope at 1,500 feet above the airport where the airplane lands after an engine fails.

(b) For the purpose of paragraph (a)(2) of this section, it is assumed that —

(1) The engine fails at the most critical point enroute;

(2) The airplane passes over the critical obstruction, after engine failure at a point that is no closer to the obstruction than the approved radio navigation fix, unless the Administrator authorizes a different procedure based on adequate operational safeguards;

(3) An approved method is used to allow for adverse winds;

(4) Fuel jettisoning will be allowed if the certificate holder shows that the crew is properly instructed, that the training program is adequate, and that all other precautions are taken to ensure a safe procedure;

(5) The alternate airport is selected and meets the prescribed weather minimums; and

(6) The consumption of fuel and oil after engine failure is the same as the consumption that is allowed for in the approved net flight path data in the Airplane Flight Manual.

EXPLANATION

In this section the one-engine inoperative "net flight path" is derived by subtracting 1.6% gradient for four-engine airplanes, 1.4% for three-engine airplanes, and 1.1% for two-engine airplanes from the actual climb performance the airplane can produce.

The provisions of §135.181 must be complied with and can be more restrictive.

CROSS REFERENCES

135.387, Large Transport Category Airplanes: Turbine Engine Powered: Landing Limitations: Alternate Airports.

ADVISORY CIRCULARS

AC 25.939-1 *Evaluating Turbine Engine Operating Characteristics* (1986).

AC 125-1 *Operations of Large Airplanes Subject to Federal Aviation Regulations Part 125* (1981).

135.383 LARGE TRANSPORT CATEGORY AIRPLANES: TURBINE ENGINE POWERED: ENROUTE LIMITATIONS: TWO ENGINES INOPERATIVE

(a) Airplanes certificated after August 26, 1957, but before October 1, 1958 (SR422). No person may operate a turbine engine powered large transport category airplane along an intended route unless that person complies with either of the following:

(1) There is no place along the intended track that is more than 90 minutes (with all engines operating at cruising power) from an airport that meets §135.387.

(2) Its weight, according to the two-engine-inoperative, enroute, net flight path data in the Airplane Flight Manual, allows the airplane to fly from the point where the two engines are assumed to fail simultaneously to an airport that meets §135.387, with a net flight path (considering the ambient temperature anticipated along the track) having a positive slope at an altitude of at least 1,000 feet above all terrain and obstructions within five statute miles on each side of the intended track, or at an altitude of 5,000 feet, whichever is higher.

For the purposes of paragraph (2) of this paragraph, it is assumed that the two engines fail at the most critical point enroute, that if fuel jettisoning is provided, the airplane's weight at the point where the engines fail includes enough fuel to continue to the airport and to arrive at an altitude of at least 1,000 feet directly over the airport, and that the fuel and oil consumption after engine failure is the same as the consumption allowed for in the net flight path data in the Airplane Flight Manual.

(b) Airplanes certificated after September 30, 1958, but before August 30, 1959 (SR422A). No person may operate a turbine engine powered large transport category airplane along an intended route unless that person complies with either of the following:

(1) There is no place along the intended track that is more than 90 minutes (with all engines operating at cruising power) from an airport that meets §135.387.

(2) Its weight, according to the two-engine-inoperative, enroute, net flight path data in the Airplane Flight Manual allows the airplane to fly from the point where the two engines are assumed to fail simultaneously to an airport that meets §135.387 with a net flight path (considering the ambient temperatures anticipated along the track) having a positive slope at an altitude for at least 1,000 feet above all terrain and obstructions within five statute miles on each side of the intended track, or at an altitude of 2,000 feet, whichever is higher.

For the purpose of paragraph (2) of this paragraph, it is assumed that the two engines fail at the most critical point enroute, that the airplane's weight at the point where the engines fail includes enough fuel to continue to the airport, to arrive at an altitude of at least 1,500 feet directly over the airport, and after that to fly for 15 minutes at cruise power or thrust, or both, and that the consumption of fuel and oil after engine failure is the same as the consumption allowed for in the net flight path data in the Airplane Flight Manual.

(c) Aircraft certificated after August 29, 1959 (SR422B). No person may operate a turbine engine powered large transport category airplane along an intended route unless that person complies with either of the following:

(1) There is no place along the intended track that is more than 90 minutes (with all engines operating at cruising power) from an airport that meets §135.387.

(2) Its weight, according to the two-engine-inoperative, enroute, net flight path data in the Airplane Flight Manual, allows the airplane to fly from the point where the two engines are assumed to fail simultaneously to an airport that meets §135.387, with the net flight path (considering the ambient temperatures anticipated along the track) clearing vertically by at least 2,000 feet all terrain and obstructions within five statute miles on each side of the intended track. For the purposes of this paragraph, it is assumed that —

(i) The two engines fail at the most critical point enroute;

(ii) The net flight path has a positive slope at 1,500 feet above the airport where the landing is assumed to be made after the engines fail;

(iii) Fuel jettisoning will be approved if the certificate holder shows that the crew is properly instructed, that the training program is adequate, and that all other precautions are taken to ensure a safe procedure;

(iv) The airplane's weight at the point where the two engines are assumed to fail provides enough fuel to continue to the airport, to arrive at an altitude of at least 1,500 feet directly over the airport, and after that to fly for 15 minutes at cruise power or thrust, or both; and

(v) The consumption of fuel and oil after the engines fail is the same as the consumption that is allowed for in the net flight path data in the Airplane Flight Manual.

EXPLANATION

Aircraft certified under SR422A and subsequent aircraft certified under SR422B and Part 25 must be able to fly for 15 minutes at cruise power after reaching the designated alternate airport. However, §135.181 must be complied with and can be more restrictive.

CROSS REFERENCES

135.387, Large Transport Category Airplanes: Turbine Engine Powered: Landing Limitations: Alternate Airports.

ADVISORY CIRCULARS

AC 25.939-1 *Evaluating Turbine Engine Operating Characteristics* (1986).

AC 125-1 *Operations of Large Airplanes Subject to Federal Aviation Regulations Part 125* (1981).

135.385 LARGE TRANSPORT CATEGORY AIRPLANES: TURBINE ENGINE POWERED: LANDING LIMITATIONS: DESTINATION AIRPORTS

(a) No person operating a turbine engine powered large transport category airplane may take off that airplane at a weight that (allowing for normal consumption of fuel and oil in flight to the destination or alternate airport) the weight of the airplane on arrival would exceed the landing weight in the Airplane Flight Manual for the elevation of the destination or alternate airport and the ambient temperature anticipated at the time of landing.

(b) Except as provided in paragraph (c), (d), or (e) of this section, no person operating a turbine engine powered large transport category airplane may take off that airplane unless its weight on arrival, allowing for normal consumption of fuel and oil in flight (in accordance with the landing distance in the Airplane Flight Manual for the elevation of the destination airport and the wind conditions anticipated there at the time of landing), would allow a full stop landing at the intended destination airport within 60 percent of the effective length of each runway described below from a point 50 feet above the intersection of the obstruction clearance plane and the runway. For the purpose of determining the allowable landing weight at the destination airport the following is assumed:

   (1) The airplane is landed on the most favorable runway and in the most favorable direction, in still air.

   (2) The airplane is landed on the most suitable runway considering the probable wind velocity and direction and the ground handling characteristics of the airplane, and considering the other conditions such as landing aids and terrain.

(c) A turbopropeller powered airplane that would be prohibited from being taken off because it could not meet paragraph (b)(2) of this section, may be taken off if an alternate airport is selected that meets all of this section except that the airplane can accomplish a full stop landing within 70 percent of the effective length of the runway.

(d) Unless, based on a showing of actual operating landing techniques on wet runways, a shorter landing distance (but never less than that required by paragraph (b) of this section) has been approved for a specific type and model airplane and included in the Airplane Flight Manual, no person may take off a turbojet airplane when the appropriate weather reports or forecasts, or any combination of them, indicate that the runways at the destination airport may be wet or slippery at the estimated time of arrival unless the effective runway length at the destination airport is at least 115 percent of the runway length required under paragraph (b) of this section.

(e) A turbojet airplane that would be prohibited from being taken off because it could not meet paragraph (b)(2) of this section may be taken off if an alternate airport is selected that meets all of paragraph (b) of this section.

EXPLANATION

When weather reports and forecasts, or any combination of them, indicate that, at the estimated time of arrival, the runways will be wet or slippery, for turbojet airplanes, the required landing runway length must be increased by 15%. For the purpose of preflight planning, a correction is not applied to the alternate airport landing runway length.

Turbojet airplanes must be able to make a full stop landing within 60% of the effective runway length at both destination and alternate airports. Turbopropeller airplanes must be able to make a full stop landing within 60% of the effective runway at the destination and 70% at the alternate airport.

CROSS REFERENCES

135.213, Weather Reports and Forecasts; 135.387, Large Transport Category Airplanes: Turbine Engine Powered: Landing Limitations: Alternate Airports.

ADVISORY CIRCULARS

AC 125-1 *Operations of Large Airplanes Subject to Federal Aviation Regulations Part 125* (1981).

135.387 LARGE TRANSPORT CATEGORY AIRPLANES: TURBINE ENGINE POWERED: LANDING LIMITATIONS: ALTERNATE AIRPORTS

No person may select an airport as an alternate airport for a turbine engine powered large transport category airplane unless (based on the assumptions in §135.385(b) that airplane, at the weight anticipated at the time of arrival, can be brought to a full stop landing within 70 percent of the effective length of the runway for turbopropeller-powered airplanes and 60 percent of the effective length of the runway for turbojet airplanes, from a point 50 feet above the intersection of the obstruction clearance plane and the runway.

EXPLANATION

To be acceptable as an alternate airport, a turbojet airplane must be able to make a full stop landing within 60 percent of the effective length of the runway and a turbopropeller airplane within 70 percent. In making the required determinations, the assumptions set forth in §135.385(b) must be used.

CROSS REFERENCES

135.385, Large Transport Category Airplanes: Turbine Engine Powered: Landing Limitations: Destination Airports.

ADVISORY CIRCULARS

AC 125-1 *Operations of Large Airplanes Subject to Federal Aviation Regulations Part 125* (1981).

135.389 LARGE NONTRANSPORT CATEGORY AIRPLANES: TAKEOFF LIMITATIONS

(a) No person operating a large nontransport category airplane may take off that airplane at a weight greater than the weight that would allow the airplane to be brought to a safe stop within the effective length of the runway, from any point during the takeoff before reaching 105 percent of minimum control speed (the minimum speed at which an airplane can be safely controlled in flight after an engine becomes inoperative) or 115 percent of the power off stalling speed in the takeoff configuration, whichever is greater.

(b) For the purposes of this section —

(1) It may be assumed that takeoff power is used on all engines during the acceleration;

(2) Not more than 50 percent of the reported headwind component, or not less than 150 percent of the reported tailwind component, may be taken into account;

(3) The average runway gradient (the difference between the elevations of the endpoints of the runway divided by the total length) must be considered if it is more than one-half of one percent;

(4) It is assumed that the airplane is operating in standard atmosphere; and

(5) For takeoff, "effective length of the runway" means the distance from the end of the runway at which the takeoff is started to a point at which the obstruction clearance plane associated with the other end of the runway intersects the runway centerline.

EXPLANATION

In the performance rules "large nontransport category airplanes" are airplanes certified under Aero Bulletin 7A, before the establishment of the transport category, and not modified or recertified in the transport category. They include Lockheed 18, the Curtis C-46, and the Douglas DC-3. Many of these aircraft have been modified by supplemental type certificates and have been recertified in the transport category. Takeoff performance for large nontransport airplanes may be based on standard temperatures without correction for ambient conditions.

Operators may only use C-46 type airplanes certified in the transport category in passenger carrying operations. [§§135.2(a) and 121.157(c).]

CROSS REFERENCES

121.157(c), Aircraft Certification and Equipment Requirements; 135.2(a), Air Taxi Operations with Large Aircraft.

ADVISORY CIRCULARS

AC 125-1 *Operations of Large Airplanes Subject to Federal Aviation Regulations Part 125* (1981).

135.391 LARGE NONTRANSPORT CATEGORY AIRPLANES: ENROUTE LIMITATIONS: ONE ENGINE INOPERATIVE

(a) Except as provided in paragraph (b) of this section, no person operating a large nontransport category airplane may take off that airplane at a weight that does not allow a rate of climb of at least 50 feet a minute, with the critical engine inoperative, at an altitude of at least 1,000 feet above the highest obstruction within five miles on each side of the intended track, or 5,000 feet, whichever is higher.

(b) Without regard to paragraph (a) of this section, if the Administrator finds that safe operations are not impaired, a person may operate the airplane at an altitude that allows the airplane, in case of engine failure, to clear all obstructions within five miles on each side of the intended track by 1,000 feet. If this procedure is used, the rate of descent for the appropriate weight and altitude is assumed to be 50 feet a minute greater than the rate in the approved performance data. Before approving such a procedure, the Administrator considers the following for the route, route segment, or area concerned:
  (1) The reliability of wind and weather forecasting.
  (2) The location and kinds of navigation aids.
  (3) The prevailing weather conditions, particularly the frequency and amount of turbulence normally encountered.
  (4) Terrain features.
  (5) Air traffic problems.
  (6) Any other operational factors that affect the operations.

(c) For the purposes of this section, it is assumed that —
  (1) The critical engine is inoperative;
  (2) The propeller of the inoperative engine is in the minimum drag position;
  (3) The wing flaps and landing gear are in the most favorable position;
  (4) The operating engines are operating at the maximum continuous power available;
  (5) The airplane is operating in standard atmosphere; and
  (6) The weight of the airplane is progressively reduced by the anticipated consumption of fuel and oil.

EXPLANATION

Any procedure approved under §135.391(b) must be set forth in the operator's manuals and training program.

The provisions of §135.181 must be complied with and can be more restrictive.

ADVISORY CIRCULARS

AC 125-1 *Operations of Large Airplanes Subject to Federal Aviation Regulations Part 125* (1981).

135.393 LARGE NONTRANSPORT CATEGORY AIRPLANES: LANDING LIMITATIONS: DESTINATION AIRPORTS

(a) No person operating a large nontransport category airplane may take off that airplane at a weight that —
  (1) Allowing for anticipated consumption of fuel and oil, is greater than the weight that would allow a full stop landing within 60 percent of the effective length of the most suitable runway at the destination airport; and
  (2) Is greater than the weight allowable if the landing is to be made on the runway —
    (i) With the greatest effective length in still air; and
    (ii) Required by the probable wind, taking into account not more than 50 percent of the headwind component or not less than 150 percent of the tailwind component.
(b) For the purpose of this section, it is assumed that —
  (1) The airplane passes directly over the intersection of the obstruction clearance plane and the runway at a height of 50 feet in a steady gliding approach at a true indicated airspeed of at least 1.3 Vso;
  (2) The landing does not require exceptional pilot skill; and
  (3) The airplane is operating in standard atmosphere.

ADVISORY CIRCULARS

AC 125-1 *Operations of Large Airplanes Subject to Federal Aviation Regulations Part 125* (1981).

135.395 LARGE NONTRANSPORT CATEGORY AIRPLANES: LANDING LIMITATIONS: ALTERNATE AIRPORTS

No person may select an airport as an alternate airport for a large nontransport category airplane unless that airplane (at the weight anticipated at the time of arrival), based on the assumptions in §135.393(b), can be brought to a full stop landing within 70 percent of the effective length of the runway.

CROSS REFERENCES

135.393, Large Nontransport Category Airplanes: Landing Limitations: Destination Airports.

ADVISORY CIRCULARS

AC 125-1 *Operations of Large Airplanes Subject to Federal Aviation Regulations Part 125* (1981).

135.397 SMALL TRANSPORT CATEGORY AIRPLANE PERFORMANCE OPERATING LIMITATIONS

(a) No person may operate a reciprocating engine powered small transport category airplane unless that person complies with the weight limitations in §135.365, the takeoff limitations in §135.367 (except paragraph (a)(3)), and the landing limitations in §§135.375 and 135.377.

(b) No person may operate a turbine engine powered small transport category airplane unless that person complies with the takeoff limitations in §135.379 (except paragraphs (d) and (f) and the landing limitations in §§135.385 and 135.387.

EXPLANATION

A small transport category airplane is an airplane, certified in the transport category, of less than 12,500 pounds maximum takeoff weight.

The performance rules for small transport category airplanes are the same as those for large transport category airplanes, except that operators of small transport category airplanes are not required to be able to show that the airplane is capable of clearing obstacles in the takeoff path in the case of the loss of an engine.

CROSS REFERENCES

135.365, Large Transport Category Airplanes: Reciprocating Engine Powered: Weight Limitations; 135.367, Large Transport Category Airplanes: Reciprocating Engine Powered: Takeoff Limitations; 135.375, Large Transport Category Airplanes: Reciprocating Engine Powered: Landing Limitations: Destination Airports; 135.377, Large Transport Category Airplanes: Reciprocating Engine Powered: Landing Limitations: Alternate Airports; 135.379, Large Transport Category Airplanes: Turbine Engine Powered: Takeoff Limitations; 135.385, Large Transport Category Airplanes: Turbine Engine Powered: Landing Limitations: Destination Airports; 135.387, Large Transport Category Airplanes: Turbine Engine Powered: Landing Limitations: Alternate Airports.

ADVISORY CIRCULARS

AC 135-7 *FAR 135: Additional Maintenance Requirements for Aircraft Type Certificated for Nine or Less Passenger Seats* (1978).

AC 135.169-1 *Small Propeller-Driven Air Taxi Airplanes that Meet §§135.169 (formerly 135.144)* (1979).

135.398 COMMUTER CATEGORY AIRPLANES PERFORMANCE OPERATING LIMITATIONS

(a) No person may operate a commuter category airplane unless that person complies with the takeoff weight limitations in the approved Airplane Flight Manual.

(b) No person may take off an airplane type certificated in the commuter category at a weight greater than that listed in the Airplane Flight Manual that allows a net takeoff flight path that clears all obstacles either by a height of at least 35 feet vertically, or at least 200 feet horizontally within the airport boundaries and by at least 300 feet horizontally after passing the boundaries.

(c) No person may operate a commuter category airplane unless that person complies with the landing limitations prescribed in §§135.385 and 135.387 of this Part. For purposes of this paragraph, §§135.385 and 135.387 are applicable to all commuter category airplanes notwithstanding their stated applicability to turbine-engine-powered large transport category airplanes.

(d) In determining maximum weights, minimum distances and flight paths under paragraphs (a) through (c) of this section, correction must be made for the runway to be used, the elevation of the airport, the effective runway gradient, and ambient temperature, and wind component at the time of takeoff.

(e) For the purposes of this section, the assumption is that the airplane is not banked before reaching a height of 50 feet as shown by the net takeoff flight path data in the Airplane Flight Manual and thereafter the maximum bank is not more than 15 degrees.

EXPLANATION

Reciprocating and turbopropeller airplanes with up to 19 passenger seats and 19,000 pounds maximum takeoff weight may be certified in the commuter category.

Commuter aircraft over 12,500 pounds maximum takeoff weight are defined as small airplanes by Part 23 for the purpose of Parts 21, 23, 36, 121, 135, and 129. They are defined as large airplanes for the purposes of Parts 61 and 91.

It should be noted that, insofar as enroute is concerned, §135.181 can be more restrictive.

CROSS REFERENCES

135.385, Large Transport Category Airplanes: Turbine Engine Powered: Landing Limitations: Destination Airports; 135.387, Large Transport Category Airplanes: Turbine Engine Powered: Landing Limitations: Alternate Airports.

135.399 SMALL NONTRANSPORT CATEGORY AIRPLANE PERFORMANCE OPERATING LIMITATIONS

(a) No person may operate a reciprocating engine or turbopropeller-powered small airplane that is certificated under §135.169 (b)(2), (3), (4), (5), or (6) unless that person complies with the takeoff weight limitations in the approved Airplane Flight Manual or equivalent for operations under this part, and, if the airplane is certificated under §135.169 (b)(4) or (5) with the landing weight limitations in the Approved Airplane Flight Manual or equivalent for operations under this part.

(b) No person may operate an airplane that is certificated under §135.169 (b)(6) unless that person complies with the landing limitations prescribed in §§135.385 and 135.387 of this part. For purposes of this paragraph, §§135.385 and 135.387 are applicable to reciprocating and turbopropeller-powered small airplanes notwithstanding their stated applicability to turbine engine powered large transport category airplanes.

CROSS REFERENCES

135.169(b)(2),(3),(4),(5), and (6), Additional Airworthiness Requirements; 135.385, Large Transport Category Airplanes: Turbine Engine Powered: Landing Limitations: Destination Airports; 135.387, Large Transport Category Airplanes: Turbine Engine Powered: Landing Limitations: Alternate Airports.

SUBPART J — MAINTENANCE, PREVENTIVE MAINTENANCE, AND ALTERATIONS

135.411 APPLICABILITY

(a) This subpart prescribes rules in addition to those in other parts of this chapter for the maintenance, preventive maintenance, and alterations for each certificate holder as follows:
   (1) Aircraft that are type certificated for a passenger seating configuration, excluding any pilot seat, of nine seats or less, shall be maintained under Parts 91 and 43 of this chapter and §§135.415, 135.417, and 135.421. An approved aircraft inspection program may be used under §135.419.
   (2) Aircraft that are type certificated for a passenger seating configuration, excluding any pilot seat, of ten seats or more, shall be maintained under a maintenance program in §§135.415, 135.417, 135.423 through 135.443.

(b) A certificate holder who is not otherwise required, may elect to maintain its aircraft under paragraph (a)(2) of this section.

EXPLANATION

Under this subpart, "certificated" means the number of passengers listed on the type data sheet or as modified by a Supplemental Type Certificate (STC). Blocking or removing passenger seats does not change the status of the aircraft.

If an operator who is not required to comply with §135.411(a)(2), elects to comply with it, the operator must demonstrate to the FAA that it has appropriate personnel and manuals to provide adequate means of compliance or the required Operations Specifications will not be issued authorizing the use of §135.411(a)(2).

For aircraft of nine seats or less used in cargo operations only there is no requirement for 100-hour inspections since §91.409(b) only applies to aircraft carrying passengers for hire.

While large and multi-engine turbine powered airplanes must meet the requirements of §91.409(e) and (f), an operator may also choose to operate under an Approved Aircraft Inspection Program. An Approved Aircraft Inspection Program can be used in lieu of compliance with §91.409 and Appendix D of Part 43.

An operator's maintenance/inspection training program should include company indoctrination and technical training, both classroom and on-the-job. Effective training is the basis for a successful maintenance/inspection program.

§135.91(a)(1)(ii) requires that equipment used for storage, generation, or dispensing of oxygen and carried aboard an aircraft must be maintained in accordance with the operator's approved maintenance program. Procedures contained in Department of Transportation regulations 49 C.F.R. Parts 100-199 are considered acceptable since Part 135 has no specific requirements for maintaining and testing pressure cylinders. Operators subject to §135.411(a)(1) are not eligible for continuing authorization to conduct ferry flights.

CROSS REFERENCES

91.401, Applicability; 91.407, Operation After Maintenance, Preventive Maintenance, Rebuilding, or Alteration; 91.409, Inspections; 135.415, Mechanical Reliability Reports; 135.417, Mechanical Interruption Summary Report; 135.419, Approved Aircraft Inspection Program; 135.421, Additional Maintenance Requirements; 135.423, Maintenance, Preventive Maintenance, and Alteration Organization; 135.443, Airworthiness Release or Aircraft Maintenance Log Entry.

NTSB DECISIONS

Respondent operated aircraft 9.8 hours beyond the due time for a 50-hour progressive Phase I inspection. Respondent admitted that the delay occurred, but said it was the result of inadvertence and was not an egregious or significant violation. The Board stated that, even if it is accepted that the delay was not deliberate, the violation nevertheless occurred. It went on to say that the operation of an aircraft "beyond inspection" is not an insignificant violation with little impact on safety. *Administrator v. Southeast Air, Inc.*, 5 NTSB 705, 708 (1985).

135.413 RESPONSIBILITY FOR AIRWORTHINESS

(a) Each certificate holder is primarily responsible for the airworthiness of its aircraft, including airframes, aircraft engines, propellers, rotors, appliances, and parts, and shall have its aircraft maintained under this chapter, and shall have defects repaired between required maintenance under Part 43 of this chapter.

(b) Each certificate holder who maintains its aircraft under §135.411(a)(2) shall —

(1) Perform the maintenance, preventive maintenance, and alteration of its aircraft, including airframe, aircraft engines, propellers, rotors, appliances, emergency equipment, and parts, under its manual and this chapter; or

(2) Make arrangements with another person for the performance of maintenance, preventive maintenance, or alteration. However, the certificate holder shall ensure that any maintenance, preventive maintenance, or alteration that is performed by another person is performed under the certificate holder's manual and this chapter.

EXPLANATION

Although Part 135 includes maintenance programs for air taxi aircraft, the performance standards for maintenance, preventive maintenance, rebuilding, and alteration are prescribed in Part 43.

Even though an operator may have maintenance performed by another person under §135.413(b)(2), the operator is still the one primarily responsible for ensuring that the work is done in accordance with the procedures outlined in the operator's manual.

A certificate holder is expected to make the same inquiries concerning a repair station's capability and performance that it does for its own facility. A repair station used by an operator to perform maintenance is an extension of the operator's organization and maintenance facility.

When a contractual arrangement exists regarding maintenance, the operator's manual must describe policies and procedures for administering the contract.

The Operations Specifications can authorize an operator to contract for an all-encompassing maintenance program. In this arrangement, all maintenance is performed in accordance with the contractor's programs, methods, procedures, and standards. The operator's equipment is considered part of the contractor's fleet for purposes of maintenance program content and maintenance intervals, including reliability control.

CROSS REFERENCES

135.411(a)(2), Applicability; 135.427, Manual Requirements.

ADVISORY CIRCULARS

AC 21-23 *Airworthiness Certification of Civil Aircraft Engine, Propellers, and Related Products* (1987).

AC 129-4 *Maintenance Programs for U.S. Registered Aircraft Under FAR Part 129* (1988).

AC 120-16C *Continuous Airworthiness Maintenance Programs* (1980).

135.415 MECHANICAL RELIABILITY REPORTS

(a) Each certificate holder shall report the occurrence or detection of each failure, malfunction, or defect in an aircraft concerning —
   (1) Fires during flight and whether the related fire-warning system functioned properly;
   (2) Fires during flight not protected by related fire-warning system;
   (3) False fire-warning during flight;
   (4) An exhaust system that causes damage during flight to the engine, adjacent structure, equipment, or components;
   (5) An aircraft component that causes accumulation or circulation of smoke, vapor, or toxic or noxious fumes in the crew compartment or passenger cabin during flight;
   (6) Engine shutdown during flight because of flameout;
   (7) Engine shutdown during flight when external damage to the engine or aircraft structure occurs;
   (8) Engine shutdown during flight due to foreign object ingestion or icing;
   (9) Shutdown of more than one engine during flight;
   (10) A propeller feathering system or ability of the system to control overspeed during flight;
   (11) A fuel or fuel-dumping system that affects fuel flow or causes hazardous leakage during flight;
   (12) An unwanted landing gear extension or retraction or opening or closing of landing gear doors during flight.
   (13) Brake system components that result in loss of brake actuating force when the aircraft is in motion on the ground;
   (14) Aircraft structure that requires major repair;
   (15) Cracks, permanent deformation, or corrosion of aircraft structures, if more than the maximum acceptable to the manufacturer or the FAA; and
   (16) Aircraft components or systems that result in taking emergency actions during flight (except action to shut-down an engine).

(b) For the purpose of this section, "during flight" means the period from the moment the aircraft leaves the surface of the earth on takeoff until it touches down on landing.

(c) In addition to the reports required by paragraph (a) of this section, each certificate holder shall report any other failure, malfunction, or defect in an aircraft that occurs or is detected at any time if, in its opinion, the failure, malfunction, or defect has endangered or may endanger the safe operation of the aircraft.

(d) Each certificate holder shall send each report required by this section, in writing, covering each 24-hour period beginning at 0900 hours local time of each day and ending at 0900 hours local time on the next day to the FAA Flight Standards District Office charged with the overall inspection of the certificate holder. Each report of occurrences during a 24-hour period must be mailed or delivered to that office within the next 72 hours. However, a report that is due on Saturday or Sunday may be mailed or delivered on the following Monday and one that is due on a holiday may be mailed or delivered on the next work day. For aircraft operated in areas where mail is not collected, reports may be mailed or delivered within 72 hours after the aircraft returns to a point where the mail is collected.

(e) The certificate holder shall transmit the reports required by this section on a form and in a manner prescribed by the Administrator, and shall include as much of the following as is available:

(1) The type and identification number of the aircraft.
(2) The name of the operator.
(3) The date.
(4) The nature of the failure, malfunction, or defect.
(5) Identification of the part and system involved, including available information pertaining to type designation of the major component and time since last overhaul, if known.
(6) Apparent cause of the failure, malfunction or defect (e.g., wear, crack, design deficiency, or personnel error).
(7) Other pertinent information necessary for more complete identification, determination of seriousness, or corrective action.

(f) A certificate holder that is also the holder of a type certificate (including a supplemental type certificate), a Parts Manufacturer Approval, or a Technical Standard Order Authorization, or that is the licensee of a type certificate need not report a failure, malfunction, or defect under this section if the failure, malfunction, or defect has been reported by it under §21.3 or §37.17 of this chapter or under the accident reporting provisions of Part 830 of the regulations of the National Transportation Safety Board.

(g) No person may withhold a report required by this section even though all information required by this section is not available.

(h) When the certificate holder gets additional information, including information from the manufacturer or other agency, concerning a report required by this section, it shall expeditiously submit it as a supplement to the first report and reference the date and place of submission of the first report.

EXPLANATION

The information received through mechanical reliability reports is used to determine safety trends in aircraft and aircraft systems.

An operator must establish a system whereby the office/person responsible for making the required reports receives the required information in sufficient time to meet the 72-hour requirement.

It should be noted that the term "flight" as used in "during flight" in this regulation differs from the way it is used in "flight time" in Part 1, i.e. "liftoff to touchdown" as opposed to "block to block."

The reporting requirement of this regulation is continuing in nature. As additional information is obtained regarding the occurrence, it must be reported to the FAA, e.g. results of a teardown of a unit.

This reporting requirement applies to all aircraft, i.e. single-, multi-engine, airplanes and helicopters.

CROSS REFERENCES

21.3, Reporting of Failures, Malfunctions, and Defects; 135.65, Reporting Mechanical Irregularities; 135.179(a)(4), Inoperable Instruments and Equipment; 135.417, Mechanical Interruption Summary Report.

ADVISORY CIRCULARS

AC 43-9B *Maintenance Records* (1984).

135.417 MECHANICAL INTERRUPTION SUMMARY REPORT

Each certificate holder shall mail or deliver, before the end of the 10th day of the following month, a summary report of the following occurrences in multi-engine aircraft for the preceding month to the FAA Flight Standards District Office charged with the overall inspection of the certificate holder:

(a) Each interruption to a flight, unscheduled change of aircraft en route, or unscheduled stop or diversion from a route, caused by known or suspected mechanical difficulties or malfunctions that are not required to be reported under §135.415.

(b) The number of propeller featherings in flight, listed by type of propeller and engine and aircraft on which it was installed. Propeller featherings for training, demonstration, or flight check purposes need not be reported.

EXPLANATION

The Mechanical Interruption Summary Report requirement applies only to multi-engine aircraft as opposed to Mechanical Reliability Reports, which apply to all aircraft.

The operators's manual should contain procedures for the timely acquisition and distribution of the reports required by this section.

This section does not limit the occurrences that must be reported to those that occur "during flight." Therefore, any mechanical irregularities or defects that appear before, during, and after a flight must be reported.

CROSS REFERENCES

135.17, Amendment of Operations Specifications; 135.21, Manual Requirements; 135.25, Aircraft Requirements; 135.417, Mechanical Interruption Summary Report.

ADVISORY CIRCULARS

AC 43-9B *Maintenance Records* (1984).

135.419 APPROVED AIRCRAFT INSPECTION PROGRAM

(a) Whenever the Administrator finds that the aircraft inspections required or allowed under Part 91 of this chapter are not adequate to meet this part, or upon application by a certificate holder, the Administrator may amend the certificate holder's Operations Specifications under §135.17, to require or allow an approved aircraft inspection program for any make and model aircraft of which the certificate holder has the exclusive use of at least one aircraft (as defined in §135.25(b)).

(b) A certificate holder who applies for an amendment of its Operations Specifications to allow an approved aircraft inspection program must submit that program with its application for approval by the Administrator.

(c) Each certificate holder who is required by its Operations Specifications to have an approved aircraft inspection program shall submit a program for approval by the Administrator within 30 days of the amendment of its Operations Specifications or within any other period that the Administrator may prescribe in the Operations Specifications.

(d) The aircraft inspection program submitted for approval by the Administrator must contain the following:

(1) Instructions and procedures for the conduct of aircraft inspections (which must include necessary tests and checks), setting forth in detail the parts and areas of the airframe, engines, propellers, rotors, and appliances, including emergency equipment that must be inspected.

(2) A schedule for the performance of the aircraft inspections under paragraph (1) of this paragraph expressed in terms of the time in service, calendar time, number of system operations, or any combination of these.

(3) Instructions and procedures for recording discrepancies found during inspections and correction or deferral of discrepancies including form and disposition of records.

(e) After approval, the certificate holder shall include the approved aircraft inspection program in the manual required by §135.21.

(f) Whenever the Administrator finds that revisions to an approved aircraft inspection program are necessary for the continued adequacy of the program, the certificate holder shall, after notification by the Administrator, make any changes in the program found by the Administrator to be necessary. The certificate holder may petition the Administrator to reconsider the notice to make any changes in a program. The petition must be filed with the representatives of the Administrator assigned to it within 30 days after the certificate holder receives the notice. Except in the case of an emergency requiring immediate action in the interest of safety, the filing of the petition stays the notice pending a decision by the Administrator.

(g) Each certificate holder who has an approved aircraft inspection program shall have each aircraft that is subject to the program inspected in accordance with the program.

(h) The registration number of each aircraft that is subject to an approved aircraft inspection program must be included in the Operations Specifications of the certificate holder.

EXPLANATION

While large and multi-engine turbine powered airplanes must meet the requirements of §91.409(e) and (f), an operator may also choose to operate under an Approved Aircraft Inspection Program.

An operator seeking approval to amend inspection or overhaul periods must justify the requested change. Justification should include the following: past operating experience; environmental conditions; inspection program provisions; at least two overhaul tear-down reports; and any other substantiating information.

A manufacturer's extension of the recommended inspection or overhaul interval does not automatically change an approved aircraft inspection program. Approval must be obtained from the Federal Aviation Administration to revise the approved program to reflect the manufacturer's recommendations.

The program must include the total aircraft, including all installed equipment such as communication and navigational equipment, cargo provisions, and emergency equipment.

CROSS REFERENCES

43.11, Content, Form, and Disposition of Records for Inspections Conducted Under Parts 91 and 125 and §§135.411(a)(1) and 135.419 of this Chapter; 91.407, Operations After Maintenance, Preventive Maintenance, Rebuilding, or Alteration; 135.17, Amendment of Operations Specifications; 135.25(b), Aircraft Requirements; 135.21, Manual Requirements.

ADVISORY CIRCULARS

AC 21-23 *Airworthiness Certification of Civil Aircraft Engine, Propellers, and Related Products* (1987).

AC 120-17A *Maintenance Control by Reliability Methods* (1978).

AC 121-16 *Maintenance Certification Procedures* (1970).

AC 121-22 *Maintenance Review Board (MRB)* (1977).

135.421 ADDITIONAL MAINTENANCE REQUIREMENTS

(a) Each certificate holder who operates an aircraft type certificated for a passenger seating configuration, excluding any pilot seat, of nine seats or less, must comply with the manufacturer's recommended maintenance programs, or a program approved by the Administrator, for each aircraft engine, propeller, rotor, and each item of emergency equipment required by this chapter.
(b) For the purpose of this section, a manufacturer's maintenance program is one which is contained in the maintenance manual or maintenance instructions set forth by the manufacturer as required by this chapter for the aircraft, aircraft engine, propeller, rotor, or item of emergency equipment.

EXPLANATION

The "manufacturer's recommended maintenance program" does not include service letters or bulletins that are not required to be complied with by an Airworthiness Directive unless they are part of the maintenance manual or maintenance instructions required by the Federal Aviation Regulations (Parts 23, 33 or 35).

An operator, who elects to comply with §135.411(b), must still comply with this section.

Carry-on oxygen equipment used for medical purposes is included in the coverage of this section. [§135.91(a)(1)(ii)]

Part 1 defines a propeller as including the controls supplied by the manufacturer.

Generally, the manufacturer's maintenance program does not include the avionics installed in the aircraft. The operator may have to develop an inspection and maintenance program for this equipment.

CROSS REFERENCES

135.427, Manual Requirements.

ADVISORY CIRCULARS

AC 135-7 *FAR 135: Additional Maintenance Requirements for Aircraft Type Certificated for Nine or Less Passenger Seats* (1978).

135.423 MAINTENANCE, PREVENTIVE MAINTENANCE, AND ALTERATION ORGANIZATION

(a) Each certificate holder that performs any of its maintenance (other than required inspections), preventive maintenance, or alterations, and each person with whom it arranges for the performance of that work, must have an organization adequate to perform the work.

(b) Each certificate holder that performs any inspections required by its manual under §135.427(b)(2) or (3), (in this subpart referred to as "required inspections"), and each person with whom it arranges for the performance of that work, must have an organization adequate to perform that work.

(c) Each person performing required inspections in addition to other maintenance, preventive maintenance, or alterations, shall organize the performance of those functions so as to separate the required inspection functions from the other maintenance, preventive maintenance, and alteration functions. The separation shall be below the level of administrative control at which overall responsibility for the required inspection functions and other maintenance, preventive maintenance, and alteration functions is exercised.

EXPLANATION

This section applies to operators using aircraft type certificated for 10 seats or more, excluding any pilot seat.

Separation of required inspections from maintenance functions is necessary to ensure that work on required inspection items is properly performed.

A person authorized to do inspections in one area is not prohibited from performing maintenance in another area. This section only provides that the person conducting the required inspection may not be the one who performs the work on the item.

An operator complying with §135.411(a)(2) may use its employees who are not certificated mechanics, but who are qualified to be certificated as repairman under §65.101 when recommended by the operator.

CROSS REFERENCES

65.101, Eligibility Requirements: General [Repairmen]; 135.411, Applicability; 135.427(b)(2) and (3), Manual Requirements.

ADVISORY CIRCULARS

AC 120-17A *Maintenance Control by Reliability Methods* (1978).

AC 121-16 *Maintenance Certification Procedures* (1970).

AC 121-22 *Maintenance Review Board (MRB)* (1977).

135.425 MAINTENANCE, PREVENTIVE MAINTENANCE, AND ALTERATION PROGRAMS

Each certificate holder shall have an inspection program and a program covering other maintenance, preventive maintenance, and alterations, that ensures that —

(a) Maintenance, preventive maintenance, and alterations performed by it, or by other persons, are performed under the certificate holder's manual;

(b) Competent personnel and adequate facilities and equipment are provided for the proper performance of maintenance, preventive maintenance, and alterations; and

(c) Each aircraft released to service is airworthy and has been properly maintained for operations under this part.

EXPLANATION

The certificate holder is the one primarily responsible for compliance with this section even when it contracts with a certificated facility/operator for the accomplishment of the work. Accordingly, it must ensure that the one performing the work has a current version of the certificate holder's manual and that the contract personnel are familiar with the procedures set forth in the manual.

The publications of a contractor may be adopted in part or in total by the operator as methods, techniques, and standards to be used. The operator's manual must specifically describe the applicability and authority of the concerned publications.

The operator's manual must describe the policies and procedures for administering contractual arrangements for maintenance, preventive maintenance, and alterations.

ADVISORY CIRCULARS

AC 120-17A *Maintenance Control by Reliability Methods* (1978).

AC 121-16 *Maintenance Certification Procedures* (1970).

AC 121-22 *Maintenance Review Board (MRB)* (1977).

AC 145-4 *Inspection, Retread, Repair and Alterations of Aircraft Tires* (1982).

135.427 MANUAL REQUIREMENTS

(a) Each certificate holder shall put in its manual the chart or description of the certificate holder's organization required by §135.423 and a list of persons with whom it has arranged for the performance of any of its required inspections, other maintenance, preventive maintenance, or alterations, including a general description of that work.

(b) Each certificate holder shall put in its manual the programs required by §135.425 that must be followed in performing maintenance, preventive maintenance, and alterations of that certificate holder's aircraft, including airframes, aircraft engines, propellers, rotors, appliances, emergency equipment, and parts, and must include at least the following:

(1) The method of performing routine and nonroutine maintenance (other than required inspections), preventive maintenance, and alterations.

(2) A designation of the items of maintenance and alteration that must be inspected (required inspections) including at least those that could result in a failure, malfunction, or defect endangering the safe operations of the aircraft, if not performed properly or if improper parts or materials are used.

(3) The method of performing required inspections and a designation by occupational title of personnel authorized to perform each required inspection.

(4) Procedures for the reinspection of work performed under previous required inspection findings ("buy-back procedures").

(5) Procedures, standards, and limits necessary for required inspections and acceptance or rejection of the items required to be inspected and for periodic inspection and calibration of precision tools, measuring devices, and test equipment.

(6) Procedures to ensure that all required inspections are performed.

(7) Instructions to prevent any person who performs any item of work from performing any required inspection of that work.

(8) Instructions and procedures to prevent any decision of an inspector regarding any required inspection from being countermanded by persons other than supervisory personnel of the inspection unit, or a person at the level of administrative control that has overall responsibility for the management of both the required inspection functions and the other maintenance, preventive maintenance, and alterations functions.

(9) Procedures to ensure that required inspections, other maintenance, preventive maintenance, and alterations that are not completed as a result of work interruptions are properly completed before the aircraft is released to service.

(c) Each certificate holder shall put in its manual a suitable system (which may include a coded system) that provides for the retention of the following information —

(1) A description (or reference to data acceptable to the Administrator) of the work performed;

(2) The name of the person performing the work if the work is performed by a person outside the organization of the certificate holder; and

(3) The name or other positive identification of the individual approving the work.

EXPLANATION

This section does not prevent an operator from having maintenance performed by persons who are not listed in the manual. The operator can have maintenance performed on an "on call" basis. §135.23(h) requires that the operator's manual include procedures for a pilot to obtain maintenance at a place where previous arrangements have not been made by the operator.

Under this section an operator is authorized to use a coded system with regard to maintenance records which eliminates the requirement for signatures and a written description of the work accomplished.

The manual is used to control and direct personnel. It must define all aspects of the maintenance operation.

The manual must have the job descriptions for those positions set forth in the organizational chart or description.

This section emphasizes the necessity for the separation of the inspection and the maintenance performance functions.

It is essential that there be appropriate procedures to ensure that inspections, maintenance, preventive maintenance, and alterations not completed as a result of a shift change or any type of work interruption are properly completed prior to the aircraft being released to service.

In designating required inspection items, it should be remembered that many maintenance tasks that are essential to a reliable and safe aircraft are not necessarily so critical that they should be required inspection items, e.g. tire changes.

CROSS REFERENCES

135.21, Manual Requirements; 135.167, Emergency Equipment: Extended Overwater Operations; 135.177, Emergency Equipment Requirements for Aircraft Having a Passenger Seating Configuration of More than 19 Passengers; 135.178, Additional Emergency Equipment; 135.423, Maintenance, Preventive Maintenance, and Alteration Organization; 135.425, Maintenance, Preventive Maintenance, and Alteration Programs; 135.429, Required Inspection Personnel; 135.437, Authority to Perform and Approve Maintenance, Preventive Maintenance, and Alterations; 135.443, Airworthiness Release or Aircraft Maintenance Log Entry.

ADVISORY CIRCULARS

AC 120-17A *Maintenance Control by Reliability Methods* (1978).

135.429 REQUIRED INSPECTION PERSONNEL

(a) No person may use any person to perform required inspections unless the person performing the inspection is appropriately certificated, properly trained, qualified, and authorized to do so.

(b) No person may allow any person to perform a required inspection unless, at the time, the person performing that inspection is under the supervision and control of an inspection unit.

(c) No person may perform a required inspection if that person performed the item of work required to be inspected.

(d) In the case of rotorcraft that operate in remote areas or sites, the Administrator may approve procedures for the performance of required inspection items by a pilot when no other qualified person is available, provided —

(1) The pilot is employed by the certificate holder;

(2) It can be shown to the satisfaction of the Administrator that each pilot authorized to perform required inspections is properly trained and qualified;

(3) The required inspection is a result of a mechanical interruption and is not a part of a certificate holder's continuous airworthiness maintenance program;

(4) Each item is inspected after each flight until the item has been inspected by an appropriately certificated mechanic other than the one who originally performed the item of work; and

(5) Each item of work that is a required inspection item that is part of the flight control system shall be flight tested and reinspected before the aircraft is approved for return to service.

(e) Each certificate holder shall maintain, or shall determine that each person with whom it arranges to perform its required inspections maintains a current listing of persons who have been trained, qualified, and authorized to conduct required inspections. The persons must be identified by name, occupational title, and the inspections that they are authorized to perform. The certificate holder (or person with whom it arranges to perform its required inspections) shall give written information to each person so authorized, describing the extent of that person's responsibilities, authorities, and inspectional limitations. The list shall be made available for inspection by the Administrator upon request.

EXPLANATION

This section relates to the inspection of those items of maintenance and alterations that are designated in the operator's manual in accordance with §135.427(b)(2).

The pilots authorized by the operator to exercise the privileges of §135.429(d), must, by reason of the training provided them, have the same level of competency as an inspector at the home base to ensure safety in all circumstances.

A remote area is considered to be an area that is out of the way, far removed from normal support services, or not easily accessible by land or sea, e.g. offshore oil derricks, villages in the tundra area of Alaska, and mining sites in the upper Sierra Nevada.

CROSS REFERENCES

135.427, Manual Requirements.

ADVISORY CIRCULARS

AC 129-4 *Maintenance Programs for U.S. Registered Aircraft Under FAR Part 129* (1988).

135.431 CONTINUING ANALYSIS AND SURVEILLANCE

(a) Each certificate holder shall establish and maintain a system for the continuing analysis and surveillance of the performance and effectiveness of its inspection program and the program covering other maintenance, preventive maintenance, and alterations and for the correction of any deficiency in those programs, regardless of whether those programs are carried out by the certificate holder or by another person.
(b) Whenever the Administrator finds that either or both of the programs described in paragraph (a) of this section does not contain adequate procedures and standards to meet this part, the certificate holder shall, after notification by the Administrator, make changes in those programs requested by the Administrator.
(c) A certificate holder may petition the Administrator to reconsider the notice to make a change in a program. The petition must be filed with the FAA Flight Standards District Office charged with the overall inspection of the certificate holder within 30 days after the certificate holder receives the notice. Except in the case of an emergency requiring immediate action in the interest of safety, the filing of the petition stays the notice pending a decision by the Administrator.

EXPLANATION

The responsibility for administering or controlling a continuing analysis and surveillance program can never be contracted out. However, contract organizations may be used to collect operational data, make analyses and recommendations, perform audits, and report information to be used by the operator in identifying deficiencies and implementing corrective actions. Programs differ depending on size and complexity of the certificate holder's operation. However, every program must have, as a minimum, monitoring of mechanical performance and audit functions.

Audits should be accomplished by other than the maintenance organization. An audit should normally be an on-the-scene observation and should be an on-going activity with periodic audits of contract agencies. The audit should look at the adequacy of equipment and facilities, storage and protection of parts, competency of maintenance personnel, and housekeeping. An approved reliability program (relating operating experience to established maintenance control) can be used to fulfill the monitoring mechanical performance functions requirement of a continuing analysis and surveillance program.

ADVISORY CIRCULARS

AC 120-16C *Continuous Airworthiness Maintenance Programs* (1980).

AC 120-17A *Maintenance Control by Reliability Methods* (1978).

135.433 MAINTENANCE AND PREVENTIVE MAINTENANCE TRAINING PROGRAM

Each certificate holder or a person performing maintenance or preventive maintenance functions for it shall have a training program to ensure that each person (including inspection personnel) who determines the adequacy of work done is fully informed about procedures and techniques and new equipment in use and is competent to perform that person's duties.

EXPLANATION

A certificate holder should ensure that proper records are maintained to demonstrate that all persons have received the appropriate training. Lack of adequate records raises the presumption that the required training was not accomplished. A certificate holder contracting out inspection/maintenance must ensure, by whatever means necessary, that the contractor provides and records the required training.

Recurrent training should include the deficiencies discovered through continuous analysis and surveillance and/or reliability programs and the corrective actions required. Special maintenance/inspection training is necessary when new, modified or different types of aircraft and/or equipment are introduced in the certificate holder's operations.

135.435 CERTIFICATE REQUIREMENTS

(a) Except for maintenance, preventive maintenance, alterations, and required inspections performed by repair stations certificated under the provisions of Subpart C of Part 145 of this chapter, each person who is directly in charge of maintenance, preventive maintenance, or alterations, and each person performing required inspections must hold an appropriate airman certificate.

(b) For the purpose of this section, a person "directly in charge" is each person assigned to a position in which that person is responsible for the work of a shop or station that performs maintenance, preventive maintenance, alterations, or other functions affecting airworthiness. A person who is "directly in charge" need not physically observe and direct each worker constantly but must be available for consultation and decision on matters requiring instruction or decision from higher authority than that of the person performing the work.

CROSS REFERENCES

Part 65, Subpart D, Mechanics and Subpart E, Repairmen.

ADVISORY CIRCULARS

AC 121-16 *Maintenance Certification Procedures* (1970).
AC 121-22 *Maintenance Review Board (MRB)* (1977).

135.437 AUTHORITY TO PERFORM AND APPROVE MAINTENANCE, PREVENTIVE MAINTENANCE, AND ALTERATIONS

(a) A certificate holder may perform, or make arrangements with other persons to perform, maintenance, preventive maintenance, and alterations as provided in its maintenance manual. In addition, a certificate holder may perform these functions for another certificate holder as provided in the maintenance manual of the other certificate holder.

(b) A certificate holder may approve any airframe, aircraft engine, propeller, rotor, or appliance for return to service after maintenance, preventive maintenance, or alterations that are performed under paragraph (a) of this section. However, in the case of a major repair or alteration, the work must have been done in accordance with technical data approved by the Administrator.

EXPLANATION

§135.37(a) authorizes maintenance arrangements between like certificate holders. There is no requirement that they operate comparable equipment.

CROSS REFERENCES

135.37(a), Management Personnel Required; 135.427, Manual Requirements.

ADVISORY CIRCULARS

AC 120-17A *Maintenance Control by Reliability Methods* (1978).

AC 121-22 *Maintenance Review Board (MRB)* (1977).

135.439 MAINTENANCE RECORDING REQUIREMENTS

(a) Each certificate holder shall keep (using the system specified in the manual required in §35.427) the following records for the periods specified in paragraph (b) of this section:
  (1) All the records necessary to show that all requirements for the issuance of an airworthiness release under §135.443 have been met.
  (2) Records containing the following information:
    (i) The total time in service of the airframe, engine, propeller, and rotor.
    (ii) The current status of life-limited parts of each airframe, engine, propeller, rotor, and appliance.
    (iii) The time since last overhaul of each item installed on the aircraft which are required to be overhauled on a specified time basis.
    (iv) The identification of the current inspection status of the aircraft including the time since the last inspection required by the inspection program under which the aircraft and its appliances are maintained.
    (v) The current status of applicable airworthiness directives, including the date and methods of compliance, and, if the airworthiness directive involves recurring action, the time and date when the next action is required.
    (vi) A list of current major alterations and repairs to each airframe, engine, propeller, rotor, and appliance.

(b) Each certificate holder shall retain the records required to be kept by this section for the following periods:
  (1) Except for the records of the last complete overhaul of each airframe, engine, propeller, rotor, and appliance the records specified in paragraph (a)(1) of this section shall be retained until the work is repeated or superseded by other work or for one year after the work is performed.
  (2) The records of the last complete overhaul of each airframe, engine, propeller, rotor, and appliance shall be retained until the work is superseded by work of equivalent scope and detail.
  (3) The records specified in paragraph (a)(2) of this section shall be retained and transferred with the aircraft at the time the aircraft is sold.

(c) The certificate holder shall make all maintenance records required to be kept by this section available for inspection by the Administrator or any representative of the National Transportation Safety Board.

EXPLANATION

When acquiring an aircraft from another party, the purchase agreement should contain a provision requiring the seller to provide all documentation it has regarding the aircraft along with the current maintenance records.

The certificate holder is responsible for ensuring that the information required by §135.439(a)(2) is complete and accurate as to all equipment used in its operation.

Prior to purchasing any aircraft or other equipment described in this section, an operator should ensure there are adequate records so the aircraft, etc. qualifies for use in its operation.

In the case of propellers, it is required that the operator's records contain the total time in service of the blades, hubs, and other control components normally supplied by the manufacturer.

As part of the record, the current status (the time remaining before retirement) of a life-limited part should be included. The record should also include any modification of the part in accordance with airworthiness directives, service bulletins, or product improvement by manufacturer or operator.

If the current status of life-limited parts records cannot be established or has not been maintained, and historical records are not available, the airworthiness of that product cannot be determined, and it must be removed from service.

Life-limited parts may not be rebuilt and certified to zero time.

If the operator has obtained prior approval for an alternative method of compliance with an airworthiness directive, the records must contain this approval.

CROSS REFERENCES

135.427, Manual Requirements; 135.443, Airworthiness Release or Aircraft Maintenance Log Entry; §902(e) of the Federal Aviation Act of 1958, as amended, [49 U.S.C. App. §1472(e)], Failure to File Reports; Falsification of Records.

ADVISORY CIRCULARS

AC 43-9B *Maintenance Records* (1984)

FAA CHIEF COUNSEL OPINIONS

A complete audit trail to the origin is not necessary for all life-limited parts. However, it is the responsibility of the operator to substantiate that its recordkeeping system produces sufficient and accurate data to determine how the current status was obtained. The requirement is merely to show with a sufficient degree of certainty that the time elapsed on a life-limited part is correct. An audit trail tracing a life-limited part back to its origin would be required only in those situations where the operator's records are so incomplete that an accurate determination of the time elapsed on the life-limited part could not be made. (6-1-92).

135.441 TRANSFER OF MAINTENANCE RECORDS

Each certificate holder who sells a United States registered aircraft shall transfer to the purchaser, at the time of the sale, the following records of that aircraft, in plain language form or in coded form which provides for the preservation and retrieval of information in a manner acceptable to the Administrator:

(a) The records specified in §135.439(a)(2).

(b) The records specified in §135.439(a)(1) which are not included in the records covered by paragraph (a) of this section, except that the purchaser may allow the seller to keep physical custody of such record. However, custody of records by the seller does not relieve the purchaser of its responsibility under §135.439(c) to make the records available for inspection by the Administrator or any representative of the National Transportation Safety Board.

EXPLANATION

If the operator allows the seller to retain physical custody of certain records as provided for in §135.441(b), the operator should include in the purchase agreement, or in a separate written agreement, a provision requiring the seller, upon request of the operator, to make such records available for inspection by the Administrator or any representative of the National Transportation Safety Board.

CROSS REFERENCES

91.419, Transfer of Maintenance Records; 135.439(a)(1)(2)and (c), Maintenance Recording Requirements.

ADVISORY CIRCULARS

AC 43-9B *Maintenance Records* (1984).

135.443 AIRWORTHINESS RELEASE OR AIRCRAFT MAINTENANCE LOG ENTRY

(a) No certificate holder may operate an aircraft after maintenance, preventive maintenance, or alternations are performed on the aircraft unless the certificate holder prepares, or causes the person with whom the certificate holder arranges for the performance of the maintenance, preventive maintenance, or alternations, to prepare —
 (1) An airworthiness release; or
 (2) An appropriate entry in the aircraft maintenance log.

(b) The airworthiness release or log entry required by paragraph (a) of this section must —
 (1) Be prepared in accordance with the procedure in the certificate holder's manual;
 (2) Include a certification that —
  (i) The work was performed in accordance with the requirements of the certificate holder's manual;
  (ii) All items required to be inspected were inspected by an authorized person who determined that the work was satisfactorily completed;
  (iii) No known condition exists that would make the aircraft unairworthy;
  (iv) So far as the work performed is concerned, the aircraft is in condition for safe operation; and
 (3) Be signed by an authorized certificated mechanic or repairman, except that a certificated repairman may sign the release or entry only for the work for which that person is employed and for which that person is certificated.

Notwithstanding paragraph (b)(3) of this section, after maintenance, preventive maintenance, or alterations performed by a repair station certificated under the provisions of Subpart C of Part 145, the airworthiness release or log entry required by paragraph (a) of this section may be signed by a person authorized by that repair station.

(c) Instead of restating each of the conditions of the certification required by paragraph (b) of this section, the certificate holder may state in its manual that the signature of an authorized certificated mechanic or repairman constitutes that certification.

EXPLANATION

The exception to the requirement of §135.433(b)(3) relating to repair stations certificated under Subpart C, Part 145 permits Part 135 operators, operating under the provisions of §135.411(a)(2), to use foreign repair stations certificated under Part 145.

Unless an operator's approved company procedures require it, use of the minimum equipment list (MEL) does not require a new airworthiness release.

Operators under an inspection program do not require an airworthiness release.

CROSS REFERENCES

135.427, Manual Requirements; 135.429, Required Inspection Personnel.

ADVISORY CIRCULARS

AC 21-23 *Airworthiness Certification of Civil Aircraft Engine, Propellers, and Related Products* (1987).

AC 120-16C *Continuous Airworthiness Maintenance Programs* (1980).

APPENDIX A

ADDITIONAL AIRWORTHINESS STANDARDS FOR 10 OR MORE PASSENGER AIRPLANES

Applicability

1. *Applicability.* This appendix prescribes the additional airworthiness standards required by §135.169.
2. *References.* Unless otherwise provided, references in this appendix to specific sections of Part 23 of the Federal Aviation Regulations (FAR Part 23) are to those sections of Part 23 in effect on March 30, 1967.

Flight Requirements

3. *General.* Compliance must be shown with the applicable requirements of Subpart B of FAR Part 23, as supplemented or modified in §§ 4 through 10.

Performance

4. *General.*
   (a) Unless otherwise prescribed in this appendix, compliance with each applicable performance requirement in §§ 4 through 7 must be shown for ambient atmospheric conditions and still air.
   (b) The performance must correspond to the propulsive thrust available under the particular ambient atmospheric conditions and the particular flight condition. The available propulsive thrust must correspond to engine power or thrust, not exceeding the approved power or thrust less —
      (1) Installation losses; and
      (2) The power or equivalent thrust absorbed by accessories and services appropriate to the particular ambient atmospheric conditions and the particular flight condition.
   (c) Unless otherwise prescribed in this appendix, the applicant must select the takeoff, enroute, and landing configurations for the airplane.
      (3) The airplane configuration may vary with weight, altitude, and temperature, to the extent they are compatible with the operating procedures required by paragraph (e) of this section.
   (e) Unless otherwise prescribed in this appendix, in determining the critical engine inoperative takeoff performance, the accelerate-stop distance, takeoff distance, changes in the airplane's configuration, speed, power, and thrust must be made under procedures established by the applicant for operation in service.
   (f) Procedures for the execution of balked landings must be established by the applicant and included in the Airplane Flight Manual.

(g) The procedures established under paragraphs (e) and (f) of this section must —
   (1) Be able to be consistently executed in service by a crew of average skill;
   (2) Use methods or devices that are safe and reliable; and
   (3) Include allowance for any time delays, in the execution of the procedures, that may reasonably be expected in service.

5. *Takeoff.*
   (a) *General.* Takeoff speeds, the accelerate-stop distance, the takeoff distance, and the one-engine-inoperative takeoff flight path data (described in paragraphs (b), (c), (d), and (f) of this section), must be determined for —
      (1) Each weight, altitude, and ambient temperature within the operational limits selected by the applicant;
      (2) The selected configuration for takeoff;
      (3) The center of gravity in the most unfavorable position;
      (4) The operating engine within approved operating limitations; and
      (5) Takeoff data based on smooth, dry, hard-surface runway.
   (b) *Takeoff speeds.*
      (1) The decision speed V_1 is the calibrated airspeed on the ground at which, as a result of engine failure or other reasons, the pilot is assumed to have made a decision to continue or discontinue the takeoff. The speed V_1 must be selected by the applicant but may not be less than —
         (i) 1.10 V_S;
         (ii) 1.10 V_{MC};
         (iii) A speed that allows acceleration to V_1 and stop under paragraph (c) of this section; or
         (iv) A speed at which the airplane can be rotated for takeoff and shown to be adequate to safely continue the takeoff, using normal piloting skill, when the critical engine is suddenly made inoperative.
      (2) The initial climb out speed V_2, in terms of calibrated airspeed, must be selected by the applicant so as to allow the gradient of climb required in §6(b)(2), but it must not be less than V_1 or less than 1.2 V_S.
      (3) Other essential take off speeds necessary for safe operation of the airplane.
   (c) *Accelerate-stop distance.*
      (1) The accelerate-stop distance is the sum of the distances necessary to —
         (i) Accelerate the airplane from a standing start to V_1; and
         (ii) Come to a full stop from the point at which V_1 is reached assuming that in the case of engine failure, failure of the critical engine is recognized by the pilot at the speed V_1.
      (2) Means other than wheel brakes may be used to determine the accelerate-stop distance if that means is available with the critical engine inoperative and —
         (i) Is safe and reliable;
         (ii) Is used so that consistent results can be expected under normal operating conditions; and
         (iii) Is such that exceptional skill is not required to control the airplane.

(d) *All engines operating takeoff distance.* The all engine operating takeoff distance is the horizontal distance required to takeoff and climb to a height of 50 feet above the takeoff surface under the procedures in FAR 23.51(a).

(e) *One-engine-inoperative-takeoff.* Determine the weight for each altitude and temperature within the operational limits established for the airplane, at which the airplane has the capability, after failure of the critical engine at V_1 determined under paragraph (b) of this section, to take off and climb at not less than V_2, to a height 1,000 feet above the takeoff surface and attain the speed and configuration at which compliance is shown with the enroute one- engine-inoperative gradient of climb specified in §6(c).

(f) *One-engine-inoperative takeoff flight path data.* The one-engine-inoperative takeoff flight path data consists of takeoff flight paths extending from a standing start to a point in the takeoff at which the airplane reaches a height 1,000 feet above the takeoff surface under paragraph (e) of this section.

6. *Climb.*

(a) *Landing climb: all-engines-operating.* The maximum weight must be determined with the airplane in the landing configuration, for each altitude, and ambient temperature within the operational limits established for the airplane, with the most unfavorable center of gravity, and out-of-ground effect in free air, at which the steady gradient of climb will not be less than 3.3 percent, with:

(1) The engines at the power that is available 8 seconds after initiation of movement of the power or thrust controls from the minimum flight idle to the takeoff position.

(2) A climb speed not greater than the approach speed established under §7 and not less than the greater of 1.05 V_{MC} or 1.10 V_{S1}.

(b) *Takeoff climb: one-engine-inoperative.* The maximum weight at which the airplane meets the minimum climb performance specified in subparagraphs (1) and (2) of this paragraph must be determined for each altitude and ambient temperature within the operational limits established for the airplane, out of ground effect in free air, with the airplane in the takeoff configuration, with the most unfavorable center of gravity, the critical engine inoperative, the remaining engines at the maximum takeoff power or thrust, and the propeller of the inoperative engine windmilling with the propeller controls in the normal position except that, if an approved automatic feathering system is installed, the propellers may be in the feathered position:

(1) *Takeoff: landing gear extended.* The minimum steady gradient of climb must be measurably positive at the speed V_1.

(2) *Takeoff: landing gear retracted.* The minimum steady gradient of climb may not be less than 2 percent at speed V_2. For airplanes with fixed landing gear this requirement must be met with the landing gear extended.

(c) *Enroute climb: one-engine-inoperative.* The maximum weight must be determined for each altitude and ambient temperature within the operational limits established for the airplane, at which the steady gradient of climb is not less than 1.2 percent at an altitude 1,000 feet above the takeoff surface, with the airplane in the enroute configuration, the critical engine inoperative, the remaining engine at the maximum continuous power or thrust, and the most unfavorable center of gravity.

7. *Landing.*
   (a) The landing field length described in paragraph (b) of this section must be determined for standard atmosphere at each weight and altitude within the operational limits established by the applicant.
   (b) The landing field length is equal to the landing distance determined under FAR 23.75(a) divided by a factor of 0.6 for the destination airport and 0.7 for the alternate airport. Instead of the gliding approach specified in FAR 23.75(a)(1), the landing may be preceded by a steady approach down to the 50-foot height at a gradient of descent not greater than 5.2 percent (3°) at a calibrated airspeed not less than 1.3 V_{S1}.

Trim

8. *Trim —*
   (a) *Lateral and directional trim.* The airplane must maintain lateral and directional trim in level flight at a speed of V_H or V_{MO}/M_{MO}, whichever is lower, with landing gear and wing flaps retracted.
   (b) *Longitudinal trim.* The airplane must maintain longitudinal trim during the following conditions, except that it need not maintain trim at a speed greater than V_{MO}/M_{MO};
      (1) In the approach conditions specified in FAR 23.161(c)(3) through (5), except that instead of the speed specified in those paragraphs, trim must be maintained with a stick force of not more than 10 pounds down to a speed used in showing compliance with §7 or 1.4 V_{S1} whichever is lower.
      (2) In level flight at any speed from V_H or V_{MO}/M_{MO}, whichever is lower, to either V_X or 1.4 V_{S1}, with the landing gear and wing flaps retracted.

Stability

9. *Static longitudinal stability.*
   (a) In showing compliance with FAR 23.175(b) and with paragraph (b) of this section the airspeed must return to within ±71/2 percent of the trim speed.
   (b) *Cruise stability.* The stick force curve must have a stable slope for a speed range of ±50 knots from the trim speed except that the speeds need not exceed V_{FC}/M_{FC} or be less than 1.4 V_{S1}. This speed range will be considered to begin at the outer extremes of the friction band and the stick force may not exceed 50 pounds with —
      (1) Landing gear retracted;
      (2) Wing flaps retracted;
      (3) The maximum cruising power as selected by the applicant as an operating limitation for turbine engines or 75 percent of maximum continuous power for reciprocating engines except that the power need not exceed that required at V_{MO}/M_{MO};

(4) Maximum takeoff weight; and
(5) The airplane trimmed for level flight with the power specified in subparagraph (3) of this paragraph.

V_{FC}/M_{FC} may not be less than a speed midway between V_{MO}/M_{MO} and V_{DF}/M_{DF}, except that, for altitudes where Mach number is the limiting factor, M_{FC} need not exceed the Mach number at which effective speed warning occurs.

(c) *Climb stability (turbopropeller powered airplanes only).* In showing compliance with FAR 23.175(a), an applicant must, instead of the power specified in FAR 23.175(a)(4), use the maximum power or thrust selected by the applicant as an operating limitation for use during climb at the best rate of climb speed, except that the speed need not be less than 1.4 V_{S1}.

Stalls

10. *Stall warning.* If artificial stall warning is required to comply with FAR 23.207, the warning device must give clearly distinguishable indications under expected conditions of flight. The use of a visual warning device that requires the attention of the crew within the cockpit is not acceptable by itself.

Control systems

11. *Electric trim tabs.* The airplane must meet FAR 23.677 and in addition it must be shown that the airplane is safely controllable and that a pilot can perform all the maneuvers and operations necessary to effect a safe landing following any probable electric trim tab runaway which might be reasonably expected in service allowing for appropriate time delay after pilot recognition of the runaway. This demonstration must be conducted at the critical airplane weights and center of gravity positions.

Instruments: Installation

12. *Arrangement and visibility.*Each instrument must meet FAR 23.1321 and in addition:

(a) Each flight, navigation, and powerplant instrument for use by any pilot must be plainly visible to the pilot from the pilot's station with the minimum practicable deviation from the pilot's normal position and line of vision when the pilot is looking forward along the flight path.

(b) The flight instruments required by FAR 23.1303 and by the applicable operating rules must be grouped on the instrument panel and centered as nearly as practicable about the vertical plane of each pilot's forward vision. In addition —

(1) The instrument that most effectively indicates the attitude must be in the panel in the top center position;
(2) The instrument that most effectively indicates the airspeed must be on the panel directly to the left of the instrument in the top center position;

(3) The instrument that most effectively indicates altitude must be adjacent to and directly to the right of the instrument in the top center position; and

(4) The instrument that most effectively indicates direction of flight must be adjacent to and directly below the instrument in the top center position.

13. *Airspeed indicating system.* Each airspeed indicating system must meet FAR 23.1323 and in addition:

(a) Airspeed indicating instruments must be of an approved type and must be calibrated to indicate true airspeed at sea level in the standard atmosphere with a minimum practicable instrument calibration error when the corresponding pitot and static pressures are supplied to the instruments.

(b) The airspeed indicating system must be calibrated to determine the system error, i.e., the relation between IAS and CAS, in flight and during the accelerate-takeoff ground run. The ground run calibration must be obtained between 0.8 of the minimum value of V_1 and 1.2 times the maximum value of V_1, considering the approved ranges of altitude and weight. The ground run calibration is determined assuming an engine failure at the minimum value of V_1.

(c) The airspeed error of the installation excluding the instrument calibration error, must not exceed 3 percent or 5 knots whichever is greater, throughout the speed range from V_{MO} to 1.3 V_{S1} with flaps retracted and from 1.3 V_{SO} to V_{FE} with flaps in the landing position.

(d) Information showing the relationship between IAS and CAS must be shown in the Airplane Flight Manual.

14. *Static air vent system.*The static air vent system must meet FAR 23.1325. The altimeter system calibration must be determined and shown in the Airplane Flight Manual.

Operating Limitations and Information

15. *Maximum operating limit speed V_{MO}/M_{MO}.* Instead of establishing operating limitations based on V_{NE} or V_{NO}, the applicant must establish a maximum operating limit speed V_{MO}/M_{MO} as follows:

(a) The maximum operating limit speed must not exceed the design cruising speed V_C and must be sufficiently below V_D/M_D, or V_{DF}/M_{DF}, to make it highly improbable that the latter speeds will be inadvertently exceeded in flight.

(b) The speed V_{MO} must not exceed 0.8 V_D/M_D or 0.8 V_{DF}/M_F unless flight demonstrations involving upsets as specified by the Administrator indicates a lower speed margin will not result in speed exceeding V_D/M_D or V_{DF}. Atmospheric variations, horizontal gusts, system and equipment errors, and airframe production variations are taken into account.

16. *Minimum flight crew.* In addition to meeting FAR 23.1523, the applicant must establish the minimum number and type of qualified flight crew personnel sufficient for safe operation of the airplane considering —

(a) Each kind of operation for which the applicant desires approval;

(b) The workload on each crewmember considering the following:

(1) Flight path control.

(2) Collision avoidance.

(3) Navigation.
(4) Communications.
(5) Operation and monitoring of all essential aircraft systems.
(6) Command decisions; and

(c) The accessibility and ease of operation of necessary controls by the appropriate crewmember during all normal and emergency operations when at the crewmember flight station.

17. *Airspeed indicator.* The airspeed indicator must meet FAR 23.1545 except that, the airspeed notations and markings in terms of V_{NO} and V_{NE} must be replaced by the V_{MO}/M_{MO} notations. The airspeed indicator markings must be easily read and understood by the pilot. A placard adjacent to the airspeed indicator is an acceptable means of showing compliance with FAR 23.1545(c).

Airplane Flight Manual

18. *General.* The Airplane Flight Manual must be prepared under FARs 23.1583 and 23.1587, and in addition the operating limitations and performance information in §§19 and 20 must be included.

19. *Operating limitations.* The Airplane Flight Manual must include the following limitations —

(a) *Airspeed limitations.*
(1) The maximum operating limit speed V_{MO}/M_{MO} and a statement that this speed limit may not be deliberately exceeded in any regime of flight (climb, cruise, or descent) unless a higher speed is authorized for flight test or pilot training;
(2) If an airspeed limitation is based upon compressibility effects, a statement to this effect and information as to any symptoms, the probable behavior of the airplane, and the recommended recovery procedures; and
(3) The airspeed limits, shown in terms of V_{MO}/M_{MO} instead of V_{NO} and V_{NE}.

(b) *Takeoff weight limitations.* The maximum takeoff weight for each airport elevation, ambient temperature, and available takeoff runway length within the range selected by the applicant may not exceed the weight at which —
(1) The all-engine-operating takeoff distance determined under §5(b) or the accelerate-stop distance determined under §5(c), whichever is greater, is equal to the available runway length;
(2) The airplane complies with the one-engine-inoperative takeoff requirements specified in §5(e); and
(3) The airplane complies with the one-engine-inoperative takeoff and enroute climb requirements specified in §§6(b) and (c).

(c) *Landing weight limitations.* The maximum landing weight for each airport elevation (standard temperature) and available landing runway length, within the range selected by the applicant. This weight may not exceed the weight at which the landing field length determined under §7(b) is equal to the available runway length. In showing compliance with this operating limitation, it is acceptable to assume that the landing weight at the destination will be equal to the takeoff weight reduced by the normal consumption of fuel and oil enroute.

20. *Performance information.* The Airplane Flight Manual must contain the performance information determined under the performance requirements of this appendix. The information must include the following:
   (a) Sufficient information so that the takeoff weight limits specified in §19(b) can be determined for all temperatures and altitudes within the operation limitations selected by the applicant.
   (b) The conditions under which the performance information was obtained, including the airspeed at the 50-foot height used to determine landing distances.
   (c) The performance information (determined by extrapolation and computed for the range of weights between the maximum landing and takeoff weights) for —
      (1) Climb in the landing configuration; and
      (2) Landing distance.
   (d) Procedure established under §4 related to the limitations and information required by this section in the form of guidance material including any relevant limitations or information.
   (e) An explanation of significant or unusual flight or ground handling characteristics of the airplane.
   (f) Airspeeds, as indicated airspeeds, corresponding to those determined for takeoff under §5(b).

21. *Maximum operating altitudes.* The maximum operating altitude to which operation is allowed, as limited by flight, structural, powerplant, functional, or equipment characteristics, and must be specified in the Airplane Flight Manual.

22. *Stowage provision for airplane flight manual.* Provision must be made for stowing the Airplane Flight Manual in a suitable fixed container which is readily accessible to the pilot.

23. *Operating procedures.*Procedures for restarting turbine engines in flight (including the effects of altitude) must be set forth in the Airplane Flight Manual.

Airframe Requirements

Flight Loads

24. *Engine Torque.*
   (a) Each turbopropeller engine mount and its supporting structure must be designed for the torque effects of:
      (1) The conditions in FAR 23.361(a).
      (2) The limit engine torque corresponding to takeoff power and propeller speed multiplied by a factor accounting for propeller control system malfunction, including quick feathering action, simultaneously with 1g level flight loads. In the absence of a rational analysis, a factor of 1.6 must be used.
   (b) The limit torque is obtained by multiplying the mean torque by a factor of 1.25.

25. *Turbine engine gyroscopic loads.*Each turbopropeller engine mount and its supporting structure must be designed for the gyroscopic loads that result, with the engines at maximum continuous r.p.m., under either —
   (a) The conditions in FARs 23.351 and 23.423; or
   (b) All possible combinations of the following:
      (1) A yaw velocity of 2.5 radians per second.
      (2) A pitch velocity of 1.0 radians per second.
      (3) A normal load factor of 2.5.
      (4) Maximum continuous thrust.

26. *Unsymmetrical loads due to engine failure.*
   (a) Turbopropeller powered airplanes must be designed for the unsymmetrical loads resulting from the failure of the critical engine including the following conditions in combination with a single malfunction of the propeller drag limiting system, considering the probable pilot corrective action on the flight controls:
      (1) At speeds between V_{MO} and V_D, the loads resulting from power failure because of fuel flow interruption are considered to be limit loads.
      (2) At speeds between V_{MO} and V_C the loads resulting from the disconnection of the engine compressor from the turbine or from the loss of the turbine blades are considered to be ultimate loads.
      (3) The time history of the thrust decay and drag buildup occurring as a result of the prescribed engine failures must be substantiated by test or other data applicable to the particular engine-propeller combination.
      (4) The timing and magnitude of the probable pilot corrective action must be conservatively estimated, considering the characteristics of the particular engine-propeller-airplane combination.
   (b) Pilot corrective action may be assumed to be initiated at the time maximum yawing velocity is reached, but not earlier than 2 seconds after the engine failure. The magnitude of the corrective action may be based on the control forces in FAR 23.397 except that lower forces may be assumed where it is shown by analysis or test that these forces can control the yaw and roll resulting from the prescribed engine failure conditions.

Ground Loads

27. *Dual wheel landing gear units.*Each dual wheel landing gear unit and its supporting structure must be shown to comply with the following:
   (a) *Pivoting.*The airplane must be assumed to pivot about one side of the main gear with the brakes on that side locked. The limit vertical load factor must be 1.0 and the coefficient of friction 0.8. This condition need apply only to the main gear and its supporting structure.
   (b) *Unequal tire inflation.* A 60-40 percent distribution of the loads established under FAR 23.471 through FAR 23.483 must be applied to the dual wheels.

(c) *Flat tire.*
   (1) Sixty percent of the loads in FAR 23.471 through FAR 23.483 must be applied to either wheel in a unit.
   (2) Sixty percent of the limit drag and side loads and 100 percent of the limit vertical load established under FARs 23.493 and 23.485 must be applied to either wheel in a unit except that the vertical load need not exceed the maximum vertical load in paragraph (c)(1) of this section.

Fatigue Evaluation

28. *Fatigue evaluation of wing and associated structure.* Unless it is shown that the structure, operating stress levels, materials and expected use are comparable from a fatigue standpoint to a similar design which has had substantial satisfactory service experience, the strength, detail design, and the fabrication of those parts of the wing, wing carry through, and attaching structure whose failure would be catastrophic must be evaluated under either —
(a) A fatigue strength investigation in which the structure is shown by analysis, tests, or both to be able to withstand the repeated loads of variable magnitude expected in service; or
(b) A fail-safe strength investigation in which it is shown by analysis, tests, or both that catastrophic failure of the structure is not probable after fatigue, or obvious partial failure, of a principal structural element, and that the remaining structure is able to withstand a static ultimate load factor of 75 percent of the critical limit load factor at V_C. These loads must be multiplied by a factor of 1.15 unless the dynamic effects of failure under static load are otherwise considered.

Design and Construction

29. *Flutter.* For multi-engine turbopropeller powered airplanes, a dynamic evaluation must be made and must include —
(a) The significant elastic, inertia, and aerodynamic forces associated with the rotations and displacements of the plane of the propeller; and
(b) Engine-propeller-nacelle stiffness and damping variations appropriate to the particular configuration.

Landing Gear

30. *Flap operated landing gear warning device.* Airplanes having retractable landing gear and wing flaps must be equipped with a warning device that functions continuously when the wing flaps are extended to a flap position that activates the warning device to give adequate warning before landing, using normal landing procedures, if the landing gear is not fully extended and locked. There may not be a manual shutoff for this warning device. The flap position sensing unit may be installed at any suitable location. The system for this device may use any part of the system (including the aural warning device) provided for other landing gear warning devices.

Personnel and Cargo Accommodations

31. *Cargo and Baggage compartments.* Cargo and baggage compartments must be designed to meet FAR 23.787(a) and (b), and in addition means must be provided to protect passengers from injury by the contents of any cargo or baggage compartment when the ultimate forward inertia force is 9g.

32. *Doors and exits.* The airplane must meet FAR 23.783 and FAR 23.807 (a)(3), (b), and (c), and in addition;
    - (a) There must be a means to lock and safeguard each external door and exit against opening in flight either inadvertently by persons, or as a result of mechanical failure. Each external door must be operable from both the inside and the outside.
    - (b) There must be means for direct visual inspection of the locking mechanism by crewmembers to determine whether external doors and exits, for which the initial opening movement is outward, are fully locked. In addition, there must be a visual means to signal to crewmembers when normally used external doors are closed and fully locked.
    - (c) The passenger entrance door must qualify as a floor level emergency exit. Each additional required emergency exit except floor level exits must be located over the wing or must be provided with acceptable means to assist the occupants in descending to the ground. In addition to the passenger entrance door;
        - (1) For a total seating capacity of 15 or less, an emergency exit as defined in FAR 23.807(b) is required on each side of the cabin.
        - (2) For a total seating capacity of 16 through 23, three emergency exits as defined in FAR 23.807(b) are required with one on the same side as the door and two on the side opposite the door.
    - (d) An evacuation demonstration must be conducted utilizing the maximum number of occupants for which certification is desired. It must be conducted under simulated night conditions utilizing only the emergency exits on the most critical side of the aircraft. The participants must be representative of average airline passengers with no previous practice or rehearsal for the demonstration. Evacuation must be completed within 90 seconds.
    - (e) Each emergency exit must be marked with the word "Exit" by a sign which has white letters 1 inch high on a red background 2 inches high, be self- illuminated or independently internally electrically illuminated, and have a minimum luminescence (brightness) of at least 160 microlamberts. The colors may be reversed if the passenger compartment illumination is essentially the same.
    - (f) Access to window type emergency exits must not be obstructed by seats or seat backs.

(g) The width of the main passenger aisle at any point between seats must equal or exceed the values in the following table:

Total seating capacity	Minimum main passenger aisle width	
	Less than 25 inches from floor	25 inches and more from floor
10 through 23	9 inches	15 inches.

Miscellaneous

33. *Lightning strike protection.* Parts that are electrically insulated from the basic airframe must be connected to it through lightning arrestors unless a lightning strike on the insulated part —
   (a) Is improbable because of shielding by other parts; or
   (b) Is not hazardous.

34. *Ice protection.* If certification with ice protection provisions is desired, compliance with the following must be shown:
   (a) The recommended procedures for the use of the ice protection equipment must be set forth in the Airplane Flight Manual.
   (b) An analysis must be performed to establish, on the basis of the airplane's operational needs, the adequacy of the ice protection system for the various components of the airplane. In addition, tests of the ice protection system must be conducted to demonstrate that the airplane is capable of operating safely in continuous maximum and intermittent maximum icing conditions as described in Appendix C of Part 25 of this chapter.
   (c) Compliance with all or portions of this section may be accomplished by reference, where applicable because of similarity of the designs, to analysis and tests performed by the applicant for a type certificated model.

35. *Maintenance information.*The applicant must make available to the owner at the time of delivery of the airplane the information the applicant considers essential for the proper maintenance of the airplane. That information must include the following:
   (a) Description of systems, including electrical, hydraulic, and fuel controls.
   (b) Lubrication instructions setting forth the frequency and the lubricants and fluids which are to be used in the various systems.
   (c) Pressures and electrical loads applicable to the various systems.
   (d) Tolerances and adjustments necessary for proper functioning.
   (e) Methods of leveling, raising, and towing.
   (f) Methods of balancing control surfaces.
   (g) Identification of primary and secondary structures.
   (h) Frequency and extent of inspections necessary to the proper operation of the airplane.
   (i) Special repair methods applicable to the airplane.

(j) Special inspection techniques, such as X-ray, ultrasonic, and magnetic particle inspection.
(k) List of special tools.

Propulsion

General

36. *Vibration characteristics.* For turbopropeller powered airplanes, the engine installation must not result in vibration characteristics of the engine exceeding those established during the type certification of the engine.
37. *In flight restarting of engine.* If the engine on turbopropeller powered airplanes cannot be restarted at the maximum cruise altitude, a determination must be made of the altitude below which restarts can be consistently accomplished. Restart information must be provided in the Airplane Flight Manual.
38. *Engines.*
   (a) *For turbopropeller powered airplanes.* The engine installation must comply with the following:
      (1) Engine isolation. The powerplants must be arranged and isolated from each other to allow operation, in at least one configuration, so that the failure or malfunction of any engine, or of any system that can affect the engine, will not —
         (i) Prevent the continued safe operation of the remaining engines; or
         (ii) Require immediate action by any crewmember for continued safe operation.
      (2) *Control of engine rotation.* There must be a means to individually stop and restart the rotation of any engine in flight except that engine rotation need not be stopped if continued rotation could not jeopardize the safety of the airplane. Each component of the stopping and restarting system on the engine side of the firewall, and that might be exposed to fire, must be at least fire resistant. If hydraulic propeller feathering systems are used for this purpose, the feathering lines must be at least fire resistant under the operating conditions that may be expected to exist during feathering.
      (3) *Engine speed and gas temperature control devices.* The powerplant systems associated with engine control devices, systems, and instrumentation must provide reasonable assurance that those engine operating limitations that adversely affect turbine rotor structural integrity will not be exceeded in service.
   (b) *For reciprocating engine powered airplanes.* To provide engine isolation, the powerplants must be arranged and isolated from each other to allow operation, in at least one configuration, so that the failure or malfunction of any engine, or of any system that can affect that engine, will not —
      (1) Prevent the continued safe operation of the remaining engines; or
      (2) Require immediate action by any crewmember for continued safe operation.

39. *Turbopropeller reversing systems.*
   (a) Turbopropeller reversing systems intended for ground operation must be designed so that no single failure or malfunction of the system will result in unwanted reverse thrust under any expected operating condition. Failure of structural elements need not be considered if the probability of this kind of failure is extremely remote.
   (b) Turbopropeller reversing systems intended for in flight use must be designed so that no unsafe condition will result during normal operation of the system, or from any failure (or reasonably likely combination of failures) of the reversing system, under any anticipated condition of operation of the airplane. Failure of structural elements need not be considered if the probability of this kind of failure is extremely remote.
   (c) Compliance with this section may be shown by failure analysis, testing, or both for propeller systems that allow propeller blades to move from the flight low-pitch position to a position that is substantially less than that at the normal flight low-pitch stop position. The analysis may include or be supported by the analysis made to show compliance with the type certification of the propeller and associated installation components. Credit will be given for pertinent analysis and testing completed by the engine and propeller manufacturers.

40. *Turbopropeller drag-limiting systems.* Turbopropeller drag-limiting systems must be designed so that no single failure or malfunction of any of the systems during normal or emergency operation results in propeller drag in excess of that for which the airplane was designed. Failure of structural elements of the drag-limiting systems need not be considered if the probability of this kind of failure is extremely remote.

41. *Turbine engine powerplant operating characteristics.*For turbopropeller powered airplanes, the turbine engine powerplant operating characteristics must be investigated in flight to determine that no adverse characteristics (such as stall, surge, or flameout) are present to a hazardous degree, during normal and emergency operation within the range of operating limitations of the airplane and of the engine.

42. *Fuel flow.*
   (a) For turbopropeller powered airplanes —
      (1) The fuel system must provide for continuous supply of fuel to the engines for normal operation without interruption due to depletion of fuel in any tank other than the main tank; and
      (2) The fuel flow rate for turbopropeller engine fuel pump systems must not be less than 125 percent of the fuel flow required to develop the standard sea level atmospheric conditions takeoff power selected and included as an operating limitation in the Airplane Flight Manual.
   (b) For reciprocating engine powered airplanes, it is acceptable for the fuel flow rate for each pump system (main and reserve supply) to be 125 percent of the takeoff fuel consumption of the engine.

Fuel System Components

43. *Fuel pumps.* For turbopropeller powered airplanes, a reliable and independent power source must be provided for each pump used with turbine engines which do not have provisions for

mechanically driving the main pumps. It must be demonstrated that the pump installations provide a reliability and durability equivalent to that in FAR 23.991(a).

44. *Fuel strainer or filter.* For turbopropeller powered airplanes, the following apply:

(a) There must be a fuel strainer or filter between the tank outlet and the fuel metering device of the engine. In addition, the fuel strainer or filter must be —

(1) Between the tank outlet and the engine-driving positive displacement pump inlet, if there is an engine-driven positive displacement pump;

(2) Accessible for drainage and cleaning and, for the strainer screen, easily removable; and

(3) Mounted so that its weight is not supported by the connecting lines or by the inlet or outlet connections of the strainer or filter itself.

(b) Unless there are means in the fuel system to prevent the accumulation of ice on the filter, there must be means to automatically maintain the fuel flow if ice-clogging of the filter occurs; and

(c) The fuel strainer or filter must be of adequate capacity (for operating limitations established to ensure proper service) and of appropriate mesh to insure proper engine operation, with the fuel contaminated to a degree (for particle size and density) that can be reasonably expected in service. The degree of fuel filtering may not be less than that established for the engine type certification.

45. *Lightning strike protection.* Protection must be provided against the ignition of flammable vapors in the fuel vent system due to lightning strikes.

Cooling

46. *Cooling test procedures for turbopropeller powered airplanes.*

(a) Turbopropeller powered airplanes must be shown to comply with FAR 23.1041 during takeoff, climb, enroute, and landing stages of flight that correspond to the applicable performance requirements. The cooling tests must be conducted with the airplane in the configuration and operating under the conditions that are critical relative to cooling during each stage of flight. For the cooling tests a temperature is "stabilized" when its rate of change is less than 2°F. per minute.

(b) Temperatures must be stabilized under the conditions from which entry is made into each stage of flight being investigated unless the entry condition is not one during which component and engine fluid temperatures would stabilize, in which case, operation through the full entry condition must be conducted before entry into the stage of flight being investigated to allow temperatures to reach their natural levels at the time of entry. The takeoff cooling test must be preceded by a period during which the powerplant component and engine fluid temperatures are stabilized with the engines at ground idle.

(c) Cooling tests for each stage of flight must be continued until —

(1) The component and engine fluid temperatures stabilize;

(2) The stage of flight is completed; or

(3) An operating limitation is reached.

Induction System

47. Air induction. For turbopropeller powered airplanes —
   (a) There must be means to prevent hazardous quantities of fuel leakage or overflow from drains, vents, or other components of flammable fluid systems from entering the engine intake systems; and
   (b) The air inlet ducts must be located or protected so as to minimize the ingestion of foreign matter during takeoff, landing, and taxiing.

48. *Induction system icing protection.* For turbopropeller powered airplanes, each turbine engine must be able to operate throughout its flight power range without adverse effect on engine operation or serious loss of power or thrust, under the icing conditions specified in Appendix C of Part 25 of this chapter. In addition, there must be means to indicate to appropriate flight crewmembers the functioning of the powerplant ice protection system.

49. *Turbine engine bleed air systems.* Turbine engine bleed air systems of turbopropeller powered airplanes must be investigated to determine —
   (a) That no hazard to the airplane will result if a duct rupture occurs. This condition must consider that a failure of the duct can occur anywhere between the engine port and the airplane bleed service; and
   (b) That, if the bleed air system is used for direct cabin pressurization, it is not possible for hazardous contamination of the cabin air system to occur in event of lubrication system failure.

Exhaust System

50. *Exhaust system drains.* Turbopropeller engine exhaust systems having low spots or pockets must incorporate drains at those locations. These drains must discharge clear of the airplane in normal and ground attitudes to prevent the accumulation of fuel after the failure of an attempted engine start.

Powerplant Controls and Accessories

51. *Engine controls.* If throttles or power levers for turbopropeller powered airplanes are such that any position of these controls will reduce the fuel flow to the engine(s) below that necessary for satisfactory and safe idle operation of the engine while the airplane is in flight, a means must be provided to prevent inadvertent movement of the control into this position. The means provided must incorporate a positive lock or stop at this idle position and must require a separate and distinct operation by the crew to displace the control from the normal engine operating range.

52. *Reverse thrust controls.* For turbopropeller powered airplanes, the propeller reverse thrust controls must have a means to prevent their inadvertent operation. The means must have a positive lock or stop at the idle position and must require a separate and distinct operation by the crew to displace the control from the flight regime.

53. *Engine ignition systems.* Each turbopropeller airplane ignition system must be considered an essential electrical load.

54. *Powerplant accessories.* The powerplant accessories must meet FAR 23.1163, and if the continued rotation of any accessory remotely driven by the engine is hazardous when malfunctioning occurs, there must be means to prevent rotation without interfering with the continued operation of the engine.

Powerplant Fire Protection

55. *Fire detector system.* For turbopropeller powered airplanes, the following apply:
    (a) There must be a means that ensures prompt detection of fire in the engine compartment. An overtemperature switch in each engine cooling air exit is an acceptable method of meeting this requirement.
    (b) Each fire detector must be constructed and installed to withstand the vibration, inertia, and other loads to which it may be subjected in operation.
    (c) No fire detector may be affected by any oil, water, other fluids, or fumes that might be present.
    (d) There must be means to allow the flight crew to check, in flight, the functioning of each fire detector electric circuit.
    (e) Wiring and other components of each fire detector system in a fire zone must be at least fire resistant.
56. *Fire protection, cowling and nacelle skin.* For reciprocating engine powered airplanes, the engine cowling must be designed and constructed so that no fire originating in the engine compartment can enter either through openings or by burning through, any other region where it would create additional hazards.
57. *Flammable fluid fire protection.* If flammable fluids or vapors might be liberated by the leakage of fluid systems in areas other than engine compartments, there must be means to —
    (a) Prevent the ignition of those fluids or vapors by any other equipment; or
    (b) Control any fire resulting from that ignition.

Equipment

58. *Powerplant instruments.*
    (a) The following are required for turbopropeller airplanes:
        (1) The instruments required by FAR 23.1305(a)(1) through (4), (b)(2) and (4).
        (2) A gas temperature indicator for each engine.
        (3) Free air temperature indicator.
        (4) A fuel flowmeter indicator for each engine.
        (5) Oil pressure warning means for each engine.
        (6) A torque indicator or adequate means for indicating power output for each engine.
        (7) Fire warning indicator for each engine.
        (8) A means to indicate when the propeller blade angle is below the low- pitch position corresponding to idle operation in flight.
        (9) A means to indicate the functioning of the ice protection system for each engine.

(b) For turbopropeller powered airplanes, the turbopropeller blade position indicator must begin indicating when the blade has moved below the flight low-pitch position.
(c) The following instruments are required for reciprocating engine powered airplanes:
   (1) The instruments required by FAR 23.1305.
   (2) A cylinder head temperature indicator for each engine.
   (3) A manifold pressure indicator for each engine.

Systems and Equipments

General

59. *Function and installation.* The systems and equipment for the airplane must meet FAR 23.1301, and the following:
(a) Each item of additional installed equipment must —
   (1) Be of a kind and design appropriate to its intended function;
   (2) Be labeled as to its identification, function, or operating limitations, or any applicable combination of these factors, unless misuse of inadvertent actuation cannot create a hazard;
   (3) Be installed according to limitations specified for that equipment; and
   (4) Function properly when installed.
(b) Systems and installations must be designed to safeguard against hazards to the aircraft in the event of their malfunction or failure.
(c) Where an installation, the functioning of which is necessary in showing compliance with the applicable requirements, requires a power supply, that installation must be considered an essential load on the power supply, and the power sources and the distribution system must be capable of supplying the following power loads in probable operation combinations and for probable durations:
   (1) All essential loads after failure of any prime mover, power converter, or energy storage device.
   (2) All essential loads after failure of any one engine on two-engine airplanes.
   (3) In determining the probable operating combinations and durations of essential loads for the power failure conditions described in subparagraphs (1) and (2) of this paragraph, it is permissible to assume that the power loads are reduced in accordance with a monitoring procedure which is consistent with safety in the types of operations authorized.

60. *Ventilation.* The ventilation system of the airplane must meet FAR 23.831, and in addition, for pressurized aircraft, the ventilating air in flight crew and passenger compartments must be free of harmful or hazardous concentrations of gases and vapors in normal operation and in the event of reasonably probable failures or malfunctioning of the ventilating, heating, pressurization, or other systems, and equipment. If accumulation of hazardous quantities of smoke in the cockpit area is reasonably probable, smoke evacuation must be readily accomplished.

Electrical Systems and Equipment

61. *General.* The electrical systems and equipment of the airplane must meet FAR 23.1351, and the following:
   (a) *Electrical system capacity.* The required generating capacity, and number and kinds of power sources must —
      (1) Be determined by an electrical load analysis; and
      (2) Meet FAR 23.1301.
   (b) Generating system. The generating system includes electrical power sources, main power busses, transmission cables, and associated control, regulation and protective devices. It must be designed so that —
      (1) The system voltage and frequency (as applicable) at the terminals of all essential load equipment can be maintained within the limits for which the equipment is designed, during any probable operating conditions;
      (2) System transients due to switching, fault clearing, or other causes do not make essential loads inoperative, and do not cause a smoke or fire hazard;
      (3) There are means, accessible in flight to appropriate crewmembers, for the individual and collective disconnection of the electrical power sources from the system; and
      (4) There are means to indicate to appropriate crewmembers the generating system quantities essential for the safe operation of the system, including the voltage and current supplied by each generator.

62. *Electrical equipment and installation.* Electrical equipment, controls, and wiring must be installed so that operation of any one unit or system of units will not adversely affect the simultaneous operation of any other electrical unit or system essential to the safe operation.

63. *Distribution system.*
   (a) For the purpose of complying with this section, the distribution system includes the distribution busses, their associated feeders, and each control and protective device.
   (b) Each system must be designed so that essential load circuits can be supplied in the event of reasonably probable faults or open circuits, including faults in heavy current carrying cables.
   (c) If two independent sources of electrical power for particular equipment or systems are required under this appendix, their electrical energy supply must be ensured by means such as duplicate electrical equipment, throwover switching or multichannel or loop circuits separately routed.

64. *Circuit protective devices.* The circuit protective devices for the electrical circuits of the airplane must meet FAR 23.1357, and in addition circuits for loads which are essential to safe operation must have individual and exclusive circuit protection.

APPENDIX B — AIRPLANE FLIGHT RECORDER SPECIFICATIONS

Parameters	Range	Installed system [1] minimum accuracy (to recovered data)	Sampling interval (per second)	Resolution[4] read out
Relative time (from recorded on prior to takeoff).	8 hr minimum	±0.125% per hour	1	1 sec.
Indicated airspeed	V_{so} to V_D (KIAS)	±5% or ±10 kts., whichever is greater. Resolution 2 kts. below 175 KIAS.	1	1%[3]
Altitude	-1,000 ft. to max cert. alt. of A/C.	±100 to ±700 ft. *(see Table 1, TSO C51-a).	1	25 to 150
Magnetic heading	360°	±5°	1	1°
Vertical acceleration	-3g to +6g	±0.2g in addition to ±0.3g maximum datum.	4 (or 1 per second where peaks, ref. to 1g are recorded).	0.03g.
Longitudinal acceleration	±1.0g	±1.5% max. range excluding datum error of ±5%.	2	0.01g.
Pitch attitude	100% of usable	±2°	1	0.8°
Roll attitude	±60° or 100% of usable range, whichever is greater.	±2°	1	0.8°
Stabilizer trim position	Full range	±3% unless higher uniquely required.	1	1%[3]
Or				
Pitch control position	Full range	±3% unless higher uniquely required.	1	1%[3]
Engine Power, Each Engine:				
Fan or N_1 speed or EPR or cockpit indicatons used for aircraft certification	Maximum range	±5%	1	1%[3]
Or				

[1] When data sources are aircraft instruments (except altimeters) of acceptable quality to fly the aircraft the recording system excluding these sensors (but including all other characteristics of the recording system) shall contribute no more than half of the values in this column.

[2] If data from the altitude encoding altimeter (100 ft. resolution) is used, then either one of these parameters should also be recorded. If however, altitude is recorded at a minimum resolution of 25 feet, then these two parameters can be omitted.

[3] Percent of full range.

[4] This column applies to aircraft manufactured after October 11, 1991.

(*Not published herein — Ed.)

APPENDIX B — AIRPLANE FLIGHT RECORDER SPECIFICATIONS

Parameters	Range	Installed system [1] minimum accuracy (to recovered data)	Sampling interval (per second)	Resolution[4] read out
Prop. speed and torque (sample once/sec as close together as practicable).			1 (prop speed) 1 (torque)	
Altitude rate[2] (need depends on altitude resolution).	±8,000 fpm	±10% Resolution 250 fpm below 12,000 ft. indicated.	1	250 fpm. below 12,000.
Angle of attack[2] (need depends on altitude resolution).	-20° to 40° or of usable range	±2°	1	0.8%[3]
Radio transmitter keying (discrete)	On/off		1	
TE flaps (discrete or analog)	Each discrete position (U, D, T/O, AAP)		1	
	Or			
	Analog 0-100% range	±3%	1	1%[3]
LE flaps (discrete or analog)	Each discrete position (U, D, T/O, APP)		1	
	Or			
	Analog 0-100% range	±3%	1	1%[3]
Thrust reverser, each engine (discrete)	Stowed or full reverse		1	
Spoiler/speedbrake (discrete)	Stowed or out		1	
Autopilot engaged (discrete)	Engaged or disengaged		1	

[1] When data sources are aircraft instruments (except altimeters) of acceptable quality to fly the aircraft the recording system excluding these sensors (but including all other characteristics of the recording system) shall contribute no more than half of the values in this column.

[2] If data from the altitude encoding altimeter (100 ft. resolution) is used, then either one of these parameters should also be recorded. If however, altitude is recorded at a minimum resolution of 25 feet, then these two parameters can be omitted.

[3] Percent of full range.

[4] This column applies to aircraft manufactured after October 11, 1991.

APPENDIX C — HELICOPTER FLIGHT RECORDER SPECIFICATIONS

Parameters	Range	Installed system [1] minimum accuracy (to recovered data)	Sampling interval (per second)	Resolution[3] read out
Relative time (from recorded on prior to takeoff).	8 hr minimum	±0.125% per hour	1	1 sec.
Indicated airspeed	V_m in to V_D (KIAS) (minimum airspeed signal attainable with installed pitot-static system).	±5% or ±10 kts., whichever is greater.	1	1 kt.
Altitude	-1,000 ft. to 20,000 ft. pressure altitude.	±100 to ±700 ft. *(see Table 1, TSO C51-a).	1	25 to 150 ft.
Magnetic heading	360°	±5°	1	1°
Vertical acceleration	-3g to +6g	±0.2g in addition to ±0.3g maximum datum	4 (or 1 per second where peaks, ref. to 1g are recorded).	0.05g.
Longitudinal acceleration	±1.0g	±1.5% max. range excluding datum error of ±5%.	2	0.03g.
Pitch attitude	100% of usable range	±2°	1	0.8°
Roll attitude	±60° or 100% of usable range, whichever is greater.	±2°	1	0.8°
Altitude rate	±8,000 fpm	±10% Resolution 250 fpm below 12,000 ft. indicated.	1	250 fpm. below 12,000.
Engine Power, Each Engine				
Main rotor speed	Maximum range	±5%	1	1%[2]
Free or power turbine	Maximum range	±5%	1	1%[2]
Engine torque	Maximum range	±5%	1	1%[2]
Flight Control—Hydraulic Pressure				
Primary (discrete)	High/low		1	

[1] When data sources are aircraft instruments (except altimeters) of acceptable quality to fly the aircraft the recording system excluding these sensors (but including all other characteristics of the recording system) shall contribute no more than half of the values in this column.

[2] Percent of full range.

[3] This column applies to aircraft manufactured after October 11, 1991.

(*Not published herein — Ed.)

APPENDIX C — HELICOPTER FLIGHT RECORDER SPECIFICATIONS

Parameters	Range	Installed system [1] minimum accuracy (to recovered data)	Sampling interval (per second)	Resolution[3] read out
Secondary-if applicable (discrete)	High/low		1	
Radio transmitter keying (discrete)	On/off		1	
Autopilot engaged (discrete)	Engaged or disengaged		1	
SAS status-engaged (discrete)	Engaged/disengaged		1	
SAS fault status (discrete)	Fault/OK		1	
Flight Controls				
Collective	Full range	±3%	2	1%[2]
Pedal position	Full range	±3%	2	1%[2]
Lat. cyclic	Full range	±3%	2	1%[2]
Long. cyclic	Full range	±3%	2	1%[2]
Controllable stabilator position	Full range	±3%	2	1%[2]

[1] When data sources are aircraft instruments (except altimeters) of acceptable quality to fly the aircraft the recording system excluding these sensors (but including all other characteristics of the recording system) shall contribute no more than half of the values in this column.

[2] Percent of full range.

[3] This column applies to aircraft manufactured after October 11, 1991.

APPENDIX D — AIRPLANE FLIGHT RECORDER SPECIFICATIONS

Parameters	Range	Accuracy sensor input to DFDR readout	Sampling interval (per second)	Resolution[4] read out
Time (GMT or frame counter) (range 0 to 4095, sampled 1 per frame).	24 Hrs	±0.125% Per Hour	0.25 (1 per 4 seconds).	1 sec.
Altitude	-1,000 ft to max certificated altitude of aircraft.	±100 to ±700 ft *(See Table 1, TSO-C51a).	1	5′ to 35′[1]
Airspeed	50 KIAS to V_{so1} and V_{so} to 1.2 V_D.	±5, ±3%	1	1 kt.
Heading	360°	±2°	1	0.5°
Normal acceleration (vertical)	-3g to +6g	±1% of max rang eexcluding datum error of ±5%.	8	0.01g
Pitch attitude	±75°	±2°	1	0.5°
Roll attitude	±180°	±2°	1	0.5°
Radio transmitter keying	On-off (discrete)		1	
Thrust/power on each engine	Full range forward	±2%	1 (per engine)	0.2%[2]
Trailing edge flap or cockpit control selection.	Full range or each discrete position.	±3° or as pilot's indicator	0.5	0.5%[2]
Leading edge flap on or cockpit control selection.	Full range or each discrete position.	±3° or as pilot's indicator	0.5	0.5%[2]
Thrust reverser position	Stowed, in transit, and reverse (discrete).		1 (per 4 seconds per engine).	
Ground spoiler position/speed brake selection.	Full range or each discrete position.	±2% unless higher accuracy uniquely required.	1	0.22[2]
Marker beacon passage	Discrete		1	
Autopilot engagement	Discrete		1	
Longitudinal acceleration	±1g	±1.5% max range excluding datum error of ±5%.	4	0.01g

[1] When altitude rate is recorded. Altitude rate must have sufficient resolution and sampling to permit the derivation of altitude to 5 feet.
[2] Percent of full range.
[3] For airplanes that can demonstrate the capability of deriving either the control input on control movement (one from the other) or all modes of operation and flight regimes, the "or" applies. For airplanes with non-mechanical control systems (fly-by-wire) the "and" applies. In airplanes with split surfaces, suitable combination of inputs is acceptable in lieu of recording each surface separately.
[4] This column applies to aircraft manufactured after October 11, 1991.

(*Not published herein — Ed.)

APPENDIX D — AIRPLANE FLIGHT RECORDER SPECIFICATIONS

Parameters	Range	Accuracy sensor input to DFDR readout	Sampling interval (per second)	Resolution[4] readout
Pilot input and/or surface position—primary controls (pitch, roll, yaw)[3]	Full range	±2° unless higher accuracy uniquely required.	1	0.2%[2]
Lateral acceleration	±1g	±1.5% max range exluding datum error of ±5%.	4	0.01g
Pitch trim position	Full range	±3% unless higher accuracy uniquely required.	1	0.3%[2]
Glideslope deviation	±400 microamps	±3%	1	0.3%[2]
Localizer deviation	±400 microamps	±3%	1	0.3%[2]
AFCS mode and engagement status	discrete		1	
Radio altitude	-20 ft to 2,500 ft	±2 Ft or ±3% whichever is greater below 500 ft and ±5% above 500 ft.	1	1 ft + 5%[2] above 500′
Master warning	discrete		1	
Main gear squat switch status	discrete		1	
Angle of attack (if recorded directly)	As installed	As installed	2	0.3%[2]
Outside air temperature or total air temperature.	-50°C to +90°C	±2°C	0.5	0.3°C
Hydraulics, each system low pressure.	discrete		0.5	or 0.5%[2]
Groundspeed	As installed	Most accurate system installed (IMS equipped aircraft only).	1	0.2%[2]

[1] When altitude rate is recorded. Altitude rate must have sufficient resolution and sampling to permit the derivation of altitude to 5 feet.

[2] Percent of full range.

[3] For airplanes that can demonstrate the capability of deriving either the control input on control movement (one from the other) or all modes of operation and flight regimes, the "or" applies. For airplanes with non-mechanical control systems (fly-by-wire) the "and" applies. In airplanes with split surfaces, suitable combination of inputs is acceptable in lieu of recording each surface separately.

[4] This column applies to aircraft manufactured after October 11, 1991.

APPENDIX D — AIRPLANE FLIGHT RECORDER SPECIFICATIONS

Parameters	Range	Accuracy sensor input to DFDR readout	Sampling interval (per second)	Resolution[4] readout
If additional recording capacity is available, recording of the following parameters is recommended. The parameters are listed in order of significance:				
Drift angle	When available, as installed	As installed	4	
Wind speed and direction	When available, as installed	As installed	4	
Latitude and longitude	When available, as installed	As installed	4	
Brake pressure/brake pedal position.	As installed	As installed	1	
Additional engine parameters:				
EPR	As installed	As installed	1 (per engine)	
N1	As installed	As installed	1 (per engine)	
N2	As installed	As installed	1 (per engine)	
EGT	As installed	As installed	1 (per engine)	
Throttle lever position	As installed	As installed	1 (per engine)	
Fuel flow	As installed	As installed	1 (per engine)	
TCAS:				
TA	As installed	As installed	1	
RA	As installed	As installed	1	
Sensitivity level (as selected by crew).	As installed	As installed	2	
GPWS (ground proximity warning system).	Discrete		1	
Landing gear or gear selector position.	Discrete		0.25 (1 per 4 seconds).	
DME 1 and 2 distance	0-200 NM	As installed	0.25	1 mi.
Nav 1 and 2 frequency selection	Full range	As installed	0.25	

[1] When altitude rate is recorded. Altitude rate must have sufficient resolution and sampling to permit the derivation of altitude to 5 feet.

[2] Percent of full range.

[3] For airplanes that can demonstrate the capability of deriving either the control input on control movement (one from the other) or all modes of operation and flight regimes, the "or" applies. For airplanes with non-mechanical control systems (fly-by-wire) the "and" applies. In airplanes with split surfaces, suitable combination of inputs is acceptable in lieu of recording each surface separately.

[4] This column applies to aircraft manufactured after October 11, 1991.

APPENDIX E — HELICOPTER FLIGHT RECORDER SPECIFICATIONS

Parameters	Range	Accuracy sensor input to DFDR readout	Sampling interval (per second)	Resolution[2] readout
Time (GMT)	24 Hrs	±0.125% per hour	0.25 (1 per 4 seconds).	1 sec.
Altitude	-1,000 ft to max certificated altitude of aircraft.	±100 to ±700ft *(See Table 1, TSO-C51a).	1	5′ to 30′
Airspeed	As the installed measuring system.	±3%	1	1 kt.
Heading	360°	±2°	1	0.5°
Normal acceleration (vertical)	-3g to +6g	±1% of max range excluding datum error of ±5%.	8	0.01g
Pitch attitude	±75°	±2°	2	0.5°
Roll attitude	±180°	±2°	2	0.5°
Radio transmitter keying	On-off (discrete)		1	0.25 sec.
Power in each engine: Free power turbine speed *and* engine torque.	0-130% (power turbine speed) full range (torque).	±2°	1 speed 1 torque. (per engine)	0.2%[1] to 0.4%[1]
Main rotor speed	0-130%	±2°	2	0.3%[1]
Altitude rate	±6,000 ft/min	As installed	2	0.2%[1]
Pilot input—primary controls (collective, longitudinal cyclic, lateral cyclic, pedal).	Full range	±3°	2	0.5%[1]
Flight control hydraulic pressure Low.	Discrete, each circuit		1	
Flight control hydraulic pressure selector switch position, 1st and 2nd stage.	Discrete		1	
AFCS mode and engagement status.	Discrete (5 bits necessary)		1	

[1] Percent of full range.
[2] This column applies to aircraft manufactured after October 11, 1991.

APPENDIX E — HELICOPTER FLIGHT RECORDER SPECIFICATIONS

Parameters	Range	Accuracy sensor input to DFDR readout	Sampling interval (per second)	Resolution[2] readout
Stability augmentation system engage.	Discrete		1	
SAS fault status	Discrete		0.25	
Main gearbox temperature low	As installed	As installed	0.25	0.5%[1]
Main gearbox temperature high	As installed	As installed	0.5	0.5%[1]
Controllable stabilator position	Full range	±3%	2	0.4%[1]
Longitudinal acceleration	±1g	±1.5% max range excluding datum error of ±5%.	4	0.01g
Lateral acceleration	±1g	±1.5% max range excluding datum error of ±5%.	4	0.01g
Master warning	Discrete		1	
Nav 1 and 2 frequency selection	Full range	As installed	0.25	
Outside air temperature	-50°C to +90C	±2°C	0.5	0.3°C

[1] Percent of full range.
[2] This column applies to aircraft manufactured after October 11, 1991.

Index